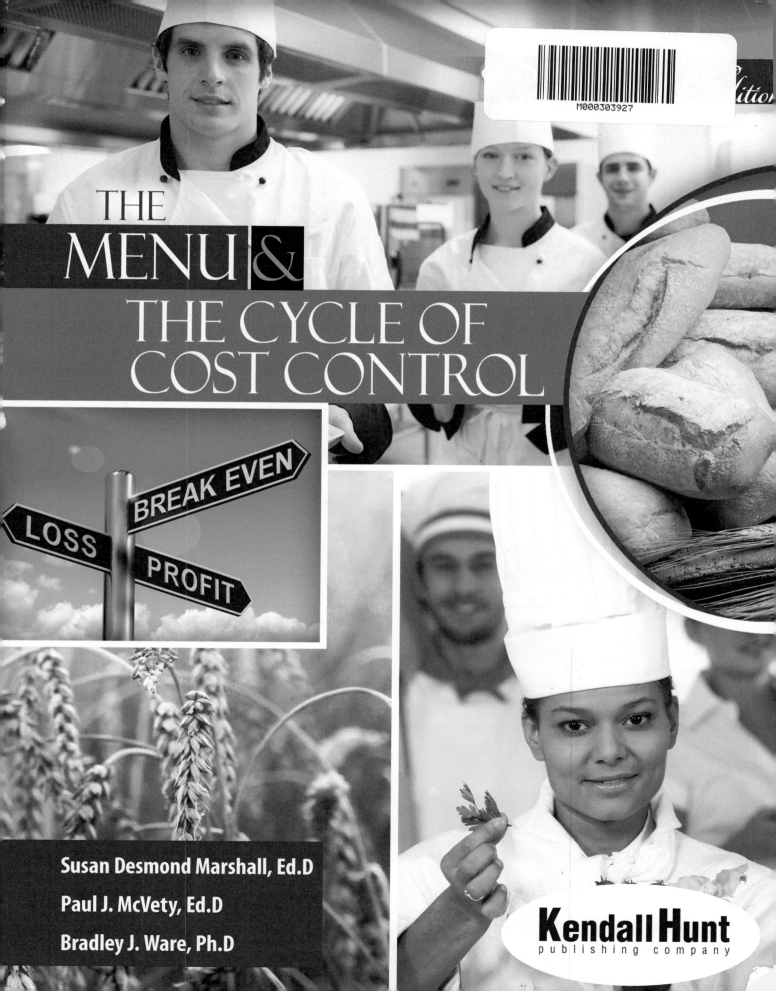

THE MENU & THE CYCLE OF COST CONTROL

BREAK EVEN

LOSS

PROFIT

Susan Desmond Marshall, Ed.D

Paul J. McVety, Ed.D

Bradley J. Ware, Ph.D

Kendall Hunt
publishing company

M000303927

Kendall Hunt
publishing company

www.kendallhunt.com
Send all inquiries to:
4050 Westmark Drive
Dubuque, IA   52004-1840

PAK ISBN: 978-1-5249-0614-6
Textbook only: 978-1-5249-0615-3

Contents

Appendices

Bibliography

Index

Preface

Success in today's foodservice industry requires a solid knowledge of industry practices. Although the techniques and mathematical processes discussed in this text are often routine for experienced foodservice professionals, novices entering the industry may find themselves a bit overwhelmed by the numerous requirements demanded by day-to-day operations. The topics discussed in this textbook include theories, practices, techniques, and applications needed for the selection of a practical concept and menu, as well as the appropriate cost control methods required to support a successful business operation. This textbook provides hospitality, culinary, baking, and pastry students with the information necessary to complete entry level management tasks and to become effective, contributing members of a management team.

Organization of the Textbook

Unit 1: The Menu

Current socioeconomic challenges have prompted restaurants to create strategies that attract customers. The selection of an appropriate concept and the creation of menu items that specifically appeal to guests' tastes and interests are imperative. Menu development and design require the ability to organize and design a menu, develop recipes, and write descriptive copy that both explains and sells the menu items. Chefs/managers must also determine the cost of recipes and individual menu items to assign a selling price that adequately covers ingredient costs and guarantees a fair and reasonable profit, as well as perceived customer value. A carefully designed menu that has attention to layout, design, descriptive copy, and costs is needed to support a concept and business plan. A well-researched business plan and a cost effective menu are the foundation to all cost control strategies.

Unit 2: The Cycle of Cost Control

After the concept and the sales menu are developed, Unit 2 goes on to provide an explanation of the cycle of cost control, including the necessary business documents and procedures needed to effectively control the movement of products and costs through the cycle of cost control. The Income Statement serves to explain how sales are generated, costs are incurred and categorized, and ultimately how profits are realized. This document has numerous uses that can help managers to forecast future sales, expenses, profits, and budgeting costs. Once completed, the profits and losses that appear on the Income Statement should be analyzed, and cost saving controls should be reassessed and improved to properly receive and store ingredients, manage inventory, and control daily production to improve company profit.

Unit 3: Sales and Labor Analysis

When the cycle of cost control is completed, sales and labor costs must be analyzed. Sales controls are put in place to track the flow of sales through a business. It is important to track sales using systems such as Point of Sales or Menu Engineering to have an accurate picture of how sales are doing. A knowledge of Labor Costs Controls, which include wages, salaries, benefits, federal taxes, hiring the right employees, tip declaration, preparing payroll, and determining payroll deductions and net pay is equally important. Managers and owners must be well versed in all of these areas to support a successful business.

The Fifth Edition

This 5th edition of *The Menu and the Cycle of Cost Control* features the most current information on industry trends and concepts as well as recent government industry-related laws, documents and requirements. An accompanying WebCom™ provides actual menus from well-known restaurants located throughout the United States, menu design techniques, and nutrition regulations, as well as review exercises, updated work and project forms, PowerPoint presentations, test bank questions, and numerous suggestions for classroom activities. The 24-hour a day accessible online website offers additional textual support tools including drag and drop menu design exercises, and recipe costing, purchasing, receiving, inventory, and yield test forms.

Acknowledgments

The authors of this text would like to thank their families for the support and encouragement they provided during this project. They also wish to recognize the contributions of two individuals without whom this textbook would never have been completed: Claudette Lévesque Ware, Ph.D., Editor, who invested countless hours crafting the words that best express the content expertise of the authors, and Deb Bettencourt, Technical Editor, who worked closely with the editor and authors to input the changes needed in producing this edition.

Susan Desmond Marshall, Ed.D
Johnson & Wales University

Paul J. McVety, Ed.D
Johnson & Wales University

Bradley J. Ware, Ph.D
Johnson & Wales University

1

The Menu

Chapter 1

The Foodservice Industry Today

Chapter 2

Concepts and the Strategic Business Plan

Chapter 3

Developing and Designing the Sales Menu

Chapter 4

Standards, Measurements, Recipes, and Formulas

Chapter 5

Determining Portion Costs and Selling Prices

Chapter 1

The Foodservice Industry Today

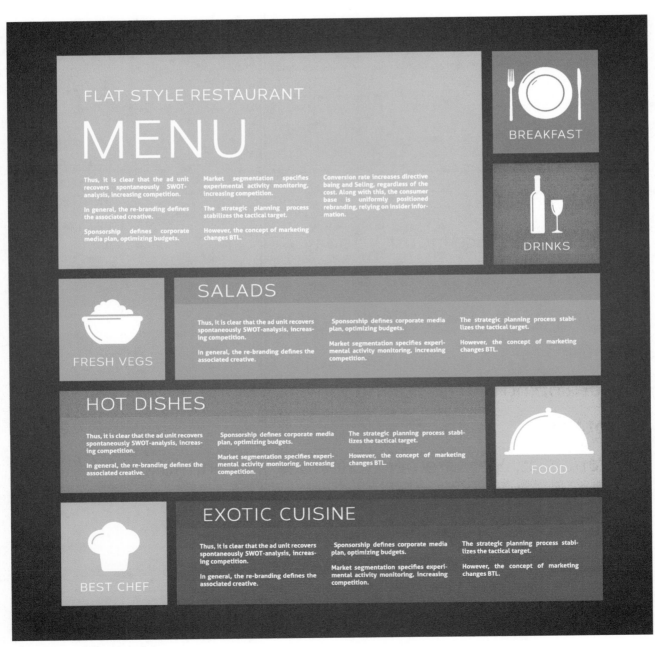

OBJECTIVES

Upon completion of this chapter, the student should be able to:

1. define and explain 10 current foodservice industry trends.
2. discuss the importance of sustainability and what restaurants are doing to support this trend.
3. discuss the causes and effects of poor "Kids' Nutrition."

KEY TERMS

Food hubs

INTRODUCTION

In the fall of 2013 the National Restaurant Association (NRA) surveyed approximately 1,300 professionals from the American Culinary Federation (ACF) who were asked to rate what they saw as the top trends in the industry. The results were then compiled and released in the "What's Hot 2014 Culinary Forecast." The top 10 topics included:

1. Locally Sourced Meats, Seafood, and Produce
2. Locally Grown Produce
3. Environmental Sustainability
4. Healthful Kids' Meals
5. Gluten-free Cuisine
6. Hyper-local Sourcing
7. Children's Nutrition
8. Non-wheat Noodles/Pastas
9. Sustainable Seafood
10. Farm/Estate Branded Items

The Top 10 Restaurant Trends

Locally Sourced Meats, Seafood, and Produce

Restaurants throughout the United States are currently using locally sourced meats, seafood, and produce on their menus in response to consumer demands for fresh and healthy products. These sourced foods are procured from local farms, dairies, and fisheries, as well as from the more recently created "food hubs." **Food hubs**, as defined by the United States Department of Agriculture, are centralized facilities where the aggregation, storage, processing, distribution, and marketing of regional food items (such as meats, seafood, fish, produce, and dairy) occur. Food items are delivered from the hub to restaurants and ultimately to customers and consumers who might not otherwise have the opportunity to enjoy such products.

In Rhode Island, for example, the Market Mobile Program hosted by Farm Aid has partnered with Farm Fresh to provide a year-round delivery system that supplies restaurants in-state and in nearby Massachusetts with products from over 50 local farms and producers. Some of the sites that participate in this program are: Narragansett Creamery (Rhode Island), Schartner Farms (Exeter, RI), Baffoni's Poultry Farm (Johnston, RI), Four Town Farm (Seekonk, MA), Cooks Valley Farm (Wrentham, MA), and Allen Farms (Westport, MA). Restaurants in Rhode Island and Massachusetts that are loyal supporters of the Market Mobile Program include: The Mooring Seafood Kitchen & Bar (Newport, RI), DeWolf Tavern (Bristol, RI), Bondir (Cambridge, MA), and the Renaissance Boston Waterfront Hotel. (Figure 1.1)

Environmental Sustainability

Although "going green" is not an easy process for most restaurants, chefs who are "sustainably minded" are realizing the advantages of offering locally sourced food items on the menu. The 2014 "What's Hot Survey" reports that 38% of the chefs surveyed believe that environmental sustainability is, and will continue to be, the most popular trend for at least another 10 years. As current as the interest in environmental sustainability may be, it is a cause to which some restaurants have been dedicated for a number of years.

The restaurant Café Normandie, in Annapolis MD, has been invested in this cause since 2008. Café Normandie partnered with the city of Annapolis to obtain a sustainability stewardship designation for its progressive green program. By adopting aggressive recycling and composting practices, the property was able to reduce waste by 90%. It installed recycled marble tops to eliminate the need for cloth tablecloths and elected to introduce biodegradable carry-out containers. The owner of the restaurant has also begun to grow produce on a farm that he owns in upper Marlboro, MD, which is used in menu items.

The InterContinental Chicago hotel is committed to the green effort as well. It has replaced the hotel roof with a green roof where the hotel's chefs have planted a garden that provides most of the herbs and produce used on premises. As of 2013, the hotel has the largest living green wall in North America. Designed by Anne Roberts Gardens Inc., this sustainable resource is able to decrease ambient temperature; improve energy efficiency and air quality; and reduce noise while protecting the structural integrity of the building and increasing its value.

Ted's Montana Grill seriously invests in the green effort and is committed to making ecologically responsible decisions for its 44 restaurants nationwide. These restaurant properties procure all-natural beef, bison, and chicken that contain no artificial ingredients or preservatives. They use energy efficient low-voltage lighting and sustainable insulation materials, as well as bamboo for constructing floors when building their properties. Their Tallahassee, FL site was the first to utilize solar power to conserve energy. Ted's Montana Grills are 90% plastic free: they print their menus on recycled paper; use drinking straws composed of eco-friendly polymer coated paper; and cover their tables with recycled brown butcher paper. Most of Ted's restaurants recycle aluminum, plastic, and steel, and collect frying oils that are then used as bio-degradable fuel.

Darden Restaurants, which has over 2,100 locations nationwide, is a leader in environmental sustainability. Employees in their restaurants form groups known as Safety & Sustainability teams, which implement programs to reduce waste energy and water usage. Whenever feasible, Darden Restaurants (LongHorn Steakhouse, Olive Garden, and Red Lobster) incorporate sustainable design in their properties by installing smarter-energy management systems that utilize 100% recycled carpeting and other recycled materials such as sustainably harvested wood. LED light bulbs replace incandescent bulbs in the dining room and compact fluorescent bulbs that use less energy illuminate the kitchen. Outdoors, low-flow faucets and nozzles are used to maintain landscaping that requires less water. Darden is also committed to sourcing local materials whenever possible.

Healthful Kids' Meals

The current rate of childhood obesity is the largest ever, and it is projected that today's children will live for a shorter life span than their parents because of their poor diets and limited physical exercise. Currently, one out of every three children is overweight or obese and runs the risk of developing diabetes, cancer, and heart disease. Parents are becoming increasingly aware of these alarming statistics and are committing themselves to providing more nutritious and healthful food items, both at home and outside the home. Changes that can be implemented to make children's meals more healthful include: reducing the size of, or replacing beverages that contain sugar with low-fat milk,100% juices, or water; incorporating vegetables, whole grains, and fruits in the diet; and reducing the intake of fried foods, sodium, butter, and cheese.

Over 4,000 restaurants are currently participating in the Kids LiveWell program that was established by the National Restaurant Association (NRA) in collaboration with Healthy Dining, to assist parents in selecting healthful menu alternatives for their children when dining out. This voluntary program asks restaurants to commit to offering healthy food items on their menus such as lean proteins, vegetables, whole grains, and low-fat dairy products. Chefs are also being asked to reduce fats and sodium in the preparation of meals. Some of the restaurants committed to this effort are: Shula's Steak House, Boudin SF, Silver Diner (located in MD, VA, and NJ), 3 Squares Restaurant (Maple Green, MN), Keystone Resort (CO), and LB Bistro & Pâtisserie at the Sheraton Chicago Hotel & Towers. Restaurants that participate in the program agree to offer and advertise select menu items that meet nutritional specifications based on the criteria set by the 2012 Dietary Guidelines.

Gluten-free Cuisine

Independent restaurants and bakeries, restaurant chains, and universities have begun to offer gluten-free menu items in response to the increasing number of cases of celiac disease (also known as gluten intolerance). This digestive disease affects one out of every 133 Americans today. Although celiac disease is most commonly linked to persons of European descent, recent studies show that it is not limited to this group. Individuals who suffer from celiac disease cannot tolerate the protein gluten found in barley, rice, and wheat. When planning to dine out, celiac sufferers should visit the restaurant's web site to peruse menu offerings to avoid being disappointed. It is

Figure 1.1
À la carte Menu—The Mooring, Newport, Rhode Island

THE MOORING

SAYER'S WHARF • NEWPORT

SEAFOOD KITCHEN & BAR

THE RAW BAR

OYSTERS* - UP TO SIX VARIETIES 2.95 PER

LITTLENECKS* 1.95 PER

CHERRYSTONES* 1.95 PER

CHILLED WHITE MEXICAN SHRIMP 3.50 PER

LOBSTER CLAW 7.00 PER

WHOLE CHILLED LOBSTER 28.00

OYSTER SHOOTER* 4.95 PER
ONE OYSTER WITH COCKTAIL SAUCE,
OUTERBRIDGES® & TRINITY I.P.A.

RAW BAR PLATTER * 41.00
3 LOBSTER CLAWS, 3 SHRIMP, 3 LITTLENECKS, 3 OYSTERS

GRAND SHELLFISH PLATTER * 69.00
6 SHRIMP, 6 LITTLENECKS, 6 OYSTERS,
WHOLE CHILLED LOBSTER, FRESH MAINE CRAB

OYSTERS & DOM PERIGNON* 75.00
6 OYSTERS & 2 GLASSES OF MÖET & CHANDON "DOM PERIGNON"

* RAW MEAT AND SHELLFISH, OR PRODUCTS NOT COOKED TO RECOMMENDED INTERNAL TEMPERATURES, CAN INCREASE YOUR RISK OF ILLNESS.
CONSUMERS WHO ARE SENSITIVE TO FOOD-RELATED REACTIONS OR ILLNESS SHOULD EAT ONLY THOROUGHLY COOKED MEATS, POULTRY & SEAFOOD.

SOUPS & SALADS

CLASSIC MOORING CLAM CHOWDER CUP...6 BOWL...8

NATIVE SCALLOP CHOWDER CUP...7 BOWL...9
AWARD-WINNING

CHOPPED SALAD
ROMAINE LETTUCE, ALFALFA SPROUTS, ORANGES, TOMATOES, BACON,
CUCUMBERS, FETA CHEESE, FINGERLING POTATOES, SUNFLOWER SEEDS,
ORANGE-BUTTERMILK DRESSING 8

MOORING CAESAR
CHOPPED ROMAINE, ROSEMARY CROUTONS, PARMIGIANO-REGGIANO,
HOUSE-MADE DRESSING 8

AUTUMN GREENS
SHAVED BUTTERNUT SQUASH, CARROTS, & WATERMELON RADISH,
MANCHEGO CHEESE, DRIED CRANBERRIES, CIDER VINAIGRETTE 8

PEAR & STILTON SALAD
FRISEE, ENDIVE, & BIBB LETTUCES, CARROTS, WALNUTS,
STILTON CHEESE, HONEY-BALSAMIC DRESSING 9

SALAD BUDDIES - GREAT COMPANIONS TO ANY SALAD
SALMON 10
LOBSTER SALAD 17
LOBSTER TAIL 17
CHICKEN 8
YELLOWFIN TUNA* 12
SHRIMP (4) 10
SCALLOPS (3) 12

APPETIZERS

MUSSELS ZUPPA
TASSO HAM, BRAISED LEEKS, TOMATO, VERMOUTH-GARLIC BUTTER,
FOCACCIA 12

PORK BELLY
SWEET & SOUR GLAZED, SESAME VEGETABLE SLAW, SZECHUAN
SPICED PEANUTS 12

GALILEE SQUID
FLASH-FRIED RINGS & TENTACLES, KALAMATA OLIVES,
PEPPERONCINI PEPPERS, TOASTED CUMIN-TOMATO DIP 11

BAG OF DOUGHNUTS
LOBSTER, CRAB & SHRIMP FRITTERS WITH CHIPOTLE-MAPLE AIOLI 12

FRIED OYSTERS & SPICY PICKLES
MARINATED VEGETABLE SALAD, CHORIZO, CHILI AIOLI 14

TUNA TARTARE*
WASABI-CUCUMBER SALAD, PICKLED ONIONS & CARROTS,
CITRUS-SOY SAUCE, WONTONS 14

ARTISAN CHEESE PLATE
CANDIED CASHEWS, PORT WINE CHERRIES, AQUIDNECK ISLAND HONEY,
CRACKERS & CROSTINI 16

CRAB CAKE
PAN-FRIED, RED PEPPER-CHIVE SAUCE, HOUSE RANCH DRESSING 12

MOORING FISH TACOS
CORNMEAL-FRIED COD, RED CABBAGE, GRILLED ONION, HOT SAUCE,
AVOCADO SOUR CREAM, CILANTRO 8

SURF & TURF SLIDERS
SHAVED SIRLOIN, LOBSTER, CHEDDAR-ALE SAUCE, ARUGULA,
CRISPY SWEET POTATOES 14

SIGNATURE SANDWICHES
SERVED WITH BOSTON SPICED FRIES

PANKO-CRUSTED COD
CAPER-PEPPER RELISH, ROASTED SHALLOT AIOLI, BRIOCHE BUN 14

SALMON WRAP
CARAMELIZED ONIONS, ROASTED PEPPERS, ARUGULA, PANCETTA,
SWEET POTATO-MASCARPONE SPREAD, SPINACH WRAP 14

GRILLED CHEESE
NARRAGANSETT CREAMERY CHEESES, PORTOBELLO MUSHROOMS,
PROSCIUTTO, COUNTRY BREAD 12

OPEN-FACED TURKEY
ROASTED TURKEY BREAST, MUENSTER CHEESE, BACON, FRIED EGG,
BASIL PESTO, TOASTED ARTISAN BREAD 12

LOBSTER CROISSANT
TRADITIONAL STEAMED, CHILLED LOBSTER MEAT,
TARRAGON DRESSING 19

BLACKENED SWORDFISH WRAP
GRILLED PINEAPPLE SALSA, AVOCADO TARTAR SAUCE, ARUGULA,
TORTILLA WRAP 15

TUNA MELT
POACHED YELLOWFIN TUNA SALAD, TOMATO, CHEDDAR CHEESE,
ARUGULA, PORTUGUESE BOLO 14

8 OZ. CERTIFIED ANGUS BURGER*
AGED CHEDDAR CHEESE, APPLEWOOD-SMOKED BACON,
CRISPY ONION STRINGS, GRILLED KAISER ROLL 12

FOR OUR GUESTS WHO PREFER GLUTEN FREE OPTIONS, WE ARE PLEASED TO OFFER A FULL MENU. PLEASE INQUIRE WITH YOUR SERVER.

THE CULINARY STAFF AT THE MOORING FEELS IT NECESSARY TO INFORM OUR GUESTS ON THE ISSUE OF MERCURY IN SEAFOOD. SOME TYPES OF SEAFOOD CAN CONTAIN ELEVATED
LEVELS OF MERCURY, WHICH CAN BE DETRIMENTAL TO THE HEALTH OF CERTAIN INDIVIDUALS. PLEASE INQUIRE WITH YOUR SERVER FOR DETAILS.

*RAW MEAT & SHELLFISH, OR PRODUCTS NOT COOKED TO RECOMMENDED INTERNAL TEMPERATURES, CAN INCREASE YOUR RISK OF ILLNESS. CONSUMERS WHO ARE SENSITIVE
TO FOOD-RELATED REACTIONS OR ILLNESS SHOULD EAT ONLY THOROUGHLY COOKED MEATS, POULTRY & SEAFOOD. PLEASE MAKE YOUR SERVER AWARE ANY FOOD ALLERGIES.

12/6/2013

ENTREES

FROM THE WATER

PORTUGUESE ROASTED COD
NATIVE LITTLENECKS, YUKON POTATOES, GREEN OLIVES, TOMATO, CHORIZO, VINHO VERDE, OLIVE OIL, FOCACCIA   28

SOLE FRANCAISE
LIGHT EGG BATTER, JASMINE RICE, TOMATO DILL PUREE, LEMON BEURRE BLANC, CAPERS   22

UPTOWN SALAD
SAUTEED LOBSTER & SHRIMP, GRILLED SALMON, GRAPE TOMATOES, CUCUMBERS, CARROTS, BALSAMIC REDUCTION   28

ATLANTIC SALMON
PAN-ROASTED, FRENCH LENTILS, GRAIN MUSTARD CREME FRAICHE, RED BEET-HORSERADISH SLAW   26

MAINE LOBSTER
STEAMED WITH WARM DRAWN BUTTER & POTATOES   1 ¼ LB 32   2 LB 60
BAKED & STUFFED WITH NATIVE SCALLOPS & SHRIMP   1 ¼ LB 42   2 LB 70

YELLOWFIN TUNA*
PAN-SEARED, ROASTED FINGERLINGS, BRAISED CARROTS, FENNEL, BOUILLABAISSE SAUCE, OLIVE PUREE   28

FISH & CHIPS
FRIED ATLANTIC BLUE COD, GUINNESS BATTER, SPICED FRIES, RED PEPPER SLAW, MOORING TARTAR SAUCE   19

GEORGES BANK SCALLOPS
PAN-SEARED, ROASTED APPLE POLENTA, AUTUMN VEGETABLE HASH, CRANBERRY GASTRIQUE   29

SEAFOOD PASTA
LOBSTER, SHRIMP, SEA SCALLOPS, TOMATO-GARLIC BUTTER SAUCE, FRESH HERBS, ANGEL HAIR PASTA   38

SWORDFISH
GRILLED, STEAK FRIES, TOMATO CONFIT, GREENS, SAFFRON BEURRE BLANC   28

SEAFOOD PIE
BAKED NATIVE FISH, SCALLOPS, SHRIMP, LOBSTER, SHERRY VELOUTE, HERB BREAD CRUMBS   32

FROM THE LAND

MURRAY'S ALL-NATURAL CHICKEN
SWEET POTATO PUREE, LOCAL KALE, ROASTED OYSTER MUSHROOMS, HERB BUTTER PAN SAUCE   22

PORK TENDERLOIN
CHEDDAR-CHIVE MASHED POTATOES, WILTED GREENS, CRISPY BACON, MAPLE-THYME GASTRIQUE   24

RICOTTA GNOCCHI
BLACK QUINOA, SEASONAL VEGETABLES, GREENS, TOMATO-OLIVE OIL SAUCE   16

BRAISED SHORTRIBS
CELERY ROOT-BROWN BUTTER PUREE, BRAISED GREENS, ROASTED CARROTS, CRISPY SQUASH   22

CERTIFIED ANGUS BEEF*
LOADED POTATO CROQUETTES, BRAISED MUSHROOMS & LEEKS, ROASTED SHALLOT DEMI-GLACE
8 OZ. FILET   37   -   WITH 1¼ LB LOBSTER   65
14 OZ. NY SIRLOIN   34   -   WITH 1¼ LB LOBSTER   62

ADDITIONAL SURF & TURF OPTIONS
LOBSTER TAIL 17   SCALLOPS 12
YELLOWFIN TUNA 12   SHRIMP 10

SEASONAL MENUS

CREATE YOUR OWN PRIX-FIXE | $30
AVAILABLE MONDAY – WEDNESDAY

3-COURSE MENU

APPETIZER
choice of cup of soup or salad

ENTREE
choice of any entree

DESSERT
choice of:
carrot cake creme brulee, coconut-apple bread pudding, or gelato

PAELLA SPECIAL - THURSDAYS
PAELLA FOR TWO SERVED WITH SANGRIA | $55
Old World-style paella with whole lobster, clams, mussels, chicken, shrimp, rice, chorizo, saffron-garlic sofrito

SIDES
EACH PREPARATION 6

SAUTEED GREENS
KALE, SPINACH, SWISS CHARD

MASHED YUKON GOLD POTATOES

BRUSSELS SPROUTS
BACON & SHALLOTS

QUINOA-VEGETABLE SUCCOTASH

ROASTED AUTUMN VEGETABLES
WHIPPED CHEVRE, FETA CRUMBLES

POTATO GRATIN
CHEDDAR BECHAMEL

THE MOORING IS COMMITTED TO PURCHASING SUSTAINABLE SEAFOOD WHENEVER POSSIBLE THROUGH A VARIETY OF SOURCES, INCLUDING *BROWN FAMILY SEAFOOD*, *FOLEY FISH*, AND *NEWPORT LOBSTER*. PLEASE INQUIRE WITH YOUR SERVER FOR TODAY'S OPTIONS SERVED WITH CHEF'S PREPARATION.

FOR OUR GUESTS WHO PREFER GLUTEN FREE OPTIONS, WE ARE PLEASED TO OFFER A FULL MENU. PLEASE INQUIRE WITH YOUR SERVER.

THE CULINARY STAFF AT THE MOORING FEELS IT NECESSARY TO INFORM OUR GUESTS ON THE ISSUE OF MERCURY IN SEAFOOD. SOME TYPES OF SEAFOOD CAN CONTAIN ELEVATED LEVELS OF MERCURY, WHICH CAN BE DETRIMENTAL TO THE HEALTH OF CERTAIN INDIVIDUALS. PLEASE INQUIRE WITH YOUR SERVER FOR DETAILS.

*RAW MEAT & SHELLFISH, OR PRODUCTS NOT COOKED TO RECOMMENDED INTERNAL TEMPERATURES, CAN INCREASE YOUR RISK OF ILLNESS. CONSUMERS WHO ARE SENSITIVE TO FOOD-RELATED REACTIONS OR ILLNESS SHOULD EAT ONLY THOROUGHLY COOKED MEATS, POULTRY & SEAFOOD. PLEASE MAKE YOUR SERVER AWARE ANY FOOD ALLERGIES.

EXECUTIVE CHEF: BOB BANKERT
SOUS CHEF: WALTER SLATER
12/6/2013

also prudent to inform the waitstaff person or a manager of this condition so that the chef might reasonably accommodate the diner and make eating out a less daunting task.

Several restaurants and bakeries in the Boston area currently offer gluten-free menu items. City Table in the Back Bay (Boston, MA) offers a special gluten-free menu, and Terramia Ristorante (Boston, MA) in the North End serves gluten-free pastas. In Cambridge, Rosie's Bakery carries blueberry muffins, oatmeal chocolate chip cookies, raspberry oat bars, and maple pecan scones that are gluten free, while Keltic Krust Bakery Café in Newton, offers gluten-free vegan breakfast bars, shortbread, sugar and chocolate chip cookies, apple and zucchini bread, and sesame white bread. Restaurant chains such as The Capital Grille and Chart House also have extensive gluten-free menus that feature appetizers, salads, entrées, sides, and desserts that are gluten-free.

Lehigh University, in Bethlehem, PA, recently created a gluten-free, allergen-free station in their campus' main dining hall. Lehigh's executive chef Joseph Kornafel has developed an extensive database of allergen-free recipes and uses the color purple to designate gluten-free food preparation equipment items, including utensils, carts, and cutting boards to alleviate any cross-contamination. All of the ingredients are also carefully labeled to prevent any accidents from occurring (Figure 1.2). Chefs who work the gluten-free station receive special training.

Hyper-local Sourcing

In recent years, chefs and restaurant operators have been participating in hyper-local sourcing. They've been growing herbs, vegetables, and fruits on rooftops or on acreages near their restaurants as well as raising pigs, poultry, and game. In Santa Rosa, CA, Duskie Estes and John Stewart, chef/owners of Zazu Kitchen + Farm, raise their own Mangalitsa pigs, chickens, ducks, turkeys, and rabbits. Their garden has expanded so rapidly that they have had to hire a full-time farmer to sustain the organic vegetables, fruits, and herbs that are used on their menu.

Chef Berglund, owner of The Bachelor Farmer, in Minneapolis, MN, produces an array of herbs and vegetables including basil, beets, bib lettuce, radishes, carrots, cucumbers, turnips, and heirloom tomatoes from a rooftop garden. Twenty-five percent of the dishes currently served at the property feature items from the on-site garden including tarragon, sage, bay leaf, Muscat grapes, Adriatic figs, golden red raspberries, spinach, arugula, fava beans, squash blossoms, and olives.

The Inn at Little Washington in Washington, VA, actually has a full-time, professional gardener who oversees more than half an acre of land and two greenhouses that adequately supply the restaurant with product almost year round. In Milton, NY, Henry's at the Farm at Buttermilk Falls Inn & Spa owns a 40-acre plot of land called Millstone Farms that produces seasonal herbs, vegetables, and fruits including: basil, beans, kale, potatoes, spinach, squash, Swiss chard, apples, blackberries, peaches, raspberries, and strawberries. They also raise heirloom chickens that produce organic eggs.

Some restaurants are growing herbs that they use in their signature cocktails and others are making their own charcuterie. Chef Richard of BLVD 16, located in Hotel Palomar in Los Angeles, was one of the first to feature an organic herb garden that was specifically designed to accommodate the drink menu. In Napa, the restaurant Oenotri makes the charcuterie that is featured on its menu.

Children's Nutrition

According to a white paper report produced by FONA International Inc., there are six areas that directly influence kids' nutrition.

1. Natural and No Additives/Preservatives Products
2. Healthy Snacking Options
3. Childhood Obesity
4. The Role of Schools—(The Problem or the Solution)
5. Healthy Options on the Menu
6. Gluten-Free and Allergy Consciousness

Food manufacturers have recently begun to listen to parents' concerns and have been developing and promoting all natural food products. A report entitled "Trends in Kids' Nutrition," prepared by Datamonitor, encourages food manufacturers to reformulate products by removing unnatural trans-fats in foods and high fructose corn syrup from drinks and snacks. They also recommend reducing or eliminating additives such as colorings and preservatives.

In June of 2010, Mintel prepared a report entitled "Kids' Snacking," which concluded that snacking in particular, needs to be scrutinized when analyzing kids' nutrition. Kids' prefer chips, pretzels, and cookies as snack favorites, followed closely in popularity by ice cream, cupcakes, and puddings with all their additives. Parents can encourage better snacking habits by limiting purchases to healthy options that kids like. Food manufacturers can contribute to these efforts by developing and promoting snacks that are both healthy and taste good. Healthy Stuff Trail Mix and Sour Orange Flavored Golden Raisins are two snacks that are healthy and currently popular with consumers.

Snacking portions must also be monitored because of the direct correlation between increased snacking and obesity and diabetes rates that have become overwhelmingly striking in the United States. To combat these problems, public and private agencies need to get involved. In 2009, the American Dietetic Association formed the "Childhood Obesity Prevention Coalition" and set up the "Kids Eat Right" initiative to support families, schools, and communities in making a consorted attempt to provide quality education and support for all children in the United States. In 2010, First Lady Michelle Obama started the "Let's Move" initiative, which has a goal of decreasing childhood obesity from 17% to 5% by the year 2030. The Mintel report on childhood obesity found that parents are either in complete denial or are just not as concerned as they should be that their child is overweight or obese.

Through federal and state initiatives and media efforts, word is finally getting out about the risks of childhood obesity. Unfortunately, one of the problems that parents face is the onslaught of advertising that sometimes manipulates the eating habits of impressionable children. A study entitled "Trends in Kids' Nutrition Opportunities and Threats in the Context of Escalating Childhood Obesity," found that about one-third of parents are worried about the foods that are being marketed directly to their children. With obesity on the rise, media and food manufacturers should take a more responsible role in combatting childhood obesity. Food manufacturers can be in the forefront by developing healthful, low-calorie food items containing less fat, sugar, and sodium that are easy to prepare and attractive to children. The Mintel report on Children and Obesity states that the Foodservice Industry is trying to tackle the obesity problem in a number of ways by reducing or removing salt, sugar, fat, high-fructose and corn syrup, and incorporating vegetables and fruits into foods whenever possible.

Elementary, secondary, and post-secondary schools play a very important role in shaping the eating habits of students. Fortunately, many schools are now accepting the challenge of becoming proactive in stressing the importance of healthy nutrition. New York City School District 41 has actually developed a cooking club made up of teachers and children who learn to make various healthy food items by visiting neighborhood restaurants. The cooking club encourages kids to try new things and to bring fresh ideas home that parents can also use. Other schools around the

Luncheon Menu—Canyon Ranch Health Resort, Tucson, Arizona

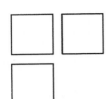

starters

CREAM OF TOMATO WITH TARRAGON SOUP GF
65.7.1.3.1.*130*

NO SALT ADDED PUREE OF BLACK EYED PEA SOUP GF,V
50.9.1.1.1.*12*

GAZPACHO SOUP GF,V 35.7.1.tr.1.*354*

MISO SOUP GF,V 40.5.2.1.1.*323*

CHICKEN NOODLE SOUP 120.16.8.3.1.*377*

HUMMUS WITH WHOLE-WHEAT CRACKERS V 155.21.5.7.4.*300*

accompaniments

MARINATED TOFU GF,V 60.1.7.4.1.*18*

TUNA GF 70.0.16.1.0.*385*

TUNA SALAD GF 120.4.12.6.tr.*261*
With bell peppers, celery, and sweet pickle relish

PLAIN GRILLED CHICKEN GF 140.0.26.3.0.*63*

PLAIN GRILLED SALMON GF 175.0.19.11.0.*69*

BAKED SWEET POTATO GF,V 140.32.3.tr.5.*31*
  Half GF,V 75.18.2.tr.3.*16*

BAKED POTATO GF,V 140.31.4.tr.3.*12*
  Half GF,V 75.17.2.tr.2.*6*

BROWN RICE GF,V 120.25.3.1.1.*4*

FRESH STEAMED VEGETABLES GF,V 65.14.3.tr.5.*73*

salad & sandwich bar

Build your own salad with organic greens, fresh vegetables, premade salad of the day, Canyon Ranch homemade salad dressings, low-fat cottage cheese, nuts, whole-wheat lavosh and gluten-free rice crackers.

Build your own cold sandwich or hot grilled Panini with your choice of assorted breads, vegetables, roasted turkey, roast beef, tuna salad, Swiss cheese and cheddar cheese.

balanced selection

PUREE OF BLACK EYED PEA SOUP GF,V
50.9.1.1.4.*12*

CHICKEN KALE SALAD GF 325.17.33.15.4.*297*

OATMEAL CRANBERRY CHOCOLATE CHIP COOKIES (2) GF 150.23.3.5.2.*111*

NUTRIENT ANALYSIS
Calories . carb grams . protein grams . fat grams . fiber grams . *sodium mg*   tr = trace (less than 1 gram)
A = Contains a trace of alcohol   V = Vegan–contains no animal product
GF = Gluten-Free–no wheat, rye or barley. Please note: Our kitchens are not gluten-free environments.

entrées

BAKED ALASKAN COD
405.36.31.15.3.*341*
Breaded and baked cod fillet served with sautéed
zucchini and tomatoes and macaroni & cheese

CHICKEN KALE SALAD GF
325.17.33.15.4.*297*
Grilled chicken breast atop kale salad with jicama,
cucumbers, tomatoes and green beans drizzled
with peanut vinaigrette and garnished with cilantro
  Substitute tofu   GF,V   320.19.19.21.6.*243*

MOZZARELLA & TOMATO BAGUETTE
390.35.24.18.7.*452*
Fresh mozzarella cheese, tomato spread, basil and
arugula on a crispy baguette, served with Indian
Raita side salad

MOROCCAN STEW   V   420.57.16.18.17.*668*
Lentils and vegetables slow simmered with cardamom,
allspice, coriander and ginger, served over bulgur wheat
with Harissa Sauce and topped with toasted almonds
  With roasted lamb   435.55.25.15.16.*752*

LOADED SOUTHWEST VEGETARIAN BURGER
Homemade spicy veggie burger patty made with fresh
vegetables, Certified Gluten-Free oats and pumpkin seeds,
served on a soft whole-wheat roll with avocado, pico de
gallo, lettuce, tomato and onion, served with a Raita Indian
side salad
  On whole-wheat roll   V   330.51.15.10.10.*485*
  On gluten-free bread   GF   430.68.17.13.13.*774*

CHILI CHEESE BAKED POTATO   GF
295.50.13.5.7.*328*
Baked potato topped with vegetarian bean chili
and Monterey Jack cheese, served with a
Raita Indian side salad

**STEAMED VEGETABLES WITH
BROWN RICE**   GF,V
215.43.6.2.6.*482*
Served with Mongolian BBQ Sauce
  With Grilled Chicken   GF   355.43.34.10.6.*545*
  With Grilled Salmon   GF   390.43.27.13.6.*551*
  With Tofu   GF,V   325.40.21.10.7.*500*

desserts

FRESH FRUIT PLATE   GF,V   120.30.2.1.6.*1*

GRAPEFRUIT SORBET   GF,V   65.17.tr.tr.tr.*1*

HOMEMADE VANILLA ICE CREAM   GF
85.16.4.1.tr.*51*
  Nonfat fudge sauce   GF,V   90.22.1.tr.4.*40*

HOMEMADE COCONUT GELATO   GF,V
100.18.tr.4.tr.*5*

CHOCOLATE CHIP COOKIES (2)   170.26.2.7.1.*124*

GLUTEN-FREE CHOCOLATE CHIP COOKIES (2)   GF
170.24.2.8.2.*118*

**OATMEAL CRANBERRY CHOCOLATE CHIP
COOKIES (2)**   GF   150.23.3.5.2.*111*

**CARROT CUPCAKE WITH
CREAM CHEESE FROSTING**
175.30.4.5.1.*237*

* Consuming raw or undercooked meats, poultry, seafood, shellfish or eggs may increase your risk of food
borne illness, especially if you have certain medical conditions.

Please let your server know your time restrictions. If you have food allergies or sensitivities,
please let your server know.

country have started to issue weight grades that indicate body mass index scores, which are then sent home to parents with information and suggestions on healthy eating. The ultimate goal of these reports is to encourage parents to get involved in helping their children to form healthy eating habits while they are still young.

Restaurants and foodservice chains throughout the country are also pitching in by including healthy options on their menus. In July 2011 the National Restaurant Association launched the "Kids Livewell" program, which has as its purpose the goal of providing parents and their children with healthier food items when they go out. McDonald's led the way by reducing the calorie count of their happy meals by 20%. Arby's followed suit and reduced the total fat of their kids' meals by 10%, the calories by 40%, and the sodium by 40%. Currently over 40,000 restaurants are participating in the Kids Livewell Initiative.

Included in the task of educating kids to eat better in order to prevent health problems, attention must be given to accommodating the growing number of individuals who have gluten intolerance and food allergies. Those who suffer from these diseases must learn how to effectively manage or control their food sensitivities by increasing their product knowledge. Mintel's Gluten-Free Food report conducted in January of 2012 found that 47% of the respondents who consumed gluten-free products wanted to see more of these products, and 44% thought that the items they had tried contained the same nutritional value as their gluten counter parts. General Mills has taken a big step in electing to transform its popular Rice Chex into a totally gluten-free product.

Non-wheat Noodles/Pastas

In recent years chefs and restaurateurs have been introducing healthy alternatives such as grains, noodles, pastas, and rice. During the 2007–08 recession the sales of these products skyrocketed by 13.1%, and further increased by 5.2% from 2008–12. Although there were a number of factors that supported this growth, the most influential was probably the introduction of gluten-free pasta, rice, noodles, soba, and grains such as quinoa, couscous, and barley. Consumers were pleased about the affordability, convenience, and health benefits related to these new alternatives until the drought of 2012, which caused the price of grains to skyrocket and their availability at restaurants to dwindle.

Vernick Food & Drink and Wokworks in Philadelphia, PA, use a variety of rices, Asian noodles, and grains on their menus. Vernick offers Ginger rice, Black Trumpet Mushrooms, and a poached egg as a small plate and an Oven-roasted Veal Loin with Israeli Couscous, Spring Beans, and Pesto as a large plate item. Wokworks provides various noodles and rice starters such as Lo-Mein noodles, rice noodles, buckwheat noodles, brown or white rice, and a red and white quinoa blend. In Los Angeles, Café Gratitude serves a dish called "the Humble" that includes Indian curried lentils with either quinoa or brown rice, oven-roasted Garnet yams, and sautéed spinach that has been drizzled with a spicy mint chutney and sweetened tamarind sauce. The entrée is then topped with chopped scallions. Another interesting dish called "the Terrific" is composed of kelp noodles pasta that is tossed in Thai almond sauce and served with carrots, red bell pepper, and shredded kale, finished with sunflower sprouts and teriyaki almonds. The restaurant also offers sides such as quinoa or rice, black beans or lentils, and flax and buckwheat crackers or tortillas.

Sustainable Seafood

In recent years restaurant chains and restaurants have begun to rethink menu offerings in an effort to sustain rapidly declining species of fish such as Cod, Sea Bass, and Tuna that have been over-fished for decades. Many fish today are farm-raised including catfish, salmon, shrimp, tilapia, cod, halibut, snapper, tuna, and turbot. Restaurants throughout the United States are purchasing and showcasing local fish and seafood on their menus that have been tested for quality and safety, as well as those that have been certified as responsibly managed, before they enter the restaurant.

Legal Sea Foods (Boston, MA) for example, tests shellfish and fish using safety standards at their own quality control center. They quarantine shellfish for 24 hours until they have tested the samples to ensure safety. Legal Sea Foods also measures parts per million of mercury in the swordfish and tuna to verify purity. The restaurant chain Rubio's, is another company committed to sustainable seafood. Their wild-caught Pollack is certified under the guidelines of FAO-Based Responsible Fisheries Management (RFM), while their tilapia is procured from sustainable farms that adhere to Best Aquaculture Practices. Throughout their menu, Rubio's has a symbol near designated dishes such as the Atlantic Salmon, Fish Tacos Especial, and their Signature Beer Battered Fish to reflect that these items are sustainable seafood items. The fast-food giant McDonald's serves fish that bears the Marine Stewardship Council eco-label and Sodexo currently displays the MSG eco-label at eleven locations in Washington, D.C.

Other restaurants serving sustainable and responsibly fished items include Uchiko: in Austin, TX, which works with suppliers to source out their fish, and Fish Story in Napa, CA. Fish Story offers sustainable ocean fresh seafood including Dungeness crab and Maine Lobster from salt water tanks, as well as shellfish and fresh fish that have been carefully sourced in compliance with the Monterey Bay Aquarium's Sea Watch program.

Farm/Estate Branded Items

The idea of farm/estate branded items grew from the farm-to-table movement that was started in the early 1970s by Alice Waters of Chez Panisse in Berkley, CA. This group encouraged local farmers to grow pesticide-free foods that were fresh and could easily be delivered to local customers. The farm-to-table movement continued to expand as did farm/estate branding. Many restaurants today have a relationship with local farms and some restaurant owners and chefs actually own farms to produce and grow food items such as meats, poultry, eggs, cheese, vegetables, and fruits that actually carry their brand names.

Chef Lee Skawinski, who co-owns Vignola Cique Terre with Dan and Michelle Kary, also happens to own Grand View Farm in Greene, ME, which supplies a number of the ingredients used in dishes on the menu such as Eggplant Millefoglie, Charcuterie, Pork and Veal Bolognese, and Pork Loin. Chef Ryan Hardy, who is also committed to the farm-to-table movement, makes cheese at the Montagna at the Little Nell in Aspen, CO. All of the chicken, lamb, meat, and eggs used at the restaurant, come directly from this farm. One of the signature entrées served at the property is the fresh Rigatoni and Rendezvous Farm Lamb Sausage.

In Austin, TX, the Eastside Café features a number of items on the menu from local farms. Locally-raised Holmes all-natural chicken breast is used on the chicken sandwich, and the Niman Ranch all-natural beef is utilized on cheeseburgers and for the Niman Ranch all-natural beef meatloaf that is accompanied with Shiner Bock Bacon and tomato sauce.

Possibly one of the most well-known farm-to-table-restaurants is Flour + Water in San Francisco, CA, which is owned by Chef Thomas McNaughton and managing partner David White. Both have a strong relationship with local farms such as Devils Gulch Ranch in Nicasio, CA, which offers eggs, lamb, pork, poultry, and rabbit, and the Country Line Harvest that grows lettuce, chicory, baby spinach, turnip, Cipolini onions, fennel, baby leeks, summer squash, basil, sage, and parsley that are all organic. Cowgirl Creamery produces organic cheeses for the restaurant.

As long as consumers have a need to know where their food comes from, the farm-to-table movement will continue to thrive in the United States for decades to come. (Figure 1.3)

Figure 1.3

Figure 1.3

Dinner Menu Greens Restaurant, San Francisco, California

Greens Restaurant

January 27, 2013

First Course

Grilled Ridgecut Gristmills Polenta with grilled wild mushrooms, crisp shallots, herb cream, shaved grana padano and arugula   12.50

Yellow Finn Potato Griddle Cakes with manchego, leeks and chives. Served with romesco, crème fraiche and Ecopia Farm herb salad   11.75

Fresh Spring Roll with grilled tofu, carrots, jicama, cucumbers, mint, rice noodles. Served with peanut sauce, beech and shitake mushroom and watermelon radish salad   10.50

Indian Sampler – Basmati rice and chick pea salad with Hamada Farm raisins and cashews; warm coral lentil dal; gingered beets; roasted cauliflower with pepper flakes and mint; apple-winter fruit chutney; roasted garlic papadams   17.00

Artisan Cheese Plate –Andante Dairy Crottin; Cowgirl Creamery Mt. Tam and Devil's Gulch; celery root and herb salad; olives; warm baguette   14.50

Warm Mariquita Farm Cauliflower Salad with crisp capers, pine nuts, mint, tarragon mustard vinaigrette and shaved pecorino fiore sardo   11.50

County Line Lettuce, Little Gems and Watercress with Brokaw avocado, Owari satsumas, cara cara oranges, spiced pumpkin seeds, citrus chili vinaigrette   11.00

Kabocha Squash and Coconut Milk Soup with Thai basil and chilies   Cup   7.50   Bowl   8.50

Main Course

Wild Mushroom Farro Risotto with hedgehog, maitake and grilled matsutake mushrooms, savoy spinach, spring onions, roasted garlic, shaved grana padano   23.00

Winter Lasagne with parsnips, butternut squash, caramelized fennel, sunchokes, roasted onions, thyme, asiago and fromage blanc custard. Served with tomato sherry sauce, broccoli di ciccio with pine nuts and pepper flakes   24.00

Tagine – Winter vegetables with tomatoes, chick peas, ginger, saffron, ras el hanout and cilantro. Served with Hamada Farm fruit and almond couscous, grilled artichoke with lemon oil and mint   23.00   Small   18.00

Goat Cheese Ravioli with Heirloom Organics chard, kale, savoy spinach, spring onions, brown butter, slow roasted almonds, grana padano and chives   23.00

Provencal Potato Pizza with spring onions, asiago, grana padano, pepper flakes, Oaks and arugula pesto   17.50

Mesquite Grilled Brochettes – mushrooms, Little Farm potatoes, peppers, yams, fennel, red onions and Hodo Soy tofu with honey miso sauce, Massa Organics brown and red rice, Asian cabbage slaw   21.00   Single Brochette   17.00

Sides 7.50
Grilled artichokes with lemon oil, mint and romesco
Grilled Ridgecut Gristmills polenta with herb butter
Broccoli di ciccio with pine nuts and pepper flakes
Hummous with grilled pita, spicy tomato jam and olives

REVIEW QUESTIONS

1. Define and explain the term "food hubs."

2. Explain why some companies are said to be at the forefront of the environmental sustainability movement.

3. Discuss why many bakeries and restaurants have begun offering gluten-free-menu items and give three examples of properties that are currently doing so.

4. Define and discuss six factors that directly influence kids' nutrition.

5. Describe how some restaurant chains and restaurants are practicing sustainable seafood methods.

Chapter 2

Concepts and the Strategic Business Plan

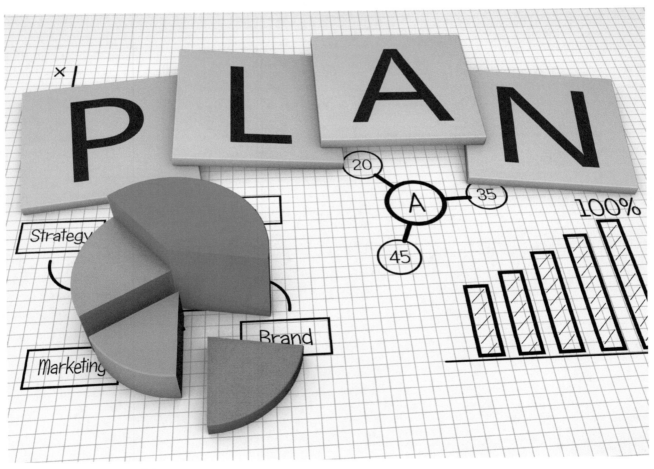

© 2014, pedrosek, Shutterstock, Inc.

OBJECTIVES

Upon completion of this chapter, the student should be able to:

1. define and explain the components of a strategic business plan.
2. evaluate the potential success of a foodservice operation in a selected community.
3. list and explain the components of a customer survey and feasibility study.

KEY TERMS

Strategic Business Plan

Concept

Customer Survey

Feasibility Study

INTRODUCTION

It is common knowledge that the foodservice business is a high-risk investment because so many operations are out of business within a year's time. This chapter examines why many foodservice operations fail and why so few actually succeed. The steps in developing a solid foodservice concept and a sound Strategic Business Plan (SBP) are discussed, as are topics that should be explored prior to selecting a business site, including: market demographics, menus, community demographics, and geography.

Developing a Concept

The concept is the foundation upon which a Strategic Business Plan (SBP) is built. It reflects the owner's business philosophy and serves as a blueprint for what needs to be accomplished to create a successful foodservice operation.

The Entrepreneur's Philosophical Approach

There are two types of entrepreneurs who attempt to start a business. One is the individual who invests time and money to create a successful business, while the other is the person who invests merely to make a maximum profit on a financial investment (see Figure 2.1).

FIGURE 2.1

Characteristics of Entrepreneurs

Entrepreneur #1

1. Has the primary investment goal of earning a maximum return on investment.
2. Considers the style and type of foodservice concept as secondary.
3. Acts mainly as a silent owner and is not typically active in daily operations.
4. Is a financial expert with a sufficient knowledge of foodservice system(s).
5. Carefully analyzes the business plan, the customer survey and feasibility study, and the strategic plan.

Entrepreneur #2

1. Has the primary investment goal of earning a maximum return on investment.
2. Considers the style and type of foodservice concept as very important.
3. Is active in the daily operations, and is willing to invest high sweat equity.
4. Is an expert in foodservice systems and has sufficient knowledge of financial system(s).
5. Does not develop a business plan or analyze a customer survey, feasibility study, or financial strategic plan.

The first type of entrepreneur typically has some knowledge of finance and financial systems. This individual is frequently referred to as a silent owner who invests "to fill the gap," or "to create a niche," by identifying what customers want and what is currently being ignored by existing competitors. He/she will usually use a customer survey or a feasibility study to analyze the current competition, and to identify the wishes and desires of individuals living in the community prior to building a business. If the analysis indicates that there are twelve French restaurants, eight steak and seafood restaurants, twenty Italian restaurants, and one Chinese restaurant, which are all very busy, the limited number of Chinese restaurants would indicate "a gap" when comparing the numbers. This type of entrepreneur would typically choose to build a Chinese restaurant based on this statistic.

The second type of entrepreneur is an active owner who is involved in the creation, development, and implementation of the concept. This person wants to reach a profitable financial goal and is willing to invest "sweat equity," (the amount of time and physical work a person performs on a specific task) to make the business successful. He/she is usually an expert in foodservice systems who elects to hire financial experts. The style of the restaurant, the concept, and the type of cuisine are all very important to this individual. If this entrepreneur enjoys French cuisine, he/she will open this type of restaurant regardless of the number of French cuisine restaurants that already exist in the same community. This type of entrepreneur does not select a concept based on customer surveys, feasibility studies, or the "filling the gap" theory, and often experiences a failed business.

Why Owners Fail

Entrepreneurs who fail within the first year of business, do so because of a lack of knowledge in one or all of these areas: finance, management, foods, beverages, and service. The main reason for this failure is an inability to generate enough money (sales/revenue) to pay the bills. Individuals who start a business often underestimate the amount of capital needed to operate a business. Businesses need a period of time to establish themselves in a community, and require adequate capital to pay expenses. Major obligations, such as having to pay purveyors in cash when deliveries arrive (COD), prior to establishing a line of credit, can be extremely burdensome.

At times, owners make poor hiring decisions as well. Inexperienced owners sometimes hire friends or family members, thinking that a great friendship makes for a great working relationship. Unfortunately, relatives or friends sometimes find it difficult to take orders, and bosses find it difficult to fire friends or family members. Many owners have difficulty saying no to their employees or not saying yes often enough, causing employees to take advantage of situations.

A lack of understanding of food, beverages, service, and foodservice systems is a third area that causes foodservice operators to fail. The great taste of food and/or beverages is the number one reason customers patronize a foodservice operation. Owners must have a working knowledge of ordering, purchasing, receiving, storing, preparing, producing, and serving food and beverages, as well as a working knowledge of health and sanitation codes (laws). Owners who do not know how to implement controls on food and beverage operate at high food and beverage costs and are more apt to serve an inconsistent quality of foods and beverages.

Owners should be knowledgeable about all three areas (finance, hiring, and food and beverage), to successfully manage a foodservice operation. Although they need not serve as the chef, bookkeeper, bartender, wait staff, and front of the house manager, it is invaluable that they have a working knowledge of all of these positions. No single individual is expected to perform all of these jobs.

Successful owners are knowledgeable about these positions, and have the following in common:

1. they enjoy eating and learning about the cuisine and beverages that they are selling.
2. they enjoy being with their target market. If you do not like children, why open a family restaurant?
3. they start at the level at which their experience indicates they should start. Most begin with a small scale foodservice concept and later expand as their experience, knowledge, and business grow.
4. they initially offer a familiar or traditional cuisine, rather than an unfamiliar style of cuisine.
5. they are willing to learn from everyone and know the direction in which they want to go. They are good leaders and understand their limitations.
6. they develop a detailed strategic business plan and follow it. They only make adjustments when absolutely necessary.

Selecting a Foodservice Concept Category

Foodservice segments can be classified in three categories: Quick Service, Casual Dining, and Fine Dining. Quick Service restaurants have low check averages and must generate a high volume of sales. Casual Dining restaurants, on the other hand, have moderate check averages and need a moderate sales volume to show a profit. Fine Dining restaurants can be successful by merely generating a lower sales volume because they have a high check average. A *check average* is the amount of money a customer spends for a meal. Once an owner decides on a foodservice category for an operation, the style of service, the restaurant décor, the menu items, and the prices must reflect that category of choice.

Quick Service concepts are designed for speed and efficiency. They typically have:

- a high turnover rate
- a check average below $7.00
- bright lights; loud noise level; seating of minimal comfort
- allotted footage of 7–12 square feet per person
- posted menus with limited descriptive copy

Casual Service concepts are designed for families and individuals with average disposable income. These properties typically have:

- a moderate turnover rate
- a check average of $15 to $30
- bright to low lighting; pleasant noise level; fairly comfortable seating
- allotted footage of 12–15 square feet per person
- moderate to extensive menu offerings with descriptive copy

Fine Dining concepts cater to individuals with higher disposable income who wish to enjoy a leisurely paced, high-quality meal. They traditionally offer:

- a limited turnover rate
- a check average of $65 to $200
- low to dim lighting; quiet and relaxing noise level; very comfortable seating
- allotted footage of 15–24 square feet per person
- moderate menu offerings with detailed descriptive copy

Once a concept category is selected, it is important to remain focused on that concept throughout the planning and design of the foodservice operation. The philosophies of two concepts do not often blend well, and their designs are incompatible. Blending concepts is difficult to accomplish and is not recommended for inexperienced foodservice operators.

The Business Plan

There are no two business plans that are exactly alike because foodservice operations are unique and have their own characteristics. A Strategic Business Plan (SBP) serves as the blueprint for a particular foodservice operation. It includes all the information needed to make a foodservice operation a successful reality. A template developed by the US Small Business Administration (U.S.S.B.A.) is included in this chapter, and may also be accessed at http://www.sba.gov. There are also several companies that can provide assistance in writing a business plan. Palo Alto Software, Inc. is one such company. Palo Alto Software Inc. has provided a business plan on WebCom for the following property: Rutabaga Sweets (a bakery that sells gourmet desserts). To view examples of some of their other business plans, e.g., Fire Fountain Grille (a family style steak house), Gabri's Restaurant & Lounge (specializes in fine dining), and Studio 67 (an organic restaurant), visit their website at www.paloalto.com. Many business schools and their entrepreneur centers offer training in business plan development.

Before developing a business plan, questions must be answered concerning the services and products that the business is selling; the manner in which the operation will be financed and managed; and the operating policies that will be put in place.

Guidelines to Developing a Business Plan

The logical steps in developing a business plan include:

1. Writing a Company Description
2. Preparing a Market Analysis
3. Developing Organizational and Management Charts
4. Delineating the Services and Products
5. Examining the Market and Potential Sales
6. Analyzing Funding
7. Making Financial Projections
8. Creating an Executive Summary

Writing a Company Description

Writing a company description involves providing a detailed review of the foodservice operation. It includes a summary of the market's needs and how the business is attempting to meet those needs with the products and services it offers. A list of the specific consumers, organizations, and businesses that are served should be included, as well as the competitive advantages that make the business a success (location, expert personnel, efficient operations, or the ability to bring value to your customers). (U.S.S.B.A., 2014.)

Preparing a Market Analysis

A market analysis begins with a description of the foodservice industry, including its current size, historic growth, and current projected growth. A manageable potential target market is selected and the critical needs of these individuals are assessed. Demographics of the market group are analyzed as well as the forecasted market growth for this group. Seasonal or cyclical purchasing trends that may impact the business are also addressed. (U.S.S.B.A.)

Developing Organizational and Management Charts

This section of the business plan includes the organizational chart and profiles of the management team. It shows the contributions and responsibilities of those individuals who will support the success of the foodservice business. (U.S.S.B.A.)

Delineating the Services and Products

The services and products that the business offers, as well as the benefits they provide to potential and current customers, are described in this section. An explanation of how these particular services and products fill the needs of customers is included, as well as any advantages they provide over those of the competition. (U.S.S.B.A.)

Examining the Market and Potential Sales

Once the service and product line has been selected the next step is to focus on marketing and sales strategies. These strategies should be part of an ongoing business-evaluation process and unique to a foodservice operation.

Marketing strategies include the potential for market penetration, a strategy for growth, distribution processes, and a plan for reaching customers.

Sales strategies consist of selecting the individual or team responsible for sales and the specific types of activities they will use to reach customers. A combination of printed matter such as brochures, catalogs, and flyers may be used, in conjunction with media advertising and personal selling to promote sales. (U.S.S.B.A.)

Analyzing Funding

When seeking funding for a business it is important to provide complete and accurate information. Funding requests should include: current funding requirements, anticipated future funding needs, funding for capital expenditures, and anticipated company changes that might affect the ability to pay back your loan.

Making Financial Projections

This section should include a projection of how the owner expects the business to perform during the next five years. It should contain data such as: income statements, balance sheets, cash flow statements, and capital expenditure budgets.

Monthly or quarterly projections for the first year, and yearly projections for years two through five, must also be discussed. It is always important that the projections and the funding requests coincide because creditors will look for inconsistencies. (U.S.S.B.A)

Creating an Executive Summary

The purpose of the executive summary is to inform readers of the essential and critical highlights of a foodservice operation. It provides information concerning the target market, foodservice concept, current finances and goals, marketing strategies, management make-up, and future plans. The executive summary serves to convince readers (especially potential investors), that the entrepreneur will succeed in this enterprise. The executive summary should not exceed two pages. It is the last component of the strategic business plan. (U.S.S.B.A.)

Customer Survey and Feasibility Analysis

A **customer survey** is used to study the market a foodservice operation will target. A feasibility analysis is a customer survey that includes additional information about the foodservice industry including: pricing and gross margin targets, competitive analysis, market share, organization and management, product line or service, marketing and sales, and financial projections.

Elements of a Customer Survey

I. Customer Demographics

Customer surveys study customer demographics to identify and learn what customers want. Customer demands range from simple to complex. Eight key demographic factors are examined when analyzing customer demographics:

1. Age
2. Gender
3. Occupation
4. Income
5. Ethnic Background
6. Household Size
7. Education
8. Food Preference

Age. Age generally indicates the amount of social, work, and life experience that an individual has. A 20-year-old customer has different demands than a 60-year-old customer. Identifying and understanding a targeted age group can help in developing a foodservice concept.

Gender. The knowledge of whether your market is predominately male or female aids in choosing the types of cuisine, the portion sizes, the balancing of calories, the nutritional elements on the menu, and the decor.

Occupation. The type of work the target group performs throughout the day contributes to establishing guidelines concerning menu offerings and portion sizes. Individuals who work and exert a considerable amount of physical energy prefer heartier food items and larger portion sizes. Customers who do less physical work may prefer food selections that have fewer calories and smaller portions.

Knowing the financial strength of companies in the area that employ restaurant patrons is also particularly beneficial. If 75% of the targeted customers work in two office complexes or textile manufacturing plants, and these companies close three months after the foodservice business opens, this change could be catastrophic for the foodservice operation.

Income. Knowing the income bracket of customers is valuable in determining the selling price of items on the menu and in forecasting annual sales. The targeted customer must have enough disposable income to support the proposed check average. Disposable income is the money that is left over after personal expenses, and city, state, and federal taxes have been paid. Typically, the higher a customer's income bracket, the greater the amount of disposable income the individual has.

Ethnic Background. Having a knowledge of the culture, race, or language of the targeted market can assist in selecting the cuisine(s) or traditional ethnic dishes to place on the menu. Understanding cultural traditions can also help in designing and decorating the front of the house.

Household Size. A knowledge of household size (the number of people living within a family), and of the number of households in a selected community, can greatly contribute to the feasibility study. There must be an adequate number of customers within the targeted geographic region to support the foodservice operation.

Education. The higher the education level the market has achieved the more open that market is to trying new foodservice operations. People who have a higher level of education usually have more disposable income and tend to dine out more frequently.

Food Preference. The purpose of studying the demographics of a target market is to gain as much insight and understanding of the likes and dislikes of that group. Understanding the foods that customers prefer assists in sales and contributes to the bottom-line profit. To determine customer food and beverage preferences, collect and compare menus of direct and indirect competition. Direct competition refers to those foodservice operations that are similar in their style of cuisine, check average, targeted market, and concept. Indirect competition includes foodservice operations that do not offer the same concepts and styles of cuisine, but compete for the same customers in the same geographical region.

Collect menus from both direct and indirect foodservice operations. Compare the same menu classifications and sub-classifications on the menus (for example, soups with soups, beef entrées with beef entrées). If ten out of ten menus offer French onion soup, it is a good indication that the customers in this community enjoy French onion soup. If only one out of ten menus features French onion soup, and the other nine feature chicken soup, it would be obvious that chicken soup is preferred. Other ways in which to research food preferences include:

- asking potential purveyors about the foods that are the most popular in the area. Purveyors keep usage charts that indicate the specific foods and quantities that foodservice operations use.
- visiting the direct competition. Observe competing businesses on a busy Friday or Saturday night. Talk with other customers, wait staff, cooks, and possibly the owner. Analyze their entire operation, including their menus and signature items.
- visiting supermarkets at which your targeted customers shop. Visit the day after a busy shopping day. Take note of which foods are left on the shelves or in the display case(s) to determine the foods that customers do not like. Talk with the store owner and counter personnel about the products that are popular.
- analyzing online the types of specialty markets that are in the community. If there are a number of successful gourmet shops and high quality pastry shops within the community, this might indicate that customers are familiar with, and appreciate quality specialty foods.

Community Geographic's Analysis

One of the most important decisions an owner makes is deciding where to locate a foodservice operation. Selecting a prime location with good visibility increases both the customer count and the number of sales. High visibility also reduces advertising expenses.

Population Growth

An examination of the population growth pattern determines whether the population is growing, declining, or maintaining its current number. If there is a great decline, it is important to examine why people are moving away. In a small community the customer base may be too small to support a foodservice operation, while in a large city a small decline may not greatly affect the operation.

Economic Growth and Financial Stability

Examine the financial condition of a city by counting the number of businesses that have "for sale" signs in their windows. Is the city is on the brink of bankruptcy? Research whether companies are relocating and if the unemployment rate is high as compared to the state and national rates. Ask about the commercial tax rates and the commercial real estate value. Observe whether there are local bank branches or bank headquarters. Analyze if the community has more jewelry and shoe stores than pharmacies and liquor stores. Evaluate the number of building permit applications and actual permits issued to assess the financial stability of the community.

Zoning, and Local and State Regulatory Restrictions

There are several types of zones, such as residential, commercial, industrial, school, hospital, no parking, tow, preservation, and environmental zones. All zones have either local, state, or federal codes associated with them. The only zone in which a commercial business cannot operate is a residential zone. All zones require permits and licenses to open a business. All states and cities/towns have other regulatory restrictions such as building codes and parking regulations.

Highway and Road Development

In surveying the community and the exact neighborhood where the foodservice operation might be located, map out roads that are under construction and those that may soon be. Find out the community's plans for road repairs and sewer development as well. Note where one-way streets, stop signs, reduced speed limits, and traffic lights are found. People tend to avoid foodservice operations that are difficult to access. Businesses located on two-way streets traditionally have higher sales than foodservice operations located on one-way streets. Easy access in and out of the foodservice operation's parking lot is also important. Stop signs, low speed limits, and traffic lights allow people, both driving and pedestrian, to have more time to look around and notice the foodservice operation.

Public Services Offered

Examining the services that the community offers to taxpaying business persons is an important consideration. Frequently, only fire, police protection, and street snow removal services are offered.

Potential Sales Generators

A sales generator is a location where potential customers gather and where sales might be generated. Some examples of sales generators are: factories, office buildings, churches, movie theaters, civic centers, busy intersections, sport arenas, and shopping malls. Locations where large groups of people congregate provide potential sales opportunities for foodservice operations. Successful owners usually identify two or more sales generators as part of their customer base profile.

Crime Rate

The crime rate of an area should also be investigated. No one is going to dine or purchase products in a foodservice operation located in a high crime neighborhood. If people fear that something bad may happen at a particular site, they will avoid going there.

School Systems

The presence of a large number and level of schools (elementary, junior high, high schools, and colleges or universities) in a community supports a stable customer base. These schools reflect a need to accommodate a large number of children, and further indicate the presence of a considerable number of families. When families own their homes, they are less likely to "just pick up" and leave town. Communities with numerous schools are positive indicators for selecting a family style foodservice concept.

Purveyors

It is always important to research the types of purveyors in the area, where they are located, and the services they offer, to evaluate the practicality of opening a business in a particular geographic location. Knowing and trusting the purveyor allows business owners to build a long-term business relationship that guarantees the delivery of quality products and services.

There is no scientific method or magical formula that promises instant success, although many financially successful foodservice operators can offer advice on how to reach this goal. Most of these individuals will encourage industry knowledge, hard work, and learning from one's mistakes. Successful foodservice operators understand the importance of developing a business plan and of planning and implementing food and beverage cost controls, as well as financial controls.

Review Questions

1. Explain the differences between quick service, casual dining, and fine dining foodservice concepts.

2. Describe the two types of entrepreneurs.

3. List three reasons why foodservice operations fail.

4. Summarize the eight components of a business plan.

5. What is the importance of conducting a customer survey?

6. Name and explain the two types of competition.

7. Why is it important to analyze both direct and indirect competition?

Chapter 3

Developing and Designing the Sales Menu

COVER

CONTENTS 1   CONTENTS 2

OBJECTIVES

Upon completion of this chapter, the student should be able to:

1. identify and discuss the major classifications on a menu.
2. select and describe menu listings based on variety, balance, and composition.
3. explain the new menu labeling requirements.
4. identify menu classifications according to the restaurant's concept.
5. highlight menu items.
6. discuss the essential elements of printing type: typeface, type size, spacing of type, weight of type, and upper and lowercase letters.
7. explain how to utilize color effectively on the menu.
8. discuss how paper selection relates to menu usage.
9. discuss how menus are printed.

KEY TERMS

Balance	Lowercase	Serif Type
Bold Print	Medium Print	Set Solid
Classifications/Headings	Menu Listings	Subclassifications/Subheadings
Composition	Normal	Texture
Descriptive Copy	Opacity	Truth-in-Menu
Grade	Padded Covers	Typeface
Italics Printing	Points	Uppercase
Laminated Cover	Proof	Variety
Leading	Ream Weight	Weight of Type
Letterspacing	Reverse Type	Wordspacing
Light Print	Sans Serif Type	
Logo	Script	

INTRODUCTION

Developing a menu takes time and careful planning. In the first part of this chapter the basic components of menu development are defined and explained: menu classifications, menu listings, variety, balance, composition, and descriptive copy. Truth-in-menu guidelines and the new menu labeling regulations are also examined.

In the second part of this chapter layout and design is discussed. The layout and design of a menu must be carefully planned in order to produce a menu that is readable and easily understood. The correct placement of headings, subheadings, and menu items; the highlighting of menu items; fundamentals of type; color presentation; paper usage; construction of covers; and printing are examined in detail. All of these elements have a direct relationship to the overall appearance of the menu and can make a favorable and lasting impression on patrons when done correctly.

Menu Classifications

The restaurant concept must first be defined in order to plan a proper menu. The number of **classifications** or **headings** on a menu depends upon the type of restaurant. Most menus have the following classifications: **appetizers, soups, salads, sandwiches, entrées, accompaniments** and **desserts**. There are, of course, other more nontraditional classifications such as: side orders and beverages, which might appear on a luncheon menu, or a pasta section on an ethnic menu. A list of menu classifications with a brief explanation of each follows.

Appetizers

The major purpose of an appetizer is to stimulate the palate before the meal. The portion size is generally small and when accompanied with wine or spirits tends to be spicy. Appetizers can be either hot or cold and include: beef, poultry, fish or seafood, fruits, and vegetables.

Soups

Soups can be either hot or cold and are usually served after the appetizer. Soups are divided into three major categories: clear or unthickened soups, thick soups, and "Specialty" soups. Clear soups consist of: bouillons, broths, consommés, and thin vegetable soups. Thick soups encompass: bisques, chowders, creams, potages, and purées. "Specialty" soups are representative of certain countries or regions and include: Minestrone, French Onion, or Gumbo. Cold soups also fall under the "National" or "Specialty" category and are often served in warmer climates: cucumber, gazpacho, fruit, and vichyssoise are a few examples of cold soups.

Salads

Salads are generally served as an accompaniment or as a main course on the menu. Salads should be fresh and served at the proper temperature whether hot or cold. Accompanying salads can be served in lieu of the appetizer or soup and are sometimes referred to as first course salads. The major purpose of the first course salad is to enliven the palate. Grilled vegetables, fish or seafood, specialty meats, or fruits can be utilized. In fine dining restaurants, the accompanying salad is served before the entrée. These salads are designed to cleanse the palate; they should be light in nature and consist of mixed greens such as Bib and Belgian endive. Main course salads or cold plates are referred to as cold entrées. Lobster salad, chicken salad with apple and walnuts, or grilled vegetable plates with aged balsamic and pecorino are a few examples of cold entrées.

Sandwiches

Sandwiches can be served cold or hot and might contain beef, poultry, fish or seafood, and vegetables. Sandwiches are generally found on the luncheon menu and can be simple to elaborate: ranging from a chicken salad sandwich, to a grilled swordfish sandwich provençale served open faced.

Entrées

Entrées are usually also separated into hot or cold sections on the menu. Hot entrées are the largest classification on the menu and are sometimes further broken down into **subclassifications** or **subheadings**. These can include: meat, poultry, and fish and seafood. Cold entrées make up a smaller classification; therefore, subclassifications are not warranted. Generally, a listing of main course salads or cold plates follows the cold entrées.

Hot Entrées

Meats. Meats are the largest subclassification on the menu and contain: beef, lamb, pork, and veal. Menu listings should be adequately represented to ensure proper cross-utilization. Cooking techniques must also be well balanced and include: braising, broiling, frying, grilling, roasting, sautéing, and smoking. An adequate representation of cooking techniques facilitates proper rotation of kitchen equipment and takes into consideration customer preferences.

Poultry. The poultry subclassification on the menu includes chicken, duck, pheasant, quail, and turkey. Poultry is relatively inexpensive to procure and can be cooked in a variety of ways: baked, barbecued, braised, fried, grilled, roasted, and smoked. Poultry can be cross-utilized with relative ease throughout the menu in appetizers, soups, salads, and entrées. Chicken and turkey, over the last decade, have risen in popularity due to health concerns over high-fat and high-cholesterol in the diet. They have become healthier alternatives to red meats.

Fish and Seafood. Fish and seafood are rich in flavor and are an excellent source of protein. Fish and seafood listings can be numerous and include freshwater fish and saltwater fish such as: flatfish, round fish, mollusks, and crustaceans. Fish and seafood can also be prepared a number of ways: baked, broiled, fried, grilled, poached, roasted, sautéed, and smoked. Unfortunately, fish and seafood are highly perishable, and therefore, should be carefully handled and served immediately.

Cold Entrées. As mentioned earlier, cold entrées generally encompass main course salads or cold plates. Main course salads might consist of: a grilled duck salad with vegetable couscous and fall greens, or Caesar salad with lobster. Cold plate listings might include herb salad with cured scallops and brioche sticks, or a fruit and cheese plate with an assortment of smoked meats. Cold entrées are a welcomed addition to the menu for patrons who prefer lighter fare.

Accompaniments

Accompaniments on the menu consist of vegetables, potatoes, rice, and pastas. Both vegetables and starches are low in calories and are relatively inexpensive to prepare. Accompaniments can be cooked in a variety of ways: baked, grilled, roasted, sautéed, and steamed. When accompaniments are prepared correctly and presented with the appropriate entrées on an à la carte menu, they can contribute considerably in increasing the overall check average.

Desserts

Desserts are relatively inexpensive to prepare, and when merchandised and served correctly, are extremely profitable. A variety of choices should be included in the dessert section of the menu: fresh cakes, cobblers or crisps, fruits, ice creams, pies, puddings, sorbets, specialty items, and tarts.

Menu Listings

Once the menu classifications have been selected, **menu listings** must be chosen. The menu listings in each classification vary depending upon the demographics, the type of restaurant, the geographical location, the accessibility of product, the equipment capacity, and the skill level of employees. All these factors must be considered when preparing menu listings. After the tentative menu listings are assembled, they should be reexamined in terms of variety, balance, and composition.

Variety

Variety refers to the diversity of product; hot and cold offerings; the cooking techniques used; and the color, configuration, taste, height, and texture of the menu items. Each component of variety must be fully addressed within each menu classification.

Hot and Cold Items. The number of hot and cold items on a menu has a direct correlation to the geographical location of the restaurant and the season. Hot or cold items can be offered in appetizer, soup, salad, sandwich, entrée, and dessert categories.

Cooking Techniques. Each classification of the menu should incorporate a variety of cooking techniques when possible, in order to facilitate equipment equalization within the kitchen, and to ensure customer satisfaction (Figure 3.1).

Figure 3.1

Menu Classifications and Cooking Techniques

Menu Classification	Cooking Techniques
Appetizers	Baking, barbecuing, frying, grilling, and smoking
Soups	Simmering
Salads	Grilling, poaching, roasting, and smoking
Sandwiches	Baking, barbecuing, broiling, frying, grilling, and roasting
Hot Entrées	
Meats	Braising, broiling, frying, grilling, roasting, sautéing, and smoking
Poultry	Braising, barbecuing, broiling, frying, grilling, roasting, sautéing, and smoking
Fish and Seafood	Baking, broiling, frying, grilling, poaching, roasting, sautéing, and smoking
Cold Entrées	Grilling, poaching, roasting, and smoking
Accompaniments	Baking, roasting, sautéing, and steaming
Desserts	Baking, poaching, and freezing

Color. A variety of vibrant, as well as earth tone colors, certainly adds eye appeal to any presentation. Scrod with bread crumbs, rice, and cauliflower is less attractive than roast ham with raisin sauce, au gratin potatoes, and French green beans with almonds. Today, patrons have come to expect an eye-appealing plate which has the proper balance of vibrant and earth tone colors. Remember, 50 percent of all sales is based on visual presentation.

Configuration. A variety of configurations of food items on a plate has a direct relationship to eye appeal. Configuration takes into consideration special cuts, slices, molds, and loose or whole food items. The rather flat configuration of a roasted tenderloin of beef entrée, served with zucchini provençale and lyonnaise potatoes, is far surpassed in attractiveness by the mixed configurations offered in a tuna steak with citrus butter, rice pilaf, and asparagus presentation.

Taste. Be careful not to overload the menu with too many spicy or bland foods. Spicy, as well as bland, foods need to be balanced throughout the menu. When composing any plate, remember this fundamental rule: spicy entrées are desirable with bland accompaniments and bland entrées are advisable with spicy accompaniments.

Height. The aesthetic qualities of each food item on the plate are enhanced through a presentation that incorporates a variety of heights. An entrée of veal schnitzel, potato pancakes, and shredded red cabbage are all fairly level in height, whereas, sirloin steak, garlic mashed potatoes, and broccoli offer diverse heights.

Texture. Menu items can contain a variety of textures. These textures include crispy, liquid, chewy, solid, and soft. A complete meal should have an abundance of textures rather than just one or two. For instance, a Chinese menu might encompass: crispy fried wantons; liquid egg drop soup; slightly chewy and crispy mandarin orange salad; solid, chewy, and soft Peking duck with pancakes; soft rice; and slightly crispy stir-fried vegetables.

Balance

Within each menu classification, there must be a proper **balance** of food items, hot and cold offerings, cooking techniques, colors, configurations, tastes, heights, and textures. Appetizers should include meats, poultry, fish, seafood, fruit, and vegetable selections. There should also be a somewhat equal number of hot and cold offerings in the appetizer classification. Cooking techniques might include: baking, barbecuing, frying, grilling, and smoking. Color, configuration, taste, height, and texture must also be examined when composing the appetizer classification. Prosciutto with Chanterelles and Tomatoes, Grilled Chicken Tortilla with Fresh Salsa, Fried Rock Shrimp with Organic Greens and Chive Mustard Sauce, and Goat Cheese Bruschetta with Pan Seared Garden Tomatoes demonstrate the fundamental principles of balance.

Composition

Composition refers to the presentation of food on a plate. Both variety and balance are an integral part of composition. When composing a plate, keep in mind traditional food combinations such as: roast ham with sweet potatoes, or au gratin potatoes and green beans; or lobster with corn on the cob, baked potato, and coleslaw. Looking to traditional combinations can greatly simplify the task of composition development.

Descriptive Copy

Descriptive copy essentially introduces the menu listings to the customers. Depending upon the menu listing, descriptive copy includes some or all of the following elements: size of portion, geographical origin, product, primary and secondary ingredients, method of preparation, and appropriate accouterments. For instance, a menu item listed as BAKED STUFFED LOBSTER might include the following descriptive copy: a two pound Maine lobster stuffed with crab meat, scallops, and seasoned Ritz® cracker crumbs, baked and served with drawn butter. When writing a descriptive copy, remember the following:

1. Keep the explanation simple, clear, and concise.
2. Exclude words such as "best," "colossal," "extraordinary," "magnificent," and "superb."
3. Use appropriate food terminology such as: chilled, glazed, flaky, grilled, medallions, sautéed, toasted, and whipped.

Truth-in-Menu

Once the major components of the menu have been developed, an examination of legal regulations should be addressed. Legally, each food item description advertised on the menu must be completely accurate. Several states have passed **truth-in-menu** legislation to deter deceptive advertising on the menu. If a restaurant violates truth-in-menu, legislation fines, court expenses, and negative publicity can result.

It is important that restaurants serve exactly what they advertise on the menu. Portion size for steaks is often described by weight. Because it is generally assumed that the stated weight of such an item is the actual weight prior to cooking, it can be legitimately listed as such on the menu. Food items from specific geographical locations must also be accurately described. Duck cannot be advertised as Long Island Duck if it is not specifically from that area. When substitutions of menu items are necessary because of availability, price or merchandising considerations, foodservice operations must specify that these changes are being made. Flounder cannot be substituted at will for sole, cod for haddock, ground beef for ground sirloin of beef, or Roquefort cheese for blue cheese.

Because the cooking method of food items is often a deciding factor in a customer's selection, the method listed on the menu must also be exactly as stated. Items that are described as smoked, grilled, barbequed, stir-fried, or poached must be prepared as indicated. When brand name items are advertised to assure patrons of a quality product, it is important that Tabasco® sauce, Godiva® chocolate, Haagen-Dazs® ice cream, 7-Up and Ritz crackers are actually used, and are not replaced by generic brands. In the intended spirit of truth-in menu, items prepared on premises must also be qualified as "made in house" rather than "home made."

Menu Labeling Regulations

The Food and Drug Administration (FDA) has recently proposed labeling regulations for "restaurants and other similar retail food establishments" that have at least 20 locations, are conducting business under the same name, and are essentially offering similar menu items. Other types of properties that sell restaurant-type food and dedicate greater than 50% of their total floor area to the sale of food would have to adhere to these labeling requirements.

The proposed regulations would require that restaurants and other food producing and processing retail establishments clearly display the calorie content of all food items with the designations "calories" or "cal" on their menus, menu boards and drive-through boards. The suggested daily caloric intake as well as a clear and succinct statement concerning the availability of additional nutritional facts would also have to be posted to assist consumers in understanding the overall importance of calorie information. The information required would include:

1. Total calories
2. Calories from fat
3. Total fat
4. Saturated fat
5. Cholesterol
6. Trans fat
7. Sodium
8. Total carbohydrates
9. Sugars
10. Dietary fiber
11. Protein

State and local governments would not be permitted to enforce different or additional nutritional requirements for foods sold at restaurants and similar food establishments under these proposed guidelines.

Implementing a Healthy Choice

Professionals in the foodservice industry have been working very hard to keep up with customers' demands for menus that offer them a choice of healthy meals. Many foodservice companies have been adapting their menus to offer a variety of healthy menu items such as appetizers, soups, entrée salads, entrées, and desserts. Customers who want to maintain a healthy life style are requesting more information on nutrition including the number of calories, the sodium and cholesterol content, and the grams of fat in dishes listed on the menu.

The challenge for foodservice managers and chefs is to serve both customers who want to maintain a healthy life style and customers who do not want to maintain a healthy life style while dining out. How do they provide the necessary information on the menu to satisfy both customers without upsetting either party?

In the past customers frowned upon menus that communicated healthy menu items by using a designated logo or symbol such as a heart. Customers who wanted to eat healthy did not want to be singled out by letting other people in their party know they wanted to eat healthy. Customers who did not want to eat healthy but knew they should eat healthier dishes found the heart label to be annoying. Today customers are demanding that companies in the foodservice industry—from limited serve to fine dining establishments—provide customers with nutritional information and a greater selection of healthy menu items so they can make an informed choice of what to eat.

Layout

Layout is nothing more than the placement of headings, subheadings, and menu items on the menu.

Identifying Menu Classifications or Headings

Generally, the classifications used on a menu reflect the type of restaurant and its offerings. When naming menu classifications, make sure that they are easily identified and not misleading to the customer. A list of menu classifications and names you might find in a casual dining restaurant follows (Figure 3.2).

Figure 3.2
Menu Classifications

Appetizers	5	Beginnings
Soups	5	Hearty Alternatives
Salads	5	Refreshing Complements
Entrées	5	Repast
Desserts	5	Finale

Occasionally, a restaurant such as a sports bar with a distinct theme, identifies menu classifications with names appropriate to a particular sport. Figure 3.3 uses menu classification names which are appropriate to baseball.

Figure 3.3

A List of Menu Classifications and Names in a Sports Bar

Appetizers	5	Singles
Soups	5	Doubles
Salads	5	Triples
Sandwiches	5	Home Runs
Entrées	5	Grand Slams
Side Orders	5	Extra Innings
Desserts	5	Bases Loaded

Sequence of Menu Classifications or Headings

The sequence of classifications on a menu should be listed in the order that they are consumed: appetizers, soups, salads, entrées, followed by desserts. Sometimes the sequence and type of menu classification varies depending on the foodservice establishment and meal period. For instance, a family restaurant that serves lunch might list appetizers, soups, salads, sandwiches, entrées, side orders, and then desserts. A white table cloth restaurant would most likely list appetizers, soups, entrées, and finish with salads (to cleanse the palate), before dessert is served.

Organizing Menu Subclassifications or Subheadings

Oftentimes subclassifications are listed under major classifications on the menu. On a typical dinner menu, below the entrée classification, the subclassifications might read: meat, poultry, fish, and seafood. These subclassifications are not subject to any particular sequence; meats for example, need not precede poultry. Once subclassifications have been finalized, the menu items must be carefully selected.

Listing Menu Items

Menu items should be grouped by the type of product. Under the entrée classification, for example, the poultry subclassification should list all chicken dishes together. Menu items should also be listed based on profitability, in lieu of price. Many restaurants list the most expensive menu items first and then proceed in descending order. When restaurants do this, customers tend to focus on the price instead of the item, and this can have a negative impact on sales. Profitable food items should be strategically placed at the top and bottom of a column. Less profitable food items can be located in the middle of a column, as patrons generally focus on the top and bottom first, and then skim the remaining food listings.

Highlighting Menu Items

After the menu items are selected, arranged, and listed, it is imperative that food items be placed in an appropriate position on the page. The type of menu a restaurant utilizes has a direct correlation to where a patron's eye focuses. On a one-page or three-page menu, customers generally look to the center upper third of the menu page. However, on a two-page menu, the eye usually focuses on the middle section of the right-hand side. Regardless of the type of menu the restaurant uses, management can utilize merchandising space to highlight specials, signature items, highly profitable food, or beverage selections.

Design

Once the placement of headings, subheadings, and menu items has been completed, attention must be given to the design process. The most important factors to consider in the design phase are readability and customer acceptance of the menu. The menu should be designed to reflect the restaurant's atmosphere and decor. For example, a fine dining menu might have a leather or suede cover with the restaurant's name and logo embossed in gold. Inside, the menu might have a light cream-colored paper with Times Roman type in black. This menu would certainly give patrons a favorable first impression and hint at what is to come throughout the meal. A menu is an overall reflection of the restaurant and can set a positive or negative mood for the entire dining experience.

Typefaces

The **typeface** or style of lettering that is selected for a menu has an impact on the patron. Typeface must be legible and compatible with the overall design of the menu. Most importantly, the selection of a particular typeface should disclose the charm and individuality of the restaurant. Commercial script typeface, for example, implies elegance and is often used on fine dining menus.

There are several different kinds of typeface or styles of lettering employed on a menu. A typeface which is frequently utilized is Serif type. **Serif type** has letters that are slightly curved, such as Palatino, and is easier to read. Serif type is often used for menu items and descriptive copy on the menu. On the other hand, **Sans serif type**, which is more difficult to read because of its blocky letters, might be utilized for headings and subheadings on the menu. Figure 3.4 offers samples of type found on a menu.

Print generally comes in four forms: normal, bold, script, and italics. **Normal** printing, such as Times Roman which is the easiest to read, can be employed for headings, subheadings, menu items, and descriptive copy on the menu. Bold print, as in the case of Bondi Regular, should only be utilized for headings and subheadings on the menu. **Script** (generally referred to as Commercial Script), due to the difficulty of its readability, should only be used for headings, subheadings, and menu items. However, in some cases, when descriptive copy is limited on the menu, Commercial Script might be employed. In **italics printing**, letters are slanted upward towards the right which also makes readability difficult. Italics is generally used for headings, subheadings, and key phrases in descriptive copy. Remember, script and italics are problematic to read and must be used sparingly on the menu. If the patron has difficulty reading a menu, it has a negative effect on sales.

Figure 3.4
Samples of Type

Serif

Times Roman

Flaky pastry shells filled with freshly chopped tomatoes sautéed in butter with parsley and shallots. Topped with poached eggs and covered with Hollandaise sauce.

Bookman

Flaky pastry shells filled with freshly chopped tomatoes sautéed in butter with parsley and shallots. Topped with poached eggs and covered with Hollandaise sauce.

Garamond

Flaky pastry shells filled with freshly chopped tomatoes sautéed in butter with parsley and shallots. Topped with poached eggs and covered with Hollandaise sauce.

Palatino

Flaky pastry shells filled with freshly chopped tomatoes sautéed in butter with parsley and shallots. Topped with poached eggs and covered with Hollandaise sauce.

Sans Serif

Avant Garde

Flaky pastry shells filled with freshly chopped tomatoes sautéed in butter with parsley and shallots. Topped with poached eggs and covered with Hollandaise sauce.

Futura

Flaky pastry shells filled with freshly chopped tomatoes sautéed in butter with parsley and shallots. Topped with poached eggs and covered with Hollandaise sauce.

Erie

Flaky pastry shells filled with freshly chopped tomatoes sautéed in butter with parsley and shallots. Topped with poached eggs and covered with Hollandaise sauce.

Helvetica

Flaky pastry shells filled with freshly chopped tomatoes sautéed in butter with parsley and shallots. Topped with poached eggs and covered with Hollandaise sauce.

Type Size

Type size on a menu should be large enough so that the patron can read the menu clearly and easily. Printing that is too small makes reading the menu problematic. On the other hand, printing that is too large can take up valuable merchandising space.

Type size on a menu is measured in **points**. On any menu, there should be a variation of point sizes. For instance, headings and subheadings can be 18 point type, menu items 12 point type, and descriptive copy 10 point type. If all of the type sizes are the same on a menu, it can be very monotonous to read and may again jeopardize sales (Figure 3.5).

Figure 3.5
Samples of Type Sizes

4-Point Type

Flaky pastry shells filled with freshly chopped tomatoes sautéed in butter with parsley and shallots. Topped with poached eggs and covered with Hollandaise sauce.

5-Point Type

Flaky pastry shells filled with freshly chopped tomatoes sautéed in butter with parsley and shallots. Topped with poached eggs and covered with Hollandaise sauce.

5 1/2-Point Type

Flaky pastry shells filled with freshly chopped tomatoes sautéed in butter with parsley and shallots. Topped with poached eggs and covered with Hollandaise sauce.

6-Point Type

Flaky pastry shells filled with freshly chopped tomatoes sautéed in butter with parsley and shallots. Topped with poached eggs and covered with Hollandaise sauce.

7-Point Type

Flaky pastry shells filled with freshly chopped tomatoes sautéed in butter with parsley and shallots. Topped with poached eggs and covered with Hollandaise sauce.

8-Point Type

Flaky pastry shells filled with freshly chopped tomatoes sautéed in butter with parsley and shallots. Topped with poached eggs and covered with Hollandaise sauce.

9-Point Type

Flaky pastry shells filled with freshly chopped tomatoes sautéed in butter with parsley and shallots. Topped with poached eggs and covered with Hollandaise sauce.

10-Point Type

Flaky pastry shells filled with freshly chopped tomatoes sautéed in butter with parsley and shallots. Topped with poached eggs and covered with Hollandaise sauce.

11-Point Type

Flaky pastry shells filled with freshly chopped tomatoes sautéed in butter with parsley and shallots. Topped with poached eggs and covered with Hollandaise sauce.

12-Point Type

Flaky pastry shells filled with freshly chopped tomatoes sautéed in butter with parsley and shallots. Topped with poached eggs and covered with Hollandaise sauce.

14-Point Type

Flaky pastry shells filled with freshly chopped tomatoes sautéed in butter with parsley and shallots. Topped with poached eggs and covered with Hollandaise sauce.

Spacing of Type

The amount of spacing between each letter in a word is referred to as **letterspacing**; and the amount of spacing between each word is known as **wordspacing**. Both influence the readability of type on the menu. Letters and words should be typeset so that they are not too condensed or too far apart to make for easier reading. Attention to the vertical spacing between the lines of type, known as **leading**, is also important. Leading, similar to type, is also measured in points. When there is no leading between lines on a menu, this is referred to as **set solid**. Generally, three point leading should be utilized on a menu to simplify reading (Figure 3.6).

Figure 3.6

Samples of Leading

Solid

Bananas Foster . . . A Brennan creation and World Famous! Bananas sautéed in butter, brown sugar, cinnamon and banana liqueur, then flamed in rum. Served over vanilla ice cream. Scandalously Delicious!

1-Point Leading

Bananas Foster . . . A Brennan creation and World Famous! Bananas sautéed in butter, brown sugar, cinnamon and banana liqueur, then flamed in rum. Served over vanilla ice cream. Scandalously Delicious!

2-Point Leading

Bananas Foster . . . A Brennan creation and World Famous! Bananas sautéed in butter, brown sugar, cinnamon and banana liqueur, then flamed in rum. Served over vanilla ice cream. Scandalously Delicious!

3-Point Leading

Bananas Foster . . . A Brennan creation and World Famous! Bananas sautéed in butter, brown sugar, cinnamon and banana liqueur, then flamed in rum. Served over vanilla ice cream. Scandalously Delicious!

4-Point Leading

Bananas Foster . . . A Brennan creation and World Famous! Bananas sautéed in butter, brown sugar, cinnamon and banana liqueur, then flamed in rum. Served over vanilla ice cream. Scandalously Delicious!

5-Point Leading

Bananas Foster . . . A Brennan creation and World Famous! Bananas sautéed in butter, brown sugar, cinnamon and banana liqueur, then flamed in rum. Served over vanilla ice cream. Scandalously Delicious!

Weight of Type

The **Weight of Type** on a menu refers to the lightness or heaviness of the print. Generally, **light print** looks gray and is difficult to read. Therefore, light print should never appear on a menu. **Medium print**, on the other hand, is darker than gray and is often utilized in books, magazines, and newspapers. Medium print should be applied to descriptive copy on the menu. **Bold print**, which is employed primarily to add emphasis, can be used for headings, subheadings, and menu items, but never for descriptive copy. Frequently, the name of a restaurant featured on the front cover is in bold print as well.

Uppercase and Lowercase Letters

Typeface can be set in either uppercase, capital letters (A, B, C), or lowercase, small letters (a, b, c). Uppercase is predominantly used for headings, subheadings, and menu items we wish to emphasize. When descriptive copy is employed on the menu, each sentence should begin with an uppercase letter, followed by lowercase letters. Also, when proper nouns are used on a menu, their first letter should be capitalized: Sauce Béarnaise or Shiitake mushrooms. On the other hand, lowercase letters are easier to read than uppercase letters and should be utilized for descriptive copy. Generally, it is advantageous to use both uppercase and lowercase type on the menu to ensure readability.

Describing Menu Items

When describing menu items, keep the explanation simple and the number of sentences to a minimum. A longer sentence may cause customers to lose their place or their concentration. The length of a sentence should not be longer than 22 picas, or about three and two-thirds inches long.

Margins

Margins on the menu should be uniform from top to bottom, and left to right. One and one half inch margins are commonplace on menus. The key is to have well-defined margins without crowding the descriptive copy. If overcrowding becomes an issue, additional pages can be added.

Color

Color also affects the readability of a menu. Black type on light-tinted paper (cream, ivory, tan, or white) is easy to read. Menus printed in colored ink or on colored paper are difficult to read. If type is printed in blue, brown, or red make sure that the print is dark and on white paper. Dark colored print on dark colored paper can also be problematic to read and should be avoided. Green print on red, or black on reddish orange paper also limits legibility. Copy in a light color on dark paper is difficult to read as well: white print on black, referred to as reverse type, should not be used.

Headings, subheadings, and menu items can be printed in a bold secondary color on the menu to distinguish them from medium colored type used for descriptive copy. Remember, the colors selected for the print and paper should complement the restaurant's decor. In a specialty restaurant with a nautical theme, blue print on white would be appropriate and easy to read.

Paper

Paper is made of a number of materials: wood pulp, fabric, chemical, and fiber compounds. Generally, most papers that are utilized for menus are wood based and coated or treated with clay, pigment, varnish, or plastic. Most restaurants select paper based on menu usage. A menu that is designated for durability is usually printed on heavy, coated paper such as heavy cover, Bristol, or tag stock, which has been coated with clay, pigment, varnish, or plastic. These menus generally last an extended period of time, despite extensive customer usage, as they are extremely durable and easy to clean. On the other hand, a menu that changes daily is usually printed on lightweight, noncoated paper that is less expensive. In many cases, menus can be printed on more than one type of paper to curtail expenditures. A strong, heavy, coated paper might be employed for the menu cover; and a lighter weight and less permanent paper for the interior pages. The menu planner must keep in mind that paper represents 30% to 50% of the total menu cost.

When selecting the paper, take into consideration the following elements: texture, opacity, color, strength, weight, and grade. Textures can vary from very smooth or coated paper, to a slightly rough surface, such as antique eggshell, or vellum finish. Since customers generally hold the menu in their hands, the **texture** or "feel" is noteworthy. Another concern when selecting paper is opacity. The **opacity** of paper refers to the inability of light to penetrate through it. Maximum opacity is important regardless of the color of the paper. Paper colors can range from white and pastels to dark solids; but as mentioned earlier, light-tinted paper is the easiest to read.

The strength of the paper is the next consideration: paper with short pulp fibers is weaker and does not hold up well. The durability of paper also depends to a lesser degree on weight. Paper is manufactured and identified according to its **ream weight**: the weight in pounds for five hundred sheets in a basic size, for that appropriate grade. **Grade** is the name given to paper, based on its intended utilization (Figure 3.7).

Figure 3.7
Types of Paper Used for Menus

Antique paper	Paper with a rough and textured surface
Bond paper	Paper utilized for forms, letterheads, and business correspondence
Book paper	Paper having attributes suitable for books, brochures, and magazines
Bristol	Cardboard which is 0.006 of an inch or more in thickness (index, mill and wedding paper are examples of Bristol
Coated	Paper of paperboard which has been treated with clay or some other pigment
Cover stock	A variety of papers utilized for the exterior cover of menus, booklets, catalogs, and magazines
Deckle edge	Paper with a feathered, uneven edge which is left untrimmed
Dull-coat	Paper coated with a low-gloss surface
Eggshell	Paper with a semi-rough exterior similar to the exterior of an egg
Enamel	Paper coated with a high-gloss surface
English finish	A book paper with a machine finish and uniform surface
Machine finish	A book paper with a medium finish, rougher than English finish, but smoother than eggshell
Matte coat	A coated paper with little or no glass surface
Offset paper	Coated or uncoated paper suitable for offset lithography printing
Vellum finish	A finish similar to eggshell, but from harder stock with a finer grained surface

Cover

The cover is the symbol of a restaurant's identity. The cover should be carefully designed, attractive, and complement the restaurant's decor and style. A fine dining menu might use leather or simulated leather with the restaurant's logo embossed in silver on the cover in order to reflect its more elegant and refined decor; whereas, a family style casual restaurant, or a dinner house, might decide on bright colors on a **laminated cover**, which is usually cardboard covered with a clear plastic coating to ensure longevity.

The selection of paper for the cover can be determined by how often the menu is used. If the menu is in the form of a place mat, light weight stock should be utilized. On the other hand, if the cover is permanent, heavy, cover stock, and Bristol or tag stock, are more appropriate. In some white table cloth restaurants, **padded covers** are popular. These permanent covers are protected with a durable plastic or other materials such as leather, simulated leather, linen, silk, suede, or velvet. These materials are often laminated onto a light board or heavy cardboard, and then packed with material, resulting in a menu cover that has a padded appearance.

Once the menu cover has been chosen, the menu planner must decide what is acceptable to put on the front and back covers. Copy on the front can include the name of the restaurant or a **logo** (an identifying symbol unique to an operation). Other information such as the address, phone number, hours of operation, credit card acceptance, reservation policy, history of the operation, management's philosophy, catering and banquet information, and takeout information can be printed on the back cover. Whenever possible, avoid placing food or beverages on the back cover as many patrons tend to overlook those items.

Printing the Menu

There are a number of options available for printing the menu. These include: **professional printers, advertising agencies/artists designers** and **desktop publishers.**

Professional Printers

The major advantage of having a menu professionally printed is the number of professionals on staff. These include: writers, artists or free-lance artists, production personnel, and designers who can assist the restaurateur in the layout and design of the menu. Once the layout and design is completed, the menu can be typeset into a computer system. The typesetting program then duplicates the type on photographic paper or transparent film. The result is a copy of the type according to specifications, called the proof or the galley. The proof must be scrutinized for punctuation, misspelled words, and incorrect phrases. All corrections are made and then fed into the computer.

Advertising Agencies/Artists Designers

Occasionally, restaurants work with advertising agencies to help generate publicity. At times, these agencies also assist in the writing, layout, and design of the menu as well. Commercial artists or graphic designers, on the other hand, are generally responsible for just the layout and design of the menu, while the writing is left up to the menu planner or menu planning consultant.

Desktop Publishers

Printing the menu in-house on a computer and utilizing a laser color printer, has a number of advantages:

1. the wine list and menu can be changed on a daily basis to meet customer demand.
2. managers and chefs can react promptly to price fluctuations in the market place.
3. the chef can take advantage of regional and seasonal items by placing them on a menu at any time.
4. the restaurant is able to print special occasion and promotional menus when necessary.
5. desktop publishing saves money on overall menu costs such as typesetting.
6. in-house publishing is convenient.

Review Questions

1. Name the seven menu classifications and create eight menu listings for each.

2. How does variety and balance play an important role in composition on a menu?

3. Write a descriptive copy for the following menu items:
   Crabcakes
   Seafood Corn Chowder
   Caesar Salad
   Grilled Swordfish with Citrus Salsa
   Brown Rice Pilaf
   Peach Crisp

4. What impact do menu labeling regulations have on restaurants?

5. Select a particular restaurant concept. List and describe the type of headings, subheadings, and menu items you would use on your menu. Write the descriptive copy for each of the menu items. Choose the typeface, size of print, and color for the headings, subheadings, menu items, and descriptive copy. Select the paper for the inside and cover of the menu. Explain the cover and design in detail.

6. What are different options available for printing a menu?

7. Define the following terms:
   Serif Type
   Sans Serif Type
   Italic Printing
   Letterspacing
   Wordspacing
   Leading
   Set Solid
   Uppercase
   Lowercase
   Reverse Type
   Opacity

Chapter 4

Standards, Measurements, Recipes, and Formulas

OBJECTIVES

Upon completion of this chapter, the student should be able to:

1. define, standard recipe, standard yield, standard portion and standard presentation.
2. understand the difference between a standard recipe and a standard formula.
3. write a standard recipe/formula.
4. convert units of measure.
5. convert standard recipes and formulas to a new standard yield.

KEY TERMS

Baker's Ratio

Conversion Rate Factor (CRF)

Method of Preparation

Standard

Standard Beverage Presentation

Standard Formula

Standard Portion

Standard Plate Presentation

Standard Procedures

Standard Recipe

Standard Yield

INTRODUCTION

Foodservice operators set the stage for efficient operations by setting standards. Standards are rules, policies, or statements set by chef/managers, to help employees perform quality tasks, produce quality products, and provide excellent service. Before chefs develop original recipes, they must practice their craft and prove that they are able to produce consistent quality products. Successful foodservice operators often state that it is easier to get customers into restaurants a first time, than it is to get them to return for a second or third visit. It would be a sound practice to set the goal of having every customer who walks into the restaurant/bakeshop become a repeat customer, who also speaks highly of the experience to hundreds of friends and business associates. Customers return when they are consistently served quality food and beverages.

Quality standards should be developed and used when purchasing food and beverages, preparing meals, writing recipe cards, answering the telephone, greeting customers, serving customers, taking inventory, performing yield tests, determining portion controls, creating plate presentations, closing out cash registers, cleaning and sanitizing equipment, hiring, and training employees. Established standards allow for consistency and cost controls. When there are no set performance standards, there is little consistency in the quality of the tasks performed and the costs of doing business are likely to increase. Customers want to experience food and service that are great at every visit.

Standards in Foodservice

The Standard Recipe/The Standard Formula

The most common resource used in foodservice kitchens is the standard recipe. A **standard recipe** is a written formula used to produce food and beverage items that are of a consistent quantity and quality. Standard recipe items are always prepared using the same preparation method and prescribed products. In the United States, the quantities of ingredients used in these recipes are usually listed using US Standard units of measure. When chefs stray from a standard recipe, the product generated is not consistent with what customers might expect. Both food menu items and beverage items need standard recipes to maintain consistency and to control costs. Many traditional and popular drinks have standardized recipes that are documented and published in bartending books. Foodservice operations sometimes have their own variations to these traditional and popular drinks for which they should also develop standard recipes. Beverage Standard Recipes state the ingredients of the beverage, the exact measurement of the ingredients, the garnish to be used, and the size and type of glass in which the product is served.

In baking and pastry kitchens, the term standard recipe is often replaced with the term **standard formula**. Standard formulas commonly use Metric units of measure to list quantities of ingredients and often include US Standard units of measure. It is imperative that when chefs create baked and pastry items, they measure ingredients precisely as indicated. If bakers stray away from a prescribed formula, the product will most often fail. It is important that both cooks and bakers use standard recipes and baking formulas to produce quality products.

Standard Yield

Quantities of ingredients in standard recipes/formulas should be stated in edible form. Edible form refers to the state of the product after it has been trimmed of unnecessary components such as the core and skin of an apple, or the fat and trim of a filet. Stating the quantity of ingredients in edible form allows for a consistent product. When recipes are prepared using the same quality and quantity of ingredients, and using a prescribed method of preparation, a consistent product results. A **standard yield** is the quantity of food generated from a standard recipe/formula. Standard yields are stated in the total quantity of food produced (3 gallons of clam chowder), or by the number of portions produced (48–8 oz. bowls). When producing standard bread formulas, a standard yield would be stated as 3 pounds of dough, or 8–6 oz. loaves.

The Standard Portion

A **standard portion** is the consistent quantity or size of product that is served to every person each time it is served. Standard Portion Control can be maintained by weight, volume, count, or the size of the container in which a product is served. Standard Portion control is not only important in maintaining a consistent quantity served to the customer, but is also necessary to ensure the expected profit on every portion of product sold. The size of portions should be prepared and separated prior to production whenever possible to ensure accuracy and speed of production time. When menu items are portioned at the time of service using standard tools such as scoops, ladles, or serving bowls, customer satisfaction and business profits are generated. The equipment used for portion control measures should be stated on the standard recipe card.

Weight. When standard portions are stated by weight, (as when the baker is preparing 10-ounce loaves of bread, or the chef is preparing a 9-ounce fillet), a scale should be used to maintain portion control. When products are advertised at a specified weight, it is generally understood that the weight stated is a pre-cooked weight. Weighing and portioning products into individual bags, or separating them with parchment paper before production, controls standard portion size and increases speed and accuracy in the production phase.

Count. Menu items are often portioned by the count. Examples of portions stated by count are: four Cocktail Shrimp, twelve Chicken Wings, or eight Mozzarella Sticks. To maintain standard counts for portion control, orders should be portioned and separated prior to cooking whenever possible.

Volume. Standard portion control for volume measures is performed by ladle, scoop, and spoon measurements, or by the size of the container in which the product is served. Volume portion control usually takes place at the end of the production phase. Standard portion control can be implemented, for example, by serving a 2-ounce ladle of hollandaise sauce over Eggs Benedict or a Number 8 Scoop of ice cream with a slice of apple pie. When portion control is maintained using containers, employees must be trained to fill these appropriately to provide consistency and cost control.

Because beverages are served in glassware, the first step in effective standard portion control is to serve beverages in the correct size glass, as stated on the standard recipe. Beverages should be served in the same type of glass each time they are prepared. "Regular customers" usually know the standard type of glass used for the beverage ordered and expect a consistent presentation as well. In addition to the glass size, portion control should also be determined concerning the amount of alcohol used to make each drink. The amount should be uniform. A jigger is a portion control tool to measure the quantity of alcohol used in a drink. As effective as jiggers are in assuring consistency and cost control, the use of a jigger often slows the process of drink making, which sometimes gets a negative response from the customer. Many foodservice operations have implemented the use of "free pour," which is based on a three count of liquor poured directly into the glass. Unfortunately, "free pours" are not as effective in controlling costs as is the use of jiggers. It takes a great deal of practice and professionalism for a bartender to become proficient at measuring by "free pour." With increased alcohol awareness as well as liquor liability, the use of jiggers is not only better for cost control but also helps to ensure that customers are not being over served.

Standard Procedures

The term **Standard Procedures** refers to processes created to guarantee that tasks are performed in the same way every time they are performed. When all employees are trained to answer the phone by first identifying the name of the establishment; providing their name; and completing the greeting with "How may I help you today?" is an example of following a standard procedure that has been established by a property. Every task an employee performs should be standardized to create the same quality message. Standard Recipes have Standard Procedures. To maintain consistent and cost efficient menu items, it is important that these items have standard methods of preparation for recipes and standard plate presentations. When recipes have standard methods of preparation, a consistent quality product is produced.

Standard Plate Presentation is the way products are consistently arranged in a set pattern. Standard plate presentation refers to how food items are arranged on plates each time a menu item is prepared. Having Standard Plate Presentations (composition) for menu items, especially in banquet settings where customers are receiving the same menu item, promotes a perceived value and a consistent product. Customers want to know that their plate has the same quantity and quality of products as the plate set in front of their dining companion. Standard Plate Presentations should be developed for all menu items. Some foodservice chains train their employees by using pictures and diagrams that illustrate how menu items should look. These pictures and diagrams are posted in the kitchen for reference.

Beverage items should also have standard presentations. Requirements of a **Standard Beverage Presentation** might include drink preparation in a standard glass size, beverages served on a napkin, or a slice of lemon presented in a water glass. Standard garnishes should be determined for all beverages and listed as ingredients in the standard recipe. Garnishes are fruits or vegetables that accompany a beverage. Set standards also help foodservice operations to meet production goals.

Reading and Writing Standard Recipes

Writing standard recipes is not an easy task, even for an experienced chef. Creating recipes from scratch is a very challenging, time consuming, and sometimes tedious process that takes critical thinking skills, practice, and experience. Recommendations for writing professional Standard Recipes include listing the recipe name, standard yield, standard portion, ingredients and their quantities, as well as the method of preparation. The use of a standardized template when writing standard recipes can guarantee that all the required information is listed and easily accessible.

Recipe Name. In professional kitchens, the recipe name serves as an organizational tool that classifies recipes into categories to assist the user to quickly locate the recipe needed. Recipes should be organized using the primary ingredient with modifiers that describe the item, followed by the name of the menu listing the recipe produces. Using this format, chefs are able to quickly find a recipe. Having access to the basic ingredients with modifiers that describe them, allows chefs to quickly determine the recipe needed. *Lasagna, meat, tomato sauce* can be easily distinguished from *Lasagna, vegetable, Béchamel.*

Standard Yield and Standard Portion. When professional chefs and recipe writers create recipes, they do not merely jot down a list of ingredients needed. The recipes include the total quantity of product produced (3 gallons) and the number of portions the recipe yields (64–6 ounce portions). When researching professional recipes, both the standard yield and the standard portion size are provided. Recipes found in magazines, or household cook books, frequently omit the standard yield or standard portion size. A general rule of thumb to determine the number of portions (standard yield), is to total the number of ounces of non-liquid ingredients, and to divide the total ounces by the serving size (in ounces) desired. To determine the standard yield, practice the preparation using portion control. Practicing recipe production leads to *culinary expertise*, which is defined as the common sense knowledge acquired through practical experience and education.

Ingredients. When writing professional recipes follow these suggestions:

1. List all ingredients and their quantities in their order of use as described by the method of preparation. Record ingredient quantities in both the English and metric units of measures. When sequencing the ingredients, also list the largest quantities (most important) of ingredients before those that are less important. If a recipe has various components, title each component clearly and list the ingredients for each component separately. For example, when making a layered cake: list the ingredients for the cake, those for the filling, then ingredients for the frosting.
2. If an ingredient is used more than once in a recipe, the total quantity of ingredient should be listed where it is first used in the method of preparation, followed by "divided,"

to indicate that the ingredient is used more than once in the recipe. Be certain to indicate the specific quantity needed at each step within the method of preparation.

3. When listing quantities of ingredients, list the quantity required, followed by the size of unit. Never put two numerals together without some indicator to clarify. An ingredient should be listed as 1 (6 ounce) package of semi-sweet chocolate morsels. It is recommended that ingredients are listed using the generic name unless brand names are absolutely necessary.

4. Spell out all units of measurement. While there are recommended professional abbreviations for units of measure, spelling out the units leaves no doubt.

5. If an ingredient needs a simple preparation before being used in the recipe, list the simple preparation after stating the quantity of the ingredient. Stating 6 Tablespoons of butter (softened), or 1/2 cup of celery (finely chopped) reminds the chef when preparing the recipe to pull the butter out of refrigeration ahead of time, and to chop the celery when preparing the *"mise en place"* for the rest of the ingredients. This professional courtesy allows even the novice chef to efficiently prepare a recipe.

Method of Preparation. The **Method of Preparation** is the step-by-step process of gathering equipment and putting ingredients together to prepare the recipe. "Methods of Preparation" also include important information about preparation methods and cooking times. Recommendations for writing effective Methods of Preparation include:

1. Listing the equipment and major tools required. List the specific size and type of pans needed to prepare, cook and serve the recipe item. Stating that a nine-inch pie plate, a large mixing bowl and a whisk are needed, allows the chef to gather the equipment prior to beginning the preparation process. Certain cooking equipment should be ready to use (oven is preheated) when the item preparation is completed.

2. Outlining the methods of preparation in steps using chronological order. When there are various components to the recipe, list the steps for each component separately. Also, place the steps in the most efficient production order.

3. Writing short, concise instructions. Steps that need to be performed together should be in the same paragraph. When there are various components to a recipe, list the production steps separately.

4. Stating exact or approximate mixing and/or cooking times. Provide cooking temperatures and any temperature adjustments that need to be made.

5. Finishing by listing serving recommendations, including the garnishes, serving temperatures and storage instructions.

Writing recipes using these professional standards allows the reader and the chef to organize ingredients and tools before the preparation begins, and to efficiently create menu items. Standard recipes/formulas guarantee a consistent product, and ultimately, customer satisfaction. There is nothing worse than going to a restaurant and enjoying a fabulous meal and returning the next week to repeat the experience only to find that the product is completely different. Having standard recipes or formulas and properly training staff to follow the standard preparation procedures prevents inconsistency.

Measurements and their Equivalents

When chefs and bakers measure the quantity of ingredients needed to prepare standard recipes/formulas, two types of measurement are used, weight and volume. Two common measurement systems used are: US Standard and Metric. Both US Standard and Metric systems of measurement have unique units of measure language and chefs/managers should be able to convert one system to the other. Appendix A provides US Standard and Metric measurement equivalents and conversion measures.

Converting Standard Recipes

Standard recipes produce a standard yield, (the quantity of product derived from producing a recipe). Production needs are met by producing more or less of a recipe as determined by business forecasts. Recipe quantities must therefore be converted to meet forecasted production needs. The process of converting a standard yield from its original standard yield, to a new desired yield, requires dividing the "new" Desired Standard Yield by the "old" Original Standard Yield to achieve a **Conversion Rate Factor (CRF)**. Appendix B reviews calculating and using percentages.

The following is a standard recipe for Gazpacho, which serves 30, (6 ounce) portions (Figure 4.1). If the chef is planning a banquet for 75 people, he/she needs to convert the Gazpacho recipe to meet those production needs.

Step 1 Formula:

Desired Standard Yield	÷	**Original Standard Yield**	=	**Conversion Rate Factor**
Example 75	÷	30	=	2.5

The Conversion Rate Factor is then multiplied by each ingredient quantity in the original standard recipe/formula to produce a new quantity of each ingredient needed for the new desired standard yield.

Step 2 Formula:

Original Ingredient/Quantity	×	**Conversion Rate Factor**	=	**New Ingredient Quantity**
Tomatoes	4 lb.	× 2.5	=	10 lb.
Cucumbers	6 ea.	× 2.5	=	15 ea.
Green Peppers	2 lb.	× 2.5	=	5 lb.
Onions	1 lb.	× 2.5	=	2.5 lb.
Olive Oil	8 oz.	× 2.5	=	20 oz. (1.25 lb.)
Garlic	4 clv.	× 2.5	=	10 clv.
Cumin	1 tsp.	× 2.5	=	2.5 tsp.

The chef then uses the new ingredient quantities to prepare the recipe to produce the desired standard yield of product. If the chef decides to serve gazpacho to a special dinner party of 15 guests, the same formula is used to reduce the recipe.

Desired Standard Yield	÷	**Original Standard Yield**	=	**Conversion Rate Factor**
Example 15	÷	30	=	0.5 (1/2)

To reduce the original recipe, multiply the original quantity of ingredients by the Conversion Rate Factor of 0.5 (1/2) to provide the new quantities of ingredients needed to produce 15 servings of gazpacho.

The Baker's Percentage

To convert the original standard yields of Standard Formulas to a new desired yield, calculate the Conversion Rate Factor, and then use the Baker's Percentage (also known as **Baker's Ratio**), to

Figure 4.1
Standard Recipe Form

Standard Recipe Card

Recipe Name:	Gazpacho		Standard Yield:	30
			Standard Portion:	6 oz.
Menu Item:	Soup		Portion Control Tool:	# 6 scoop

Recipe Quantity	Unit	Ingredient
4	lb.	Tomatoes, diced
6	ea.	Cucumbers, Peeled, diced
2	lb.	Green Peppers, seeded, diced
2	lb.	Red Peppers, seeded, diced
1	lb.	Onions, peels, diced
8	oz.	Olive Oil
4	clv.	Garlic
1	tsp.	Cumin Ground
1	tsp.	salt, to taste
1	tsp.	pepper, to taste

Method of Preparation
1. Combine all ingredients.
2. Blend slightly till desired consistency
3. Place in non-metal storage container, cover tightly, refrigerate 24 hours.

Equipment Required
Large mixing bowl, blender, non-metal storage container.

calculate the quantities of ingredients needed to produce new desired yields for bread products. The Baker's Percentage illustrates standardized relationships between flour and other foundational ingredients. Foundational ingredients are usually flour, water, salt and yeast, although other ingredients may be included. Because baking is a science, baking formulas use scaled metric weight measurements to guarantee that the relationships between ingredients are constant. Metric weight measurements are more precise than U.S. Standard volume and weight measurements.

Standardized baking formulas should also include the name of the item, yield, portion size, ingredients, and their quantities and the method of preparation. Professionally written baking formulas often include the ingredients in both Metric and U.S. Standard units of measure as well as the Baker's Percentages. A *Baker's Percentage* indicates the percentage each ingredient repre-sents as compared to total weight of flour. Flour is always 100%. The following formula is for 16 baguette loaves.

Baguette	Standard Yield:	16 loaves	
Ingredient	**U.S. Standard**	**Metric**	**%**
Flour	**10 lb.**	**4540 g**	**100.0%**
Water	6.6 lb.	2996 g.	66.0%
Salt	1.6 oz.	45.4 g.	1.0%
Instant Dry Yeast	1.28 oz.	36.3 g.	0.8%

The weight of the flour is multiplied by each ingredient's Baker's Percentage to determine the quantity of ingredients needed to produce the standard yield. Different bread products will have different Baker's Percentages for ingredients, but the process of calculating ingredients is the same.

To convert a Standard Formula to a new desired yield, a Conversion Rate Factor is calculated (CRF). Using the baguette formula, the baker needs to produce 8 baguettes. The new standard yield (8) is divided by the original standard yield (16) to determine the CRF (0.5). The CRF (0.5) is multiplied by the original quantity of flour to determine the quantity of flour needed to produce the desired yield. The baker then multiplies new quantity of flour by each ingredient's baker's per-centages to provide the quantity of all other ingredients needed to produce 8 baguettes.

Baguette	Standard Yield:	8 loaves	
Ingredient	**U.S. Standard**	**Metric**	**%**
Flour	**5 lb.**	**2270 g.**	**100.0%**
Water	3.3 lb.	1498 g.	66.0%
Salt	0.8 oz.	22.7 g.	1.0%
Instant Dry Yeast	0.64 oz.	18.2 g.	0.8%

Professional baking formulas often list the quantities of ingredients in both Metric and U.S. Stan-dard units of measure, as well as baker's percentages for all ingredients listed. Baker's percentages are useful for successfully converting baking formulas to desired standard yields.

Standards provide consistency, control costs, and serve as the basis to all cost control proce-dures. Chapters in this book address how standards are utilized in menu and recipe development, recipe costing, and the cycle of cost control.

Review Questions

1. Define:

   Standard Portion   Standard Procedure
   Standard Yield   Standard Presentation

2. Explain the difference between a Standard Recipe and a Standard Formula.

3. Using the three recipes in question #5; identify the portion control tools needed to present each menu item.

4. Determine the Conversion Rate Factors for the following:

	Original Yield	Desired Yield
French Onion Soup	50	125
Shrimp Scampi	20	30
Ratatouille	20	10
Wild and White Rice	10	50
Baked Scrod	50	15

5. Calculate the new quantities of ingredients needed to produce 40 portions of the following recipes.

   Recipe #1: Baked Scrod with Lemon Butter
   Yield: 50   Standard Portion: 6 oz.

Qty./Unit	Ingredient
19 lb.	Scrod Fillets
6 oz.	Fish Stock
1/2 cup	Wine, White
10	Lemons
2 1/2 lb.	Clarified Butter
2 1/2 lb.	Bread Crumbs
1 bunch	Fresh Parsley

   Recipe #2: White and Wild Rice with Mushrooms
   Yield: 10   Standard Portion: 4 oz.

Qty./Unit	Ingredient
6 oz.	Clarified Butter
6 oz.	Onions
6 oz.	Wild Rice
10 oz.	White Rice
1 qt.	Chicken Stock
1	Bay Leaf
10 oz.	Mushrooms
1/2 bunch	Parsley

   Recipe #3: Ratatouille
   Yield: 20   Standard Portion: 6 oz.

Qty./Unit	Ingredient
8 oz.	Olive Oil
8 oz.	Onions
2 lb.	Green Peppers
1 lb.	Tomatoes
1.5 lb.	Eggplant
1.5 lb.	Zucchini
1.5 lb.	Green Beans
8 oz.	Tomato Purée
2 oz.	Garlic

6a. A standard formula for pizza dough includes the following ingredients and baker's percentages. Calculate the quantity needed for each ingredient if the quantity of flour is 7.5 lb.

Water	68.0%	Salt	3.0%
Fresh Yeast	.3%	Olive Oil	2.0%

6b. Convert each of the US Standard units of measure calculated to Metric units of measure (grams).

7a. A standard formula for pretzels includes the following ingredients and baker's percentages. Calculate the quantity for each ingredient needed if the quantity of flour is 920 grams

Water	60.0%
Fresh yeast	2.0%
Salt	2.0%

7b. Convert each Metric unit of measure calculated, to US Standard units of measure (ounces).

8. Using the Standard Recipe/Standard Formula Template found on WebCom or Appendix F, and the professional recipe writing guidelines in this chapter, write a recipe/formula for your favorite family appetizer, entrée, or dessert.

Chapter 5

Determining Portion Costs and Selling Prices

© 2014, doupix art, Shutterstock, Inc.

OBJECTIVES

Upon completion of this chapter, the student should be able to:

1. define the terms "As Purchased" and "Edible Portion" when used to cost recipes.
2. determine Standard Portion Cost using the methods of Cost per Unit, Yield Test, Cooking Loss Test, and Recipe Costing.
3. calculate and use Cost Factors.
4. calculate a Preliminary Selling Price using methods of "Desired Cost %" and "Pricing Factor."
5. set the selling price of a menu item to ensure a profit as well as to maintain customer satisfaction.

KEY TERMS

As Purchased	Edible Yield %	Standard Portion
Cooking Loss Tests	Mark up	Standard Portion Cost
Cost Factor	Menu Selling Price	Standard Recipes
Desired Beverage Cost %	Preliminary Selling Price	Standard Yield
Desired Cost %	Pricing Factor	Standard
Desired Food Cost %	Q Factor	Yield Test
Edible Portion	Standard Plate Cost	

INTRODUCTION

Once the concept and business plan have been decided; the menu has been created; the Standard Recipes for the menu have been determined and documented in Standard Recipe forms, it is time to determine the cost of each menu item by calculating the total cost to produce a recipe/formula as well as the cost of a single serving. A single portion cost of a recipe/formula may have to be calculated several times for a menu item because of the numerous recipes/formulas required to produce the menu item. Once the portion costs of all the recipes/formulas needed to prepare a menu item have been calculated, all the portion costs are combined to determine the Standard Plate Cost and a selling price for the item. Determining the standard cost of a menu item and a profitable selling price is vital to the success of a foodservice operation.

Determining the Standard Portion Cost

The process of calculating the Standard Portion Cost of a menu item is used by foodservice operations to determine how much the prepared menu item actually cost the business to purchase and to present on a plate. Prior to setting a selling price for a menu item, it is extremely important that the chef/manager know exactly how much the food or beverage item costs the business to prepare. As defined in Chapter 6, "Food Cost" is the total dollar amount spent to purchase the products needed to produce a food item. "Beverage Cost" is the total dollar amount spent to purchase the products needed to produce a beverage item. Food and Beverage Costs combined are referred to as "Cost of Sales." How does a chef determine the cost of preparing a menu item when some items are made from scratch using standard recipes, and other items are purchased ready to sell? A combination of practices must sometimes be used to arrive at the cost. There are four methods that can help a chef/manager to calculate Standard Portion Costs of both food and beverage menu items. The four methods of determining a standard portion cost are: Cost per Unit Method; Yield Test; Cooking Loss Test; and the Standard Recipe/Formula. One or more of these methods can be used to determine a standard plate cost. A standard plate cost is the total cost of the product needed to produce a menu listing.

The "Cost per Unit" Method

Because of improved product processing and the preparation of food and beverage items by suppliers, an increasing number of products are now purchased in ready to use, edible portion form. Edible portion is defined as the form in which the product is served. Little or nothing needs be done to prepare a product in its edible portion form. Examples of edible portions that might be purchased include: a prepared cheese cake that needs only to be sliced; a case of 8 oz. chicken breasts that only have to be cooked; or a case of 24–10 oz. bottles of sparkling water that merely has to be opened. These products are already in their "edible portion," servable form. The only procedure a chef needs to perform to "make ready" this product is to portion the product; cook the product; or perhaps open and serve the product.

The formula to determine the portion cost of a prepared item purchased in its edible portion form using the Cost/Unit method is:

Purchase Unit Cost ÷ Number of Portions = Standard Portion Cost

Example: The chef purchases a prepared cheesecake for $18.00. Using the 12-slice portion marker, the Standard Portion Cost is calculated as follows:

Purchase Unit Cost	÷	**Number of Portions**	=	**Standard Portion Cost**
$18.00	÷	12	=	$1.50

Example: The chef purchases a case of twenty-four, 8 oz. boneless chicken breasts that cost $38.50. The Standard Portion Cost of each chicken breast is determined as follows:

Purchase Unit Cost	÷	**Number of Portions**	=	**Standard Portion Cost**
$38.50	÷	24	=	$1.60

Example: The bar manager purchases a case of twenty-four, 10 oz. bottles of sparkling water at a cost of $16.80. The Standard Portion Cost is calculated in this way:

Purchase Unit Cost	÷	**Number of Portions**	=	**Standard Portion Cost**
$16.80	÷	24	=	$0.70

With the current advanced processing technology, purchasing prepared food and beverage products is becoming commonplace at many types of foodservice operations. Restaurants often purchase products in an edible portion form, and use the product as an ingredient in their Standard Recipes. Using the Cost per Unit method to determine the standard portion cost of a prepared item within a standard recipe is often just one step in the process of recipe costing. The process of determining the Standard Portion Cost of a Standard Recipe is more thoroughly explained later in this chapter.

The Yield Test

A **yield test** is a process in which raw product purchased in an "As Purchased" form is broken down into edible product and waste. **As Purchased** is defined as the form of the purchased product that needs some preparation before it is ready to be served in its edible portion form. The preparation needed is usually that of trimming waste from the product and separating it from the usable product. Although yield tests are commonly performed on raw product, they may also be used on prepared products. A cooking loss test, which is a similar method of breaking product into edible product and waste, is used to determine the "Standard Portion Cost" of products that need to be cooked before portioning. The purpose of a yield test is to determine the yield, the cost per pound, and the cost per portion of a product purchased in an "As Purchased" form.

A yield test can be performed on a variety of food and beverage items: fresh produce (a case of green beans), poultry (a turkey), seafood or meat (a 10 lb. beef tenderloin), canned items (#10 can chopped tomatoes), bottled products (14 oz. artichoke hearts), and frozen items (5 gallons ice cream) that have been prepared prior to purchasing. Many of these products are not 100% usable as they include some waste. The purpose of the yield test is to break down the product into useable product and non-usable waste.

Preparation of the Yield Test Form

The information required to perform a yield test includes the As Purchased Cost (the cost of the product when purchased), the As Purchased Weight (the weight of the product when purchased), and the Standard Portion Size (the size of the serving in ounces). The Standard Recipe and appropriate purchasing documents can supply this information. Figure 5.1 illustrates how a yield test would be performed on a 24 lb. case of fresh green beans.

Figure 5.1
Yield Test Form: Case of Green Beans

Yield Test Standard Portion Cost Form   Menu Listing: Accompaniment

Product: Green Beans   Standard Portion Size in oz.: 3

As Purchased Cost: $38.00   As Purchased Weight in Lbs: 24   As Purchased Cost/Lb. $1.58

Product Use	Weight Lbs	Yield %	Number of Portions	Edible Cost/Lb.	Edible Cost/Portion	Cost Factor per Lb.	Cost Factor per Portion
Total Weight:	24	100.0%					
Trim Loss:	2	8.3%					
Edible Product:	22	91.7%	117	$1.73	$0.32	1.095	0.203

As Purchased Cost per Pound

The formula to calculate the As Purchased Cost per Pound is:

As Purchased Cost ÷ **As Purchased Weight** = **As Purchased Cost per Pound**
Green Beans: $38.00 ÷   24 lb.   = $1.58/lb.

Product Break Down

Although a yield test is normally performed in a kitchen or laboratory setting, the resulting information is also used by management to both cost and purchase products. Once the product is broken down into edible product and waste, the edible yield % for the specification of the product can be determined.

Edible Yield %

The Edible Yield % represents the part of the product that is useable. If the chef/manager maintains quality standards when purchasing, the edible yield should remain fairly consistent. The Edible Yield % is important in both the costing and purchasing processes. The formula to calculate the Edible Yield % is:

[(Edible Weight ÷ **As Purchased Weight)** × **100]** = **Edible Yield %**

Example:
Green Beans: [(22 lb. ÷   24 lb.)   ×   100]   =   91.7%

As indicated in the breakdown of the case of green beans, the case of green beans was not 100% useable. The chef had to separate the waste from the edible product to be able to determine not only how many portions the case of green beans would yield, but also to be able to determine a "true portion cost." The chef must be certain that waste and the edible yield % have been taken into consideration to ensure an adequate amount of product and profit.

The Edible Cost per Pound

It is important that the chef/manager calculate the Edible Cost per Pound. The Edible Cost per Pound refers to how much a foodservice operation has to pay for each pound of edible product when it is purchased in the As Purchased (AP) form. For example, if the chef/manager determines that the process of cleaning and trimming a case of fresh green beans is too labor intensive, he/she may consider purchasing green beans in a frozen, prepared form, where no cleaning and trimming is needed.

When looking at the "As Purchased Cost" of $38.00 for the case of Green Beans and the "As Purchased Weight" of 24 lb., we can determine an "As Purchased Cost per Pound" of $1.58 per Pound. However, as identified in the product breakdown, the case of green beans does not yield an edible yield of 24 lb., it only yields 22 lb. due to "waste." The formula for calculating the Edible Cost per Pound is:

As Purchased Cost ÷ **Edible Weight** = **Edible Cost per Pound**
Green Beans: $38.00 ÷   22 lb.   = $1.73/lb.

The chef/manager can now compare the Edible Cost per Pound of $1.73 to the As Purchased cost per pound of $1.58 for green beans in the frozen, prepared form. This is a type of "cost analysis." Once the "cost analysis" has been done, the chef/manager must also consider the quality of the product and its preparation time. The Edible Cost per Pound provides the chef/manager with the information necessary to make important food cost decisions.

Number of Portions

After the product has been broken down and the edible yield has been determined, the number of edible portions can be determined. The case of green beans yielded 22 lb. of edible product. If the chef were to serve 3 oz. Standard Portions, how many portions would be available? Determining the number of portions is a two-step process:

Step A

Formula:

Pounds of Edible Weight	×	**16 oz.**	=	**Total Ounces**
Green Beans: 22 lb.	×	16 oz.	=	352 oz.

Step B

Formula:

Total Ounces	÷	**Portion Size**	=	**Number of Portions**
Green Beans: 352 oz.	÷	3 oz.	=	117 (117.333)

Step A illustrates that the case of green beans yields 352 ounces of edible product. Step B shows that if the chef serves 3 oz. portions, the case of green beans should provide 117 portions of product.

The Edible Cost per Portion

The Edible Cost per Portion is the cost of each portion when the product has been purchased in AP form. As previously determined, the Edible Cost per Pound tells the chef/manager how much 1 lb. (1 lb. = 16 oz.) of the edible product costs the business to purchase. Because the chef is selling the green beans in 3 oz. portions rather than 16 oz. portions, he/she must calculate the cost per 3 oz. portion. To calculate the Edible Cost per Portion, the chef uses the number of portions previously determined.

Formula:

As Purchased Cost	÷	**Number of Portions**	=	**Edible Cost per Portion**
$38.00	÷	117	=	$0.32/portion

By preparing a yield test on a case of fresh green beans, we determine that a 3 oz. portion costs $0.32 to prepare. The portion cost of the green beans can be added as an accompaniment cost to a standard plate presentation or used to calculate an a la carte selling price.

Calculating Cost Factors

Cost factor is a ratio that illustrates the relationship between the "Edible Cost" and the original "As Purchased" price. The Cost Factor can be illustrated either in decimal or percentage form. There are two types of cost factors: the Cost Factor per Pound and the Cost Factor per Portion.

The Cost Factor per Pound illustrates the relationship between the Edible Cost per Pound and the As Purchased Cost per Pound.

Formula:

Edible Cost per Pound ÷ **As Purchased**   =   **Cost Factor**
                                     Cost per Pound   **per Pound**

Example:
    Green Beans: $1.73   ÷ $1.58   =   1.095 (109.5%)

The Edible Cost per Pound is 1.095 times greater than the As Purchased Cost per Pound, or the Edible Cost per Pound is 109.5% of the As Purchased Cost per Pound. The Cost Factor per Portion illustrates the relationship between the Edible Cost per Portion and the As Purchased Cost per Pound.
Formula:

Edible Cost per Portion ÷ **As Purchased**   =   **Cost Factor**
                                       Cost per Pound   **per Portion**

Example:
    Green Beans: $0.32   ÷ $1.58   =   .203 (20.3%)

The Edible Cost per Portion is 0.203 times the original As Purchased Cost per Pound, or 20.3% of the original As Purchased Cost per Pound. "As Purchased Costs" increase and decrease on a regular basis, due to seasonal variations, supply and demand, and the changing popularity of products. It is therefore impossible to prepare a yield test on a case of green beans every time the As Purchased Cost fluctuates. To recalculate the Edible Cost, without performing a new yield test whenever the "As Purchased Cost" changes, it is important to understand the relationship between the "Edible Cost" and the "As Purchased Cost" originally paid.

Using the Cost Factors

Another case of green beans is purchased at a new price of $42.00 per case. Using the calculations derived in Figure 5.1 and changing the "As Purchased Cost per Pound" to $1.75 per pound ($42.00 ÷ 24 lb.), determine the new Edible Cost per Pound and the new Edible Cost per Portion. The formula to calculate the new Edible Cost per Pound is:

Cost Factor   × **New As Purchased Cost** = **New Edible Cost**
    per Pound   **per Pound**   **per Pound**
    Green Beans: 1.095   × $1.75   = $1.92/lb.

Using the cost factor per pound to calculate the new edible cost per pound provides the chef/manager with a tool to quickly calculate the increase in the As Purchase Price and how it affects the Edible Cost per pound. This process can assist the chef/manager in deciding which purchase form (AP or EP) is most cost effective for the business.
    The formula to calculate the new Edible Cost per Portion is:

Cost Factor   × **New As Purchased Cost** = **New Edible Cost**
    per Portion   **per Pound**   **per Portion**
    Green Beans: 0.203   × $1.75   = $0.36/portion

Even though the increase in cost may only be a few cents, these few cents represent money that was once in the profit column. The chef/manager must pay attention to the effect that an increase or decrease of As Purchase Costs has on the foodservice operation's food cost. Cost Factors allow chefs/managers to determine changes without having to perform additional yield tests.

The Cooking Loss Test

Unlike the yield test, where the number of portions and the costs are determined prior to the restaurant's cooking process, the cooking loss test is performed on products that need to be cooked before portioning and serving. Cooking Loss Tests are most often used on whole roasts (lamb, beef, and pork) and poultry (turkey and chicken). The breakdown of the number of portions and their costs are determined after the cooking process. The actual procedure of the cooking loss test is performed in a kitchen or laboratory setting. The information is then provided to the chef/manager to allow him/her to determine the edible yield %, the number of portions, the Edible Cost per Pound, the Edible Cost per Portion, and the cost factors of the cooked product. Most of the steps in preparing the Cooking Loss Test are very similar to those applied in preparing a Yield Test.

Figure 5.2

Cooking Loss Standard Portion Cost Form

Cooking Loss Standard Portion Cost Form

Menu Listing: Roasted Lamb with Rosemary

Product: Leg of Lamb

Standard Portion Size in oz.: 6

As Purchased Cost: $32.25   As Purchased Weight in Lbs: 8   As Purchased Cost/Lb. $4.03

Product Use	Weight in Lbs	Yield %	Number of Portions	Edible Cost/Lb.	Edible Cost/Portion	Cost Factor per Lb.	Cost Factor per Portion
Total Weight:	8.00	100.00%					
Trim Loss:	3.00	37.5%					
Pre-Cooked Weight	5.00	62.5%					
Loss in Cooking	1.25	15.6%					
Trim After Cooking	0.25	3.1%					
Edible Product:	3.50	43.8%	9	$9.21	$3.58	2.285	0.888

Preparation of the Cooking Loss Test Form

The first step is to examine the required information given in the Standard Recipe, and the purchasing information provided. Additional information concerning cooking time is also needed when preparing a cooking loss test. Many chefs perform several tests on the same type of product, cooking them at different temperatures and for different lengths of time, to evaluate the product yield. Figure 5.2 illustrates the results of a Cooking Loss Test performed on a 8 lb. leg of lamb.

As Purchased Cost per Pound

The As Purchased Cost per Pound refers to how much the product costs per pound. The following formula is used to calculate the As Purchased Cost per Pound:

As Purchased Cost ÷ **As Purchased Weight** = **As Purchased Cost per Pound**
Leg of Lamb: $32.25 ÷ 8 lb. = $4.03/lb.

Product Breakdown

The Product Breakdown consists of weighing, trimming, and cooking; and weighing and trimming again after cooking to achieve the edible product weight.

Edible Yield %

The Edible Yield % is the percent of the product that is servable. When looking at the total cost and weight of the leg of lamb, we are led to believe that the 8 lb. leg of lamb is going to yield 8 lb. of edible product. But as we have identified in Figure 5.2, the leg of lamb only yields 3.5lb of servable product after it is boned, trimmed and cooked. Only a little more than one-third of the product's "As Purchased Weight" is available for use. The formula to calculate the Edible Yield % for the Leg of Lamb is:

Edible Weight in Pounds	÷	**As Purchased Weight**	=	**Edible Yield %**
Lamb: 3.5 lb.	÷	8 lb.	=	0.438 (43.8%)

The Edible Yield % listed in the specification of the product purchased will usually assist the chef/manager in determining how much product is needed to feed a prescribed number of customers.

The Edible Cost per Pound

The Edible Cost per Pound is derived by dividing the "As Purchased Cost" of the product by the edible weight. Knowing the Edible Cost per Pound helps the chef/manager to determine whether or not the "As Purchased" form of the product is the most cost effective form to purchase. Formula:

As Purchased Cost	÷	**Edible Weight**	=	**Edible Cost per Pound**
Lamb: $32.25	÷	3.5 lb.	=	$9.21/lb.

Number of Portions

Once it is known that the 8 lb. Leg of Lamb produces 3.5 lb. of edible product, the next step is to determine the number of portions derived from the Leg of Lamb. A 6 oz. Standard Portion size is used in the following example. There are two steps to this process.

Step A
Formula:

Pounds of Edible Weight	×	**16 oz.**	=	**Total Ounces**
Lamb: 3.5 lb.	×	16 oz.	=	56 oz.

Step B
Formula:

Total Ounces	÷	**Portion Size**	=	**Number of Portions**
56 ounces	÷	6 oz.	=	9 portions (9.333)

The Edible Cost per Portion

Knowledge of the Edible Cost per Portion ensures that the chef/manager knows exactly how much each portion of product served actually costs to prepare. To calculate the Edible Cost per Portion, the chef divides the As Purchased Cost by the Number of Portions.

Formula:

As Purchased Cost	÷	Number of Portions	=	Edible Cost per Portion
Lamb: $32.25	÷	9	=	$3.58 per portion

When determining the standard portion cost of a menu item, it is imperative that the chef/manager takes into consideration the product's waste and loss through cooking.

Calculating Cost Factors

Cost Factors show the relationship between the Edible Cost per Pound or the Edible Cost per Portion and the original As Purchased Cost per Pound. Because the costs of products fluctuate, determining Cost Factors can help the chef/manager to adjust costs as needed.

The Cost Factor per Pound illustrates the relationship between the Edible Cost per Pound and the As Purchased Cost per Pound.
Formula:

Edible Cost per Pound	÷	As Purchased Cost per Pound	=	Cost Factor per Pound
Lamb: $9.21	÷	$4.03	=	2.285 (228.5%)

The Edible Cost is 2.285 times greater than the original As Purchased Cost per Pound. The boneless lamb's Edible Cost per Pound is 228.5% of the As Purchased Cost per Pound.

The Cost Factor per Portion illustrates the relationship between the Edible Cost per Portion and the As Purchased Cost per Pound.
Formula:

Edible Cost per Portion	÷	As Purchased Cost per Pound	=	Cost Factor per Portion
Lamb: $3.58	÷	$4.03	=	0.888 (88.8%)

The Edible Cost/Portion is .888 times the original As Purchased Cost per Pound, or 88.8% of the As Purchased Cost per Pound.

Using the Cost Factors

If a chef/manager purchases another Leg of Lamb weighing 8 lb. with an As Purchased Cost of $35.85, the new As Purchased Cost per Pound can be determined at $4.48 per pound ($35.85 ÷ 8 lbs.). Using the Cost Factors previously determined, the chef/manager can calculate the new Edible Cost per Pound and the new Edible Cost per Portion. The formula to determine the new Edible Cost per Pound follows.

Cost Factor per Pound	×	New As Purchased Cost per Pound	=	New Edible Cost per Pound
Lamb: 2.285	×	$4.48/lb.	=	$10.24/lb.

The new Edible Cost per Pound can then be used to perform a cost analysis when purchasing other cuts of lamb. The formula to determine the new Edible Cost per Portion is:

Cost Factor per Portion	×	New As Purchased Cost per Pound	=	New Edible Cost per Portion
Lamb: 0.888	×	$4.48/lb.	=	$3.98/portion

Using the Cost Factor per Portion allows the chef/manager to quickly identify any significant changes in portion cost and to adjust menu prices as needed.

Recipe Costing

Most foodservice establishments have developed standard recipes for the menu items offered. These recipes include the name of the menu item, the standard yield, the standard portion, the name and quantity of ingredients needed, and the standard procedures involved in preparing the recipe. Because most recipes include several ingredients, it is often a time consuming process to calculate how much a recipe costs to prepare. But the process is necessary, especially for the inexperienced foodservice employees.

Chefs/managers use Recipe Costing to determine the Standard Portion Cost of a menu item. By knowing the entire cost of the recipe, a business can determine the standard portion cost as well as an adequate selling price that ensures a profit. Figure 5.3 illustrates the Standard Costing form for a side order of Three Bean Salad. The recommended steps to determine the Standard Portion Cost of a Standard Recipe follow.

Step 1: Readying the Costing Form

Fill in the required information such as the name of the recipe, the standard yield, the standard portion and the exact quantities of ingredients (including garnishes) used in the standard recipe. The latest "As Purchased Cost" of each ingredient should be posted in the Invoice Cost per Unit column.

Step 2: Calculate the Individual Ingredient Cost

The "individual ingredient cost" informs the chef/manager of the price of each ingredient in the standard recipe. By knowing the cost of each ingredient, the chef/manager can identify the high cost items that need special tracking. The formula to calculate the Individual Ingredient Cost is:

Ingredient Quantity × Price = Individual Ingredient Cost

Calculating the "Individual Ingredient Cost" is a simple multiplication process, however, there are several procedures to consider before performing the calculation.

Edible Yield %. It is important to understand that most standard recipes are written in an edible portion form. To achieve the correct standard yield using the stated standard portion size, the quantity of ingredients listed must be measured in edible portion form (rather than As Purchased form). Writing Standard Recipes in edible portion form ensures a consistent product. The recipe in Figure 5.3 calls for 3 lb. of green beans that have already been cleaned and snipped. Because Standard Recipes are written in edible portion quantities, the standard yield and the standard portion are guaranteed. Three pounds of edible product is 3 lb. of edible product, no matter who prepares the recipe. When calculating the Individual Ingredient Cost, the chef/manager must decide whether to use the Edible Yield % to determine the actual "As Purchased amounts." At this point, it should be quite obvious that 3 lb. of As Purchased green beans do not yield 3 lb. of edible green beans. It would take more than the 3 lbs., but how much more?

The more familiar a chef is with preparing the menu item ingredients, the more accurate the chef usually is at estimating how much edible product is derived from an "As Purchased" product. Chefs may also ask purveyors to provide the edible yield % of products or can refer to published guidelines prepared by the US Department of Agriculture. Appendix A provides a partial list of recommended Edible Yield % from the USDA.

Figure 5.3
Three Bean Salad Costing Form

Standard Recipe Cost Card

Recipe Name: Three Bean Salad

Standard Yield: 30

Standard Portion: 6 oz

Portion Control Tool: #6 scoop

Recipe Quantity	Unit	EY%	As Purchased Quantity	Unit	Ingredient	Invoice Cost	Unit	Recipe Cost	Unit	Individual Ingredient Cost
3	lb.	91.7%	3.50	lb.	Beans, fresh yellow	$1.95	lb.	$1.95	lb.	$6.83
3	lb.	91.7%	3.50	lb.	Beans, fresh green	$38.00	24 lb.	$1.58	lb.	$5.53
2	lb.	100.0%	2.00	lb.	Beans, red kidney	$3.90	#10	$0.60	lb.	$1.20
1	lb.	80.0%	1.25	lb.	Peppers, red	$2.75	lb.	$2.75	lb.	$3.44
4	hd.	100.0%	4.00	hd.	Lettuce, green leaf	$24.50	24 hd.	$1.02	hd.	$4.08
2	qt.	100.0%	2.00	qt.	Olive oil	$10.81	gal.	$2.70	qt.	$5.40
1	qt.	100.0%	1.00	qt.	Vinegar, red wine	$12.60	4 gal.	$0.79	qt.	$0.79
4	oz.	100.0%	4.00	oz.	Sugar, granulated	$24.40	50#	$0.03	oz.	$0.12
1	bun.	100.0%	1.00	bun.	Basil	$39.00	12 bun.	$3.25	bun.	$3.25
1	bun.	100.0%	1.00	bun.	Oregano	$12.75	12 bun.	$1.06	bun.	$1.06
0.5	tsp.	100.0%	0.50	tsp.	Marjoram	$1.06	bun		tsp.	$0.00
3	clv.	100.0%	3.00	clv.	Garlic	$2.10	lb.		clv.	$0.00
1	tsp.	100.0%	1.00	tsp.	Salt	$0.55	26 oz.		tsp.	$0.00
1	tsp.	100.0%	1.00	tsp.	Pepper	$8.05	lb.		tsp.	$0.00

Total Ingredient Cost:	$31.70
Q Factor %: 5.0%	$1.59
Recipe Cost:	$33.29
Portion Cost:	$1.11
Additional Cost:	
Additional Cost:	
Additional Cost:	
Total Plate Cost:	$1.11
Desired Cost %:	30.0%
Preliminary Selling Price:	$3.70
Actual Selling Price:	$3.95
Actual Cost %:	28.1%

Please note:
As Purchased Quantities have been rounded up to the .5 unit
Costs have been rounded to the nearest cent.

In the yield test example, a 24 lb. case of green beans was broken down into edible product and waste, and an edible yield % was calculated. The edible yield % is that part of an "As Purchased" product that is usable. The edible yield % of 91.7% previously determined in the yield test was calculated by taking the 22 lb. of usable product and dividing that number by the 24 lb. total weight.

When an edible yield % is determined for an ingredient, post it to the Edible Yield % column. Next calculate how much product must be purchased to yield the quantity of product stated in the original recipe. It is important to understand that the "As Purchased" quantity should be used to calculate the Individual Ingredient cost of each recipe ingredient. The foodservice operation must purchase that amount to achieve the necessary quantity of edible product.

As Purchased Quantity. The following formula is used to determine how many pounds of green beans are needed to yield the 3 lb. required in the recipe.

Recipe Amount ÷ **Edible Yield %** = **As Purchased Quantity**
Green Beans: 3 lb.   ÷   91.7% (.917)   =   3.5 lb. (3.27)

In order to obtain the yield and portion size of the standard recipe, it must be understood that the Recipe Quantity is stated in the edible portion form. The chef must purchase 3.5 lb. of green beans to yield the 3 lb. called for in the recipe. The cost of the 3.5 lb. purchased must be used in calculating the individual ingredient cost.

Invoice Cost per Unit. Most foodservice operators use the current market price of ingredients when posting the purchase price and unit of each ingredient to the Invoice Cost per Unit column. These prices are typically taken from the invoice that accompanies the order when delivered (Chapter 8), and are based on the purchase unit stated on the product specification (Chapter 7).

Recipe Cost per Unit. Before calculating the "Individual Ingredient Cost," the preparer should be certain that the quantity needed and price of each ingredient are stated in the same unit. If the quantity and the price are already in the same unit of measure, multiply these two numbers to derive the Individual Ingredient cost. In Figure 5.3, both the Recipe Quantity and the Invoice Cost of the Yellow Beans are stated in the same unit of measure. Simply multiply 3.5 lb. × $1.95 per pound = $6.83.

If the quantity and cost are not stated in the same unit, the preparer can use the Recipe Cost per Unit column to convert the Invoice Cost per Unit to the Recipe Unit that is called for in the Standard Recipe. The Recipe Cost per Unit column is only used when the Invoice Cost per Unit is different from the Recipe Quantity per Unit. To convert the Invoice Cost per Unit to the Recipe Cost per Unit, the chef/manager must be familiar with measurement equivalents in weight and volume including container sizes (Appendix A).

If the Invoice Cost per Unit is $38.00 per 24 lb. case, and the recipe quantity per unit is also in pounds, merely calculate the cost per pound.
Formula:

	Invoice Cost	÷	Invoice Quantity	=	Recipe Cost per Unit
Green Beans:	$38.00	÷	24 lb.	=	$1.58/lb.

Post the new Recipe Cost per Unit and proceed to solve the Individual Ingredient Cost by multiplying the As Purchased Quantity by the Recipe Cost per Unit.
Formula:

As Purchased Quantity per Unit	×	Recipe Cost per Unit	=	Individual Ingredient Cost
Green Beans: 3.5 lb.	×	$1.58/lb.	=	$5.53

In examining the example of Red Kidney Beans that come in a #10 can, the chef/manager must know the yield of the product from various size cans (Appendix A). A #10 can typically yields between 6.0 and 7.5 lb. of product. To solve for the Recipe Cost per Unit, the chef/manager would divide the invoice cost by the invoice quantity.
Formula:

	Invoice Cost	÷	Invoice Quantity	=	Recipe Cost per Unit
Red Kidney Beans:	$3.90	÷	6.5 lb.	=	$0.60/lb.

Now the chef/manager can multiply the 2 lb. Recipe Quantity by the Recipe Cost per Unit, to arrive at the Individual Ingredient Cost for Red Kidney Beans.
Formula:

	Recipe Quantity	×	Recipe Cost per Unit	=	Individual Ingredient Cost
Red Kidney Beans:	2 lb.	×	$.60 per Pound	=	$1.20

Remember that if the Recipe Amount per Unit is in the same unit as the Invoice Cost per Unit, a figure is not needed in the Recipe Cost per Unit column.

Calculating the Individual Ingredient Cost. Calculate the Individual Ingredient Cost by multiplying the Ingredient Quantity (Recipe Quantity or As Purchased Quantity if needed) by the Cost (Invoice Cost per Unit or the Recipe Cost per Unit). Both the quantity and cost must be in the same unit of measure when calculating the Individual Ingredient Cost.

Once all the Individual Ingredient Costs are calculated, the chef/manager can review these to determine if the costs are realistic and profitable for the foodservice operation. If a cost is identified as excessive, the chef/manager may look to a lower cost ingredient as an alternative that might reduce the cost of the item without altering quality. The calculation Individual Ingredient Costs calls for a great deal of knowledge about food products. Although time consuming, it is extremely important to determine the Individual Ingredient Cost to guarantee that a foodservice operation is charging an adequate price to cover product costs.

Step 3: Totaling the Individual Ingredient Costs

Once the individual ingredient costs are calculated, total the Individual Ingredient Cost column. The Total Ingredient Cost is the total cost of all the ingredients for which the chef/manager is able to determine a cost.

Step 4: Calculating the "Q Factor" (the Questionable Ingredient Cost)

There are certain ingredients to which an actual cost cannot be assigned due to the small quantity used. In fact, in some cases, the ingredients are actually immeasurable. It is in these cases that a "Q Factor" must be utilized. A **Q Factor** is an immeasurable ingredient cost that is assigned to Standard Recipe ingredients that are impossible, or too time consuming, to calculate. It is important to remember that even though an individual ingredient cost cannot be determined, the ingredient still costs the business money to purchase and to use. This cost must be accounted for even if it is assigned as estimated cost.

A "Q Factor" can be utilized in the following cases:

1. when pinches, dashes, or "to taste" type of measurements are needed;
2. if a recipe ingredient (such as salt) calls for a very small quantity (.25 tsp.). This quantity is measurable, however salt is a low cost item. It is difficult to calculate an actual cost for such a small quantity, so chefs and managers cover their costs by including them in the Q Factor. The purchase of salt costs the business money, and that cost must be considered so that it may be passed on to the consumer.
3. to cover excessive costs caused by an incorrect measurement, or even to absorb some of the costs due to seasonal fluctuations.
4. to account for the cost of condiments used. Condiments are often included in the Q Factor rather that in the Individual Ingredient Cost. Since condiments are often placed on tables for customer use, it is much more practical to use the Q Factor than to determine how much each customer uses and what the cost per portion of each condiment is to the foodservice operation.

The "Q Factor" is usually calculated based on a percentage of the Total Ingredient Cost of those costs that are measurable. Chefs/managers usually choose a percentage between 1% and 15% of the Total Ingredient Cost. The more accurate the calculation of each ingredient cost, the lower the percentage commonly added to the recipe. The less accurate the calculation, the higher the percentage used. Some chefs elect not to determine the individual ingredient cost of spices and herbs in a recipe. Instead they increase the Q Factor % to compensate. Other chefs think that this practice is outrageous, and take the time to determine the exact cost of all small ingredients.

The choice of using the Q Factor percentage is up to the chef/manager who is costing the recipe. The Q Factor is used to ensure that the costs of all ingredients are covered, while maintaining a fair price for the customer.

It is common practice to include a Q Factor in the cost of the Recipe even if there are no immeasurable ingredients in the recipe. Some foodservice operations use the same Q Factor % for every recipe, while others assign a Q Factor % based on the individual ingredients in each standard recipe.

The Q Factor is calculated by multiplying the Total Ingredient Cost by the Q Factor % chosen. In Figure 5.3, a Q factor of 5% has been selected. The Q Factor $ amount is calculated as follows:

Total Ingredient Cost	×	**Q Factor %**	=	**Q Factor $ Amount**
Three Bean Salad: $31.70	×	5% (.05)	=	$1.59

The Q Factor $ can range from a few cents to a few dollars, depending upon the Q Factor Cost % and the Standard Yield of the recipe. Including a Q Factor in the recipe costing process rarely increases a Standard Portion Cost by more than a few cents, but those "few cents" add up to a noticeable overall food cost increase.

Step 5: Calculating the Recipe Cost

The Recipe Cost is the total cost of measurable ingredients and the estimated immeasurable ingredients. It is an educated estimate of how much the Standard Recipe costs the foodservice operation to prepare.

Formula:

Total Ingredient Cost	+	**Q Factor Dollars**	=	**Recipe Cost**
Three Bean Salad: $31.70	+	$1.59	=	$33.29

Step 6: Calculating the Standard Portion Cost

In Step 5 (Calculating the Recipe Cost), it is illustrated how much it costs the restaurant to prepare the entire recipe. Because it is unusual to sell menu items by the recipe as a whole, the Standard Portion Cost of a Standard Recipe must also be calculated.

Formula:

Recipe Cost	÷	**Standard Yield**	=	**Standard Portion Cost**
Three Bean Salad: $33.29	÷	30	=	$1.11

Once those six major steps are completed to determine the Standard Portion Cost of a standard recipe, Portion costs of the other recipes used in the menu item can be combined to achieve the Standard Plate Cost (Total Cost of the Menu Item).

All of the previously mentioned costing methods must be used when the chef sets the Standard Plate Cost for a single menu item. Example: A menu item of boneless Leg of Lamb is accompanied by scalloped potatoes, fresh green beans, and applesauce. The chef has to perform a cooking loss test to determine the portion cost of the leg of lamb; cost out a recipe to determine the portion cost for the scalloped potatoes; perform a yield test to get a portion cost for green beans; and calculate the cost per unit of the applesauce.

It is important when Menu Costing to consider each and every item provided to the customer. The cost of rolls, butter, and garnishes must be included. The more the chef/manager uses the prescribed methods, the more refined his/her skills will become in costing menu items.

Setting the Preliminary Selling Price

It is extremely important and strongly recommended that before setting a selling price for a menu item, one of the aforementioned Standard Portion Costing methods is utilized. If the Standard Portion Cost of a product or menu item is unknown, it is nearly impossible to successfully set a Menu Selling Price that ensures a profitable menu and a successful foodservice operation. Once the Standard Plate Cost of a menu item is calculated, the chef/manager can start to consider how much to actually charge for the menu item.

To determine the actual selling price stated on the menu, we must first determine the "Preliminary Selling Price." The **Preliminary Selling Price** is the least amount of money that a foodservice operation can charge for a menu item in order to guarantee that all costs are covered (food, beverage, labor overhead, and profit). There are several mathematical approaches that can be used when setting the Preliminary Selling Price. Two methods will be discussed.

Desired Cost %

The **Desired Cost %** is the overall cost percentage that a restaurant is striving to achieve (by setting control standards throughout the cycle of food and beverage cost control). It is the ideal cost percentage attainable when all standards have been maintained and the purchase prices have remained constant. Commonly, the Desired Cost Percentage is 2 to 4 percentage points below the Actual Cost Percentage. The Actual Cost Percentage is the cost percentage that is determined by implementing the Cost of Sales formula. The Desired Cost Percentage can serve as a goal for a restaurant operation.

When setting the Preliminary Selling Price for a food item, the **Desired Food Cost %** is used. When setting the Preliminary Selling Price for a beverage item, the **Desired Beverage Cost %** is used. Restaurateurs often have different Desired Cost %'s for the various categories of menu items. They may want the Soups at a 20% Desired Food Cost %, and the Entrées at 28% Desired Food Cost %. Historical data and the chef's/manager's knowledge and experience, are valuable when setting Desired Cost % goals.

The examples below include Standard Portion Costs that have already been determined in the costing explanation in this chapter. These costs will be used to illustrate the Desired Cost % method of calculating a Preliminary Selling Price. The formula for setting the Preliminary Selling Price using the Desired Cost % method is:

Standard Portion Cost ÷ **Desired Cost %** = **Preliminary Selling Price**

Example: If a side order of Three Bean Salad has a portion cost of $1.11 to prepare, and the Desired Food Cost % is 30%, the Preliminary Selling Price for the 3 oz. portion is $3.70.

The price is determined as follows:
Formula:

Standard Portion Cost	÷	Desired Food Cost %	=	Preliminary Selling Price
Three Bean Salad: $1.11	÷	30% (.3)	=	$3.70

Example: If a slice of cheesecake has a Standard Portion Cost of $1.50 and the chef wants to maintain a 25% Desired Food Cost, the Preliminary Selling Price for the slice of cheesecake is $6.00.

Formula:

Standard Portion Cost	÷	Desired Food Cost %	=	Preliminary Selling Price
Cheesecake: $1.50	÷	25% (.25)	=	$6.00

How does the Desired Cost % method ensure that all costs are covered? An example and explanation follow.

Three Bean Salad	One Sold	10 Sold	100 Sold
Sales	$3.70	$37.00	$370.00
Food Cost	$1.11	$11.00	$111.00
Gross Profit	$2.59	$25.90	$259.00

When breaking down the sales price into Food Cost and Gross Profit, (Labor, Overhead, and Profit), we conclude that every portion of Three Bean Salad sold contributes $2.59 to the Gross Profit of the foodservice operation. Gross Profit is the amount of money remaining after the business pays the Cost of Sales (Food and Beverage Cost). Although the Gross Profit from one menu item may not seem like much, the gross profit from the sale of 100 portions or from the total of menu items, is sizable. It is simple to ensure that all the costs are covered when cost control standards are in place.

Pricing Factor

The second method used to determine the Preliminary Selling Price is known as the **Pricing Factor**. Divide 100% by the Desired Food Cost % to arrive at the Pricing Factor (Figure 5.4).

Figure 5.4
Pricing Factors

		Desired Food Cost %		Pricing Factor
100%	÷	40%	=	2.5
	÷	38%	=	2.632
	÷	36%	=	2.778
	÷	35%	=	2.857
	÷	34%	=	2.941
	÷	32%	=	3.125
	÷	30%	=	3.333
	÷	28%	=	3.571
	÷	26%	=	3.845
	÷	25%	=	4.0
	÷	24%	=	4.167
	÷	22%	=	4.545
	÷	20%	=	5.0
	÷	18%	=	5.556
	÷	16%	=	6.25
	÷	15%	=	6.667

Using the previous examples, we see that the Three Bean Salad generates a 30% Desired Food Cost % and the Cheesecake a 25% Desired Food Cost %. The formula for determining the Pricing Factor for each of the Desired Food Cost %s previously stated is:

100%		**÷**	**Desired Food Cost %**	**=**	**Pricing Factor**
Three Bean salad:	100%	÷	30%	=	3.333
Cheesecake:	100%	÷	25%	=	4.000

In a restaurant that wishes to maintain a 30% or 25% Desired Food Cost, the chef/manager would multiply the Standard Portion Cost by the 3.33 or 4 pricing factor to arrive at a preliminary selling price.

Formula:

Standard Portion Cost		**×**	**Pricing Factor**	**=**	**Preliminary Selling Price**
Three Bean Salad:	$1.11	×	3.333	=	$3.70
Cheesecake:	$1.50	×	4	=	$6.00

The Pricing Factor provides the foodservice operator with the same Preliminary Selling Price as does the Desired Food Cost % method. Some chefs/managers prefer the Pricing Factor method because it makes more sense to multiply to achieve a selling price than to divide. The Preliminary Selling Price is the smallest amount a business might charge to reach its Desired (Food or Beverage) Cost %, assuming again, that all cost control standards are met.

Determining the Menu Selling Price

Once the chef/manager has determined the Preliminary Selling Price, it is time to set the price that will be stated on the menu. The **Menu Selling Price**, unlike the Preliminary Selling Price, is not only determined mathematically. Considerations concerning potential profit and customer price acceptance must also be evaluated. Chefs/managers want to charge as much as possible so that the business makes a maximum profit from every menu item sold. When a manager says that a restaurant is maintaining a 30% food cost, it must be understood that not every menu item is working at a 30% food cost. The overall menu average is 30%, but some menu items generate a 20% food cost, and others a 35% or 40% food cost. The Preliminary Selling Price guarantees that the Desired Cost % is achieved. Menu items have different cost %'s, due to the **mark up** (or mark down) that takes place after the Preliminary Selling Price has been determined. Chefs/managers must select a Menu Selling Price that ensures a profit, without being unfair to customers. Charging prices that are too expensive for the target market will cause customers to go elsewhere, while a price decrease might mean an inadequate Gross Profit to pay expenses. When setting a Menu Selling Price, there are also other considerations to evaluate such as: labor, competition, clientele, atmosphere, location, and the psychology of pricing.

Labor

Chefs/managers often mark up the Preliminary Selling Price of menu items that are labor intensive. Products that are labor intensive require more time, care, and skill to prepare than the average product. A Caesar's Salad prepared table side is an example of a labor intensive item. If the chef were to compare the cost of the ingredients used in a Caesar's Salad prepared tableside to the food cost of the same salad prepared in the kitchen, the food cost would be the same. Restaurants charge so much for a Caesar's Salad prepared table side because tableside service requires more time and skill. People enjoy watching the table side preparation of the Caesar's Salad and are willing to pay more.

Competition

Competition is good. Foodservice operators often review the menus of competitors to see what they are charging for similar items, to use these figures as a guide for locking in their Menu Selling Prices. Although competitors often appear to have similar menu items, it is important to examine the quality of the ingredients and the portion sizes.

Clientele

The clientele of a foodservice operation plays an important part in setting the Menu Selling Price. Foodservice operators who have a large percentage of customers who pay with credit cards, often mark up the Menu Selling Prices to pay for service charges. Foodservice operations that cater to business professionals often charge more than those that cater to families because business professionals are thought to have more disposable income or an expense account from which to draw.

Atmosphere

More formal style foodservice operations typically charge higher prices because of Product Differentiation. Product Differentiation refers to the uniqueness of a product. A local pub may be serving a 10 oz. New York Sirloin for $15.50; while a fine dining restaurant just next door offers a 10 oz. New York Sirloin for $24.95. Chances are that the cost of the New York Sirloin is the same to both restaurants, but each has developed its own product differentiation. Traditionally, fine dining foodservice operations charge more than family style dining operations.

Location

Location can contribute to higher Menu Selling Prices. Various cities and regions of the country have different cost of living standards. Foodservice operations located in a city can often charge more for a product than those located in a rural community because of the increased disposable income available and the competition.

Psychology of Pricing

The Psychology of Pricing refers to how a customer reacts to the prices on a menu. How does the customer react to a price of $4.95 as compared to one of $5.00? When chefs/managers raise their selling prices, they often hesitate to move into a new dollar category. A price of $13.95 that is raised to $14.25 has a bigger increase perception than one of $14.25 that is raised to $14.75, even though the first increase is only $0.30 and the second is $0.50. Start Menu Selling Prices on the lower end of the dollar category so that when prices have to be adjusted, they can be adjusted once, or maybe twice, without entering into the next dollar category. A starting price of $22.25 can go to $22.50, $22.75, or $22.95 before entering a new dollar category.

The most important aspect in setting a menu item's selling price is covering the costs of operating the business. Start by using one of the mathematical methods presented to set the Preliminary Selling Price. Once the Preliminary Selling Price has been determined, adjust the selling price to make sure that it is contributing to the profit of the business and that the price is fair and reasonable to the customer.

Determining a Standard Portion Cost is important to the success of foodservice operations. Using the methods of Cost per Unit, the Yield Test, the Cooking Loss Test, and Recipe Costing, a chef/manager can determine how much the products cost the foodservice operation to produce. Once the Standard Portion Cost is determined, then and only then, should the chef/manager create a Menu Selling Price. The Menu Selling Price must cover all costs; contribute to the profit of the business; and be fair to the customer. The determination of a Standard Portion Cost and the setting of a Menu Selling Price are major components of the cycle of cost control because they serve as the basis of every other function in the cycle (Purchasing, Receiving, Storage/Inventories, Production, Sales, and Analysis).

Review Questions

1. Determine the Standard Portion Cost using the Cost per Unit Method.
   a. The chef/manager purchases a case of 84–3 oz. fruit filled Danish for $86.40.
   b. The chef/manager purchases a case of 100 Maine Baking potatoes for $24.40 per case.
   c. The chef/manager purchases a pound of bacon at $2.44 per pound. The pound of bacon has sixteen slices, what is the cost per slice?

2a. Using the information given and the Yield Test Form in Appendix F, perform a Yield Test to calculate the following:

   Beef Tenderloin, No. 189
   As Purchased Cost: $85.50   Portion Size: 8 oz.
   As Purchased Weight: 10 lb.
   Edible Weight (lb.):   8 lb.
   Waste: 2 lb.

   a. As Purchased Price per Pound
   b. Edible Yield %
   c. Number of Portions
   d. Edible Cost per Pound
   e. Edible Cost per Portion
   f. Cost Factor per Pound
   g. Cost Factor per Portion

2b. If another beef tenderloin is purchased at an As Purchased Cost of $9.95 per pound, calculate the following:
   a. New Edible Cost per Pound
   b. New Edible Cost per Portion

3a. Post the following information to the Cooking Loss Form found on WebCom or Appendix F. Perform a Cooking Loss Test using the information given:

   Turkey
   As Purchased Cost: $31.25   Portion Size: 5 oz.
   As Purchased Weight: 25 lb.
   Edible Weight after Cooking: 10 lb.
   Waste: 15 lb.
   (Trim, bones)

   Calculate:
   a. As Purchased Cost per Pound
   b. Edible Yield %
   c. Number of Portions
   d. Edible Cost per Pound
   e. Edible Cost per Portion
   f. Cost Factor per Pound
   g. Cost Factor per Portion

3b. A second turkey was purchased at an As Purchased Cost of $1.35 per pound. Determine the:
   a. New Edible Cost per Pound
   b. New Edible Cost per Portion

4. Using the Standard Recipe Costing Form on WebCom or Appendix F, determine the Standard Portion Cost for these three recipes. Use the Edible Yield % as given, and use a 3% Q Factor for each recipe. Round off Purchase Amounts up to the next whole purchase unit, and round costs to the nearest cent.

Recipe #1: Baked Scrod with Lemon Butter   Yield: 50   Standard Portion: 6 oz.

Qty./Unit	Edible Yield %	Ingredient	Invoice Cost per Unit
19 lb.		Scrod Fillets	$6.25/lb.
As Needed		Fish Stock	n/c
1/2 cup		Wine, White	$30.54/cs. 4–1.5 liters*
10		Lemons	$111.20/cs.–165
2 1/2 lb.	67%	Clarified Butter	$2.10/lb.
2 1/2 lb.		Bread Crumbs	$0.92/lb.
1 bunch		Fresh Parsley	$0.65/bun.
To Taste		Salt	$0.55–26 oz.
To Taste		White Pepper	$14.18/lb.

*1 liter = 33.8 ounces

Recipe #2: White and Wild Rice with Mushrooms   Yield: 10   Standard Portion: 4 oz.

Qty./Unit	Edible Yield %	Ingredient	Invoice Cost per Unit
6 oz.	67%	Clarified Butter	$2.10/lb.
6 oz.	88%	Onions	$19.50/50 lb.
6 oz.		Wild Rice	$7.10/28 oz.
10 oz.		White Rice	$2.20/lb.
1 qt.		Chicken Stock	n/c
1		Bay Leaf	$5.00/lb.
10 oz.	98%	Mushrooms	$1.75/lb.
1/2 bunch		Parsley	$0.65/bun.
To Taste		Salt	$0.55/26 oz.
To Taste		Pepper	$14.18/lb.

Recipe #3: Ratatouille   Yield: 20   Standard Portion: 6 oz.

Qty./Unit	Edible Yield %	Ingredient	Invoice Cost per Unit
8 oz.		Oil	$10.69/gal.
8 oz.	88%	Onions	$19.50/50 lb.
2 lb.	80%	Green Peppers	$1.58/lb.
1 lb.	99%	Tomatoes	$26.50/25# cs.
1.5 lb.	81%	Eggplant	$56.75/24# cs.
1.5 lb.	94%	Zucchini	$1.10/lb.
1.5 lb.	91%	Green Beans	$38.00/24# cs.
8 oz.		Tomato Purée	$18.50/6–#10 cans
2 oz.		Garlic	$2.10/lb.
To Taste		Salt	$0.55/26 oz.
To Taste		White Pepper	$14.18/lb.

5. Assuming that the Standard Portion Costs in Question #4 are from an à la carte menu, calculate the Preliminary Selling Price using a Desired Food Cost % of 30%. Round out the answer to the nearest cent.

6. Assuming that the Standard Portion Costs in Question #4 are from a table d'hôte menu, total the Standard Portion Costs and calculate the Preliminary Selling Price using the price factor for maintaining a 28% Food Cost. Round out your answer to the nearest cent.

7. List and explain considerations described in the text that might help the chef/manager to set the Menu Selling Price. What other considerations might play a part in setting the Menu Selling Price?

8. Using a spreadsheet package of your professor's choice, create a work sheet to calculate a yield test.

9. Using a spreadsheet package of your professor's choice, create a work sheet to calculate a cooking loss test.

10. Using a spreadsheet package of your professor's choice, create a work sheet to determine the standard portion cost of a Standard Recipe.

2 The Cycle of Cost Control

Chapter 6

Analyzing and Budgeting Sales and Costs

© 2014, Keepsmiling4u, Shutterstock, Inc.

OBJECTIVES

Upon completion of this chapter, the student should be able to:

1. state the purpose of an income statement.
2. prepare an income statement.
3. define, explain, and calculate sales.
4. define and calculate gross profit.
5. describe and distinguish between controllable and non-controllable costs.
6. forecast sales and budget costs using a simplified income statement.

KEY TERMS

Average Sale per Cover

Budgeting Costs

Controllable Costs

Cost of Beverage Sales/Beverage Cost

Cost of Food Sales/Food Cost

Cost of Sales

Fixed Cost

Forecasting Sales

Gross Profit

Income Statement

Labor Cost

Net Profit before Taxes

Non-Controllable Cost

Operating Expenses

Overhead Costs

Profit

Sales

Seating Capacity

Seating Capacity Method of Forecasting Sales

Semi-Variable Cost

Simplified Income Statement

Turnover Rate

Variable Cost

INTRODUCTION

The concept and the menu are the basis of all cost control measures taken by a foodservice operation to ensure that the operation is successful. This chapter is designed to give an overall picture of how a business operates. Dollars brought in (sales/revenues), minus the dollars paid out to operate the business (costs/expenses), determine the profit of a foodservice operation. Knowing how a foodservice operation makes money is the foundation of success. The ability to analyze historical data and to forecast future business is very important. This chapter begins with a review of an operation's income statement, which provides a statement of the financial condition of a business.

Income Statement

The **income statement**, also referred to as the profit and loss statement, lists the income and expenses that a foodservice operation has incurred during a specified time of business operation. The income statement provides historical data, which is actual business data that has been previously collected for a pre-determined period of time. Typically, the period of time is a year or a month and is expressed on the income statement as "for the year ending December 31, 20XX" or "for the month ending April 30, 20XX."

The income statement provides management with a summary of how well a business has performed during a specified length of time. The historical data found on an income statement can also be used to help a manager forecast future sales, expenses, and profit. The use of an income statement to help a manager forecast future financial information is discussed later in this chapter.

Components of the Income Statement

The income statement is composed of four parts: sales, cost of sales, operating expenses, and profit. These four areas on the income statement will be explained in detail. A sample income statement is illustrated in Figure 6.1.

Sales

The term **Sales** refers to the revenue that foodservice operations generate by selling goods and services to customers. Simply stated, sales are the monies that an operation brings into the business. While there are many types of sales that foodservice operations may collect (merchandise, gift certificates, etc.), the focus of this text is food and beverage sales. "Food sales" refer to the amount of revenue generated from the sale of food items, and "beverage sales" refer to the revenue generated from the sale of beverage items. The procedures used by foodservice operators to track total sales are explained in Chapter 11. Adding total food sales to total beverage sales equals total sales (often referred to as gross sales). Total Sales (Gross Sales) is the total dollar amount of revenue brought into the restaurant that is available to pay expenses.

Food Sales	+	**Beverage Sales**	=	**Total Sales**
$700,000	+	$300,000	=	$1,000,000

Businesses will often determine the percent of sales represented by each type of revenue collected. To determine the percent of each type of sale, the following formulas may be used:

Food Sales	÷	**Total Sales**	=	**Food Sales %**
$700,000	÷	$1,000,000	=	70%

Beverage Sales	÷	**Total Sales**	=	**Beverage Sales %**
$300,000	÷	$1,000,000	=	30%

Similar types of businesses will often generate similar sales category percentages for food or beverage sales. Food service managers frequently use sales percentages to forecast future sales and costs. Which types of foodservice operations might show percentages similar to those illustrated in Figure 6.1?

Figure 6.1

Income Statement

University Inn
For the year ending December 31, 20XX

Sales

Food Sales	$700,000	70.00%
Beverage Sales	$300,000	30.00%
Total Sales	$1,000,000	100.00%

Cost of Sales

Food Cost	$231,000	33.00%
Beverage Cost	$63,000	21.00%
Total Cost of Sales	$294,000	29.40%

Gross Profit	$706,000	70.60%

Expenses

Salaries and Wages	$250,000	25.00%
Employee Benefits	$65,300	6.53%
Direct Operating Costs	$62,000	6.20%
Music & Entertainment	$11,200	1.12%
Marketing	$32,500	3.25%
Utility Services	$55,000	5.50%
Repairs & Maintenance	$15,000	1.50%
Occupancy Costs	$90,000	9.00%
Depreciation	$13,000	1.30%
General and Administrative	$43,400	4.34%
Interest	$5,000	0.50%
Total Operating Expenses	$642,400	64.24%

Net Profit Before Income Taxes	$63,600	6.36%

Cost of Sales

Cost of Sales is the total dollar amount spent to purchase the food and beverages needed to produce sales. The cost of sales includes both the costs incurred for food (food cost) and beverages (beverage cost).

Cost of Food Sales (food cost) is defined as the total dollar amount spent to purchase food and any beverage product used in producing food menu items that are sold. The Cost of Food Sales found on an income statement is determined by using the cost of food sales formula (see Chapter 9). Information needed to calculate the Cost of Food Sales involves taking a periodic food inventory at the beginning of the month; tracking the costs of food purchases during the month; and taking a periodic food inventory at the end of the month (beginning of the following month).

In this example the Food Cost (Cost of Food Sales) is calculated at $231,000 or 33%. The Food Cost percentage is determined by dividing the cost of food sales ($231,000), by total food sales ($700,000), to equal 33%.

Food Cost	÷	**Food Sales**	=	**Food Cost %**
$231,000	÷	$700,000	=	33%

Cost of Beverage Sales (beverage cost) is defined as the total dollar amount spent to purchase alcoholic beverage items, non-alcoholic beverage items, and food items needed to produce beverage items sold. The Cost of Beverage Sales found on an income statement is determined by using the cost of beverage sales formula (Chapter 9). The cost of beverage sales is derived by taking a periodic beverage inventory at the beginning of the month; tracking the costs of beverage purchases during the month; and taking a periodic beverage inventory at the end of the month. In this example the Beverage Cost was calculated at $63,000, or 21%. To determine the Beverage Cost percentage, divide the cost of beverages ($63,000), by beverage sales ($300,000), to equal 21%.

Beverage Cost	÷	**Beverage Sales**	=	**Beverage Cost %**
$63,000	÷	$300,000	=	21%

Total Cost of Sales. The total cost of sales is the sum of the cost of food sales and the cost of beverage sales. Add the Food Cost of $231,000 and the Beverage Cost of $63,000, to equal the Total Cost of Sales.

Food Cost	+	**Beverage Cost**	=	**Total Cost of Sales**
$231,000	+	$63,000	=	$294,000

To determine the **cost of sales percentage,** divide the total cost of sales by total sales.

Cost of Food Sales $	÷	**Total Sales $**	=	**Cost of Sales %**
$294,000	÷	$1,000,000	=	29.40%

Gross Profit is the amount of revenue that remains after calculating the dollars spent to purchase the food and beverage items sold. By calculating the gross profit, a business knows the amount of money available to pay operating expenses. Gross Profit is calculated by subtracting the total cost of sales from total sales.

Total Sales	–	**Total Cost of Sales**	=	**Gross Profit**
$1,000,000	–	$294,000	=	$706,000

The gross profit percentage is determined by dividing the gross profit dollar by the total sales.

Gross Profit $	÷	**Total Sales $**	=	**Gross Profit %**
$706,000	÷	$1,000,000	=	70.60%

Gross profit serves as a guide in estimating if there is adequate money to make a net profit. The greater the gross profit margin, the better the chances of generating a net profit.

Operating Expenses

Operating Expenses consists of all labor and overhead costs. Labor Cost is defined as the total dollar amount spent to pay employee wages, salaries, benefits, and payroll taxes. Methods of tracking and determining labor cost are explained in Chapter 12. **Overhead Costs** are the combined expenses that a business incurs excluding food, beverage, and labor. Overhead costs include items such as linens, glassware, occupancy costs, utilities, advertising, etc. Businesses often use the Uniform System of Accounts for Restaurants, as recommended by the National Restaurant Association, to track and classify the different types of costs. A Sample Chart of Accounts in **Appendix C** provides a list of expense categories that a food service operation might incur. Foodservice managers must develop a system to track costs in order to determine the total expenditures within each cost category. The sum of the total dollar amount spent to pay both labor and overhead costs will equal Total Operating Expenses.

In the example, the total operating expenses equal $642,000. To calculate the total operating expense %, divide Total Operating Expenses by Total Sales.

Total Operating Expenses $ ÷ **Total Sales $** = **Operating Expense %**
$642,400   ÷ $1,000,000   =   64.24%

Profit

Profit is the amount of revenue remaining after paying costs or expenses. When evaluating profit, both the gross profit and the net profit before taxes must be considered. Total Sales minus the Cost of Sales determines Gross Profit. Once the Total Operating Expenses have been determined, the Total Operating Expenses are subtracted from the Gross Profit to determine **Net Profit before Taxes**. Net Profit before Taxes is the amount of income left after the business pays all of its expenses (food, beverage, labor, and overhead).

Gross profit – **Total Operating Expenses** = **Net Profit**
$706,000   – $642,400   = $63,600

To calculate the Net Profit %, divide the Net Profit dollar divided by Total Sales dollar.

Net Profit $ ÷ **Total Sales $** = **Net Profit %**
$63,600   ÷ $1,000,000   =   6.36%

When using percentage analysis to calculate percentages on an income statement remember to compare food cost to food sales, beverage cost to beverage sales, and every other cost to total sales. Appendix B provides additional information and practice exercises on percentage analysis. Percentage analysis allows a business to more easily determine how well it is doing in controlling the costs of operation.

What percentages of total sales should be represented by each cost for a successful food service operation? While every foodservice is unique, the percentages that follow provide a general guideline that may prove to be helpful in the sales and cost analysis process.

Sales %	100%
Cost of Sales %	35%–45%
Food Cost % = 20%–35%	
Beverage Cost % = 15%–20%	
Total Operating Expenses %	50%–60%
Labor Cost = 25%–35%	
Overhead Cost = 15%–25%	
Profit %	5%–10%

Foodservice operation percentages that fall within these ranges have a fairly good chance of succeeding. Foodservice operators who implement the controls suggested in this text will have a solid foundation to reach profit goals.

The income statement is the financial statement that identifies whether or not a business has made a profit. It is a valuable tool that helps businesses to identify how well sales are being generated and how well costs are being controlled. Businesses use the income statement in addition to other financial statements to make important management decisions. A direct relationship exists between sales, expenses, and profit. When sales are greater than expenses, there is a profit. When sales are less than expenses, there is a loss. If sales are equal to expenses, and there is no profit or loss, a business is said to break-even. Knowledge of the break-even point assists managers in proactively managing sales and expenses. Calculating the break-even point and knowing how to use it to make decisions is explained in Chapter 11.

Analyzing Expenses in a Different Way

Businesses also analyze costs by using categories other than food, beverage, labor, and overhead costs. Costs may be analyzed based on management's ability to control costs or by enhancing the relationship between the costs and sales.

Costs Analyzed Based on Management's Ability to Control. Expenses are often expressed in two categories: controllable and non-controllable. The costs are classified based on management's ability to control or not control them. **Controllable costs** are identified as the costs that management can affect by implementing a control tool or procedure that allows cost maintenance or a reduction of waste. Controllable expenses include: food, beverage, wages, utilities (gas, electricity, and water), and supplies (paper, plastic, glassware, china, silverware, linen, laundry, and uniforms). Managers can control food cost by using proper purchasing techniques to acquire the best price or by using portion control tools to reduce over-portioning or waste. Properly scheduling employees can also reduce costs, an example of a controllable cost.

A **non-controllable cost** is one that cannot be controlled by management. Once a cost has been determined, little or nothing can be done to reduce that cost. Non-controllable expenses include items such as: salaries, insurance, real estate taxes, mortgages, or rent. These costs are considered non-controllable costs because once decided, the cost cannot be controlled or changed by implementing a control tool or procedure.

Costs Analyzed Based on Their Relationship to Sales. Expenses are often analyzed by their relationship to sales and are defined as either fixed, variable, or semi-variable. A **fixed cost** (fixed expense) does not fluctuate in relationship to sales. Examples of fixed costs include rent or a mortgage payment. Once the rent or mortgage is agreed upon, the expense is locked in and does not increase or decrease as sales increase or decrease. Salaries, which are a part of labor costs, are also considered a fixed cost. Once a salary is decided upon, sales successes or failures do not affect the amount of money that must be paid to the employee. Fixed costs usually fit the criteria of non-controllable costs.

A **variable cost** (variable expense) fluctuates in relationship to sales. As sales increase, variable costs increase. As sales decrease, the variable costs decrease. Food costs and beverage costs are examples of variable costs. The cost of food sales (food cost) and the cost of beverage sales (beverage cost) are the only truly variable costs in the industry. As food sales increase the amount of food cost increases because the business is using more food product to produce greater food sales. As beverage sales decrease the beverage cost also goes down because less beverage product is being used. The relationship (percent) between sales and expenses (costs) remains the same.

A **semi-variable cost** (expense) often shows characteristics of both fixed costs and variable costs. A semi-variable cost is a cost that fluctuates as sales fluctuate, but only to a maximum and a minimum level. When sales rise, more staff is needed, and wage expenses increase. Even on a busy night when all work stations are already scheduled, there is a maximum amount of wages that can be expended. A minimum limit also exists when sales are down. Restaurants must have a skeleton staff to open their doors, and they must incur some expense to open. A semi-variable cost fluctuates within limits. Business operations should always closely monitor their costs. The method employed to monitor costs should be the one that best accommodates the needs of a business.

Forecasting Sales and Budgeting Costs

Sales forecasting is a calculated prediction of the amount of potential sales that a food service operation might achieve in the future. Forecasting sales can assist the business manager in **budgeting costs** appropriately. It can be done on an annual, monthly, weekly, daily, or even a meal period basis. Management often utilizes the income statement as a tool to forecast sales and estimate costs. The use of the income statement to forecast allows management to better: project targeted profits, expenses, and sales; compare the actual sales and expenses with the forecasted sales and expenses so that business decisions can be made along the way; and be proactive instead of reactive in managing food, beverage, labor, and expense budgets.

Forecasting Sales. A common method used to forecast sales is the **seating capacity method**. This method can be employed either by businesses that have historical data, or by those that are just starting up. The seating capacity method is based on a foodservice operation's seating capacity and its sales potential. **Seating capacity** refers to the number of seats in dining areas. The forecasted sales are calculated one meal period at a time. If a foodservice operation offers three meal periods (breakfast, lunch, and dinner), the potential sales for each meal period are calculated separately; and then added to determine daily sales. There are four steps to the seating capacity method:

Step 1: Determining the Number of Covers per Meal Period

The process to determine the potential number of covers for the meal period that is being evaluated requires two pieces of information: the seating capacity and the average turnover rate. The Seating Capacity is the number of seats in the dining room. The **Turnover rate** is the number of times a dining room is seated in a given meal period and is calculated by taking the total number of covers (customers served), and dividing that number by the seating capacity. A turnover rate for a meal period will vary based on the fluctuation of daily business. Using an average turnover rate can provide a more accurate forecast. The Average Turnover Rate per Meal Period is determined by averaging daily turnover rates for the meal period. The seating capacity is then multiplied by the average turnover rate to equal the Covers per Meal Period (the number of people served). Formula:

Seating Capacity × **Average Turnover Rate per Meal Period** = **Covers per Meal Period**

Step 2: Determining the Total Number of Covers per Meal Period

Covers Per Meal Period plus Additional Covers (take-out orders, the number of guests who may choose to dine at the bar, etc.), equals Total Covers Served.

Formula:

Covers per Meal Period   +   Additional Covers   =   Total Covers Served

Step 3: Estimated Daily Sales per Meal Period

Total Covers multiplied by the Average Sale per Cover equals Daily Sales. The **average sale per cover** is the amount of money spent by each customer while dining. Foodservice managers can determine the average sale per cover by using previously recorded total sales for the meal period divided by the number of covers served to produce those sales. Although most businesses regularly include both food and beverage sales in the average sale per cover, some elect to focus on one or the other. If the foodservice manager knows how much the typical average customer historically spends for a meal it is possible to predict the number of covers. The manager can then use the two pieces of information to forecast sales for the meal period.
Formula:

Total   Covers Served   ×   Average Sale per Cover   =   Meal Period Sales

Step 4: Estimated Annual Sales per Meal Period

Meal Period Sales multiplied by the Number of Days Open per Year equals the Annual Meal Period Sales.
Formula:

Daily Meal Period Sales   ×   Number of Days Open per Year   =   Annual Meal Period Sales*

*The sales for each meal period served are calculated separately.

Step 5: Estimated Total Annual Sales Potential

Once the sales for each meal period are calculated, combine the totals to determine the Annual Forecasted Sales potential for the business operation.

Example: Forecasting Annual Sales for the University Inn

The University Inn is a quaint, Victorian inn located in a bustling city that is the home to several colleges. The Inn is open for dinner and lunch 360 days per year. The dining room has a seating capacity of 80. In the dining room, the Average Turnover Rate for dinner is 200%, while the Average Turnover Rate for lunch is 250%. Additional covers average 20 customers for dinner and 20 customers for lunch, consisting of both take-out orders and customers who choose to dine in the cozy bar area. The average sale per cover for the dinner meal period is $68.00, while the average sale per cover for the lunch meal period is $22.50.

Calculating Forecasted Annual Sales for a Dinner Meal Period
The annual sales for a Dinner Meal Period is calculated in the following manner:

Step 1

Seating Capacity	×	Average Turnover Rate per Dinner Period	=	Covers per Meal Period
80	×	200% (or 2.0)	=	160

Step 2

Covers per Meal Period	+	Additional Covers	=	Total Covers Forecasted
160	+	20	=	180

Step 3

Total Covers Forecasted	×	Dinner Average Sale per Cover	=	Forecasted Daily Dinner Sales
180	×	$68.00	=	$12,240

Step 4

Forecasted Daily Dinner Sales	×	Number of Days Open per Year	=	Forecasted Annual Dinner Sales
$12,240	×	360	=	$4,406,400

If the University Inn served dinner only, the foodservice operation would have annual sales equaling $4,406,400. To continue working toward the total Forecasted Annual Sales, also use the luncheon information to calculate the Forecasted Annual Lunch Sales.

Calculating Forecasted Annual Sales for a Lunch Meal Period

Step 1

Seating Capacity	×	Average Lunch Turnover Rate	=	Covers per Lunch Period
80	×	250% (or 2.5)	=	200

Step 2

Covers per Lunch Period	+	Additional Covers	=	Total Covers Served
200	+	20	=	220

Step 3

Total Lunch Covers	×	Lunch Average Sale per Cover	=	Forecasted Daily Lunch Sales
220	×	$22.50	=	$4,950

Step 4

Forecasted Daily Lunch Sales	×	Number of Days Open per Year	=	Forecasted Annual Lunch Sales
$4,950	×	360	=	$1,782,000

Step 5

Once the annual meal period sales have been calculated for each meal period, each of the forecasted annual meal period sales are combined with the Total Annual Forecasted Sales. In this University Inn example, the Annual Forecasted Sales would be:

Dinner Meal Period Annual Sales	$4,406,400
Lunch Meal Period Annual Sales	+ $1,782,000
Total Annual Sales	$6,188,400

To get the best forecast, calculate the annual sales for each meal period individually. If a full menu is offered in a lounge or at the bar, a separate collection of data should be kept as well. The seating capacity and the number of days open per year are often the same for all meal periods, but not always. Average turnover rate, additional customers, and average sale per cover usually vary by meal period, due to the nature of each. Using actual data makes forecasting more accurate. By keeping track of food and beverage sales separately, it is easier to manage sales and to understand and control sales that fall below projected goals.

Budgeting Costs. Once sales have been forecasted for a desired time period, costs can be budgeted using a simplified income statement. A **simplified income statement** is a tool that is used to help a business determine an estimated budget for each of the major costs. The simplified income statement has the same major categories as an income statement, but with less detail. To budget each cost category, the percentages for each major cost category should be discussed and decided upon by management. Forecasted/budgeted costs can be calculated by using the desired cost percentage goals of a business and reviewing the percentages previously determined on the business's income statement to forecast the percent of sales desired for each major cost category. It is important to remember that sales always represent 100%, and the combined total of each category percent must add up to 100%.

SIMPLIFIED INCOME STATEMENT

Sales	$6,188,400	100%
Cost of Sales		40.0%
Labor Cost		32.0%
Overhead Cost		22.0%
Desired Profit		6.0%

Using the total sales forecasted from the previous example ($6,188,400), the forecasted budgeted cost for each major cost category can be calculated by multiplying Total Sales by the desired cost %:

Total Sales	×	**Cost of Sales %**	=	**Cost of Sales $**
$6,188,400	×	40% (.40)	=	$2,475,360

Total Sales	×	**Labor Cost %**	=	**Labor Cost $**
$6,188,400	×	32% (.32)	=	$1,980,288

Total Sales	×	**Overhead Cost %**	=	**Overhead Cost $**
$6,188,400	×	22% (.22)	=	$1,361,488

Total Sales	×	**Profit %**	=	**Profit $**
$6,188,400	×	6% (.06)	=	$ 371,304

SIMPLIFIED INCOME STATEMENT

Sales	$6,188,400	100.0%
Cost of Sales	$2,475,360	40.0%
Labor Cost	$1,980,288	32.0%
Overhead Cost	$1,361,488	22.0%
Desired Profit	$ 371,304	6.0%

Remember that the cost percentages should add up to 100%, and the budgeted cost dollars should add up to the forecasted sales. Management can use the budgeted forecast as a guide for a business operation. Once the annual costs are budgeted, the budgeted cost dollars can be broken down in specific time periods and compared to the current cost data of that same time period. More specific budgeting cost techniques are discussed in Chapter 10.

Review Questions

1. Explain the difference between sales and costs (expenses).

2. Businesses often classify costs in two ways: (1) their relationship to sales and (2) management's ability to control. Keeping this in mind, define the terms variable, semi-variable, fixed, controllable, and non-controllable costs. Once defined, identify the category of cost for each cost listed below.

Salaries	Wages	Food	Occupancy
Insurance	Beverage	Utilities	Advertising

3. Using the seating capacity method, use the information provided to forecast meal period sales.

	a.	b.	c.
Seating Capacity	120	75	300
Turnover Rate	4	2	3
Additional Covers	35	10	0
Average Sale per Cover	$32.00	$65.00	$18.50
Days Open per Year	363	260	313

4. Utilizing the forecasted sales results for the examples in question 3, set up a simplified income statement using the following percentages for each cost category:

   Cost of Sales   38%   Labor Cost   32%   Overhead Cost   25%   Profit 5%

5. Using the Income Statement template on WebCom or Appendix F and the following information, complete an Income Statement for each month.

	January	April	October
Food Sales	$250,000	$276,250	$348,500
Beverage Sales	$ 50,000	$ 48,750	$ 75,750
Food Cost	$ 90,000	$ 96,687	$ 111,520
Beverage Cost	$ 11,500	$ 12,188	$ 16,665
Salaries/Wages	$ 75,000	$ 75,250	$108,750
Employee Benefits	$ 21,500	$ 22,650	$ 25,455
Direct Operating	$ 18,550	$ 22,750	$ 33,940
Music/Entertainment	$ 7,000	$ 6,500	$ 5,000
Marketing/Advertising	$ 6,000	$ 8,125	$ 11,935
Utilities	$ 15,000	$ 13,000	$ 16,900
Repairs/Maintenance	$ 6,000	$ 5,000	$ 8,485
Occupancy Costs	$ 17,000	$ 19,500	$ 27,570
Depreciation	$ 1,500	$ 5,400	$ 1,300
General/Admin	$ 12,000	$ 16,250	$ 14,850
Interest	$ 900	$ 1,300	$ 2,100

Chapter 7
Purchasing Controls

© 2014, Tyler Olson, Shutterstock, Inc.

OBJECTIVES

Upon completion of this chapter, the student should be able to:

1. identify the person who is responsible for the purchasing function within different size foodservice operations.
2. perform the three steps of decision making in the purchasing function: the identification of the product and service; the determination of how much to purchase; and the procurement decisions.
3. organize and prepare specification forms to be utilized in the purchasing function.
4. perform the steps in choosing the best purveyor to meet operational needs.
5. differentiate among the methods of procurement and when each should be utilized.
6. calculate how much to purchase based on business needs and customer demands.
7. develop and set up business forms necessary in purchasing controls.

KEY TERMS

Cash and Carry

Contract Buying

Edible Portions per Purchase Unit

Identification Stage

Large Independent

Lead Time

Maximum Par

Medium Independent

Minimum Par

Multi-Unit Operations

Non-competitive Procurement

One Stop Shopping

Par Stock System

Procurement

Purchase Order

Purchase Unit

Purveyor Bid Sheet

Shelf-Life

Small Independent

Specification

Standing Orders

Stock Out

Stockless Purchasing

INTRODUCTION

When a novice thinks of the purchasing function, it is in reference to the process of buying products from a supplier. Although buying is a very important part of the purchasing function, it is not the entire picture. Purchasing is:

1. the identification of the quality and quantity of products or services needed by the foodservice operation.
2. the determination of the quantity of purchase units that must be ordered.
3. the procurement of the product/service at the most favorable price.

The **Identification stage** occurs when the chef/manager determines the quality and quantity standards of a product or service. It is the step at which a decision is made concerning the product/service that best meets the needs and standards of the business operation. Determining the quantity of purchase units needed is based on usage, delivery times, and the space available to store the product. Procurement is the process during which a supplier is identified, and an order is placed with the purveyor who offers the best price for products or services.

There are many decisions that must be made during the purchasing function, including: **Who** should make the buying decisions and perform the purchasing function; **what** should be purchased; **where** to buy the products; **how much** to buy; and **when** to make the purchase. The answers to each of these questions are discussed in detail within this chapter.

Who Should Do the Purchasing?

The person who has the responsibility and the authority for purchasing is the **Purchasing Agent.** The style and size of a business operation determines who actually performs this task.

John M. Stefanelli, in his book *Purchasing: Selection and Procurement for the Hospitality Industry* (Stefanelli 2012, Wiley & Sons, Inc.), suggests that foodservice operations be divided into two classifications: independent operations and multi-unit/chain operations. Most foodservice operations fit into variations of these two classifications; and the employee who performs the role of purchasing agent varies depending on the size and style of the operation.

The Independent Foodservice Operation

Stefanelli states that Independent operations can be divided into three categories depending on the size and volume of the business: the Small Independent, the Medium Independent, and the Large Independent.

A **Small, Independent** Operation can be thought of as a restaurant business that seats less than 75 customers. The purchasing function is usually performed by a single individual who often owns the foodservice operation. In many small independent operations, the owner not only owns the business, but also works within the business either as the General Manager or Chef. The owner/general manager is the person who makes the purchasing decisions about what to buy, how much to buy, and from whom to purchase. He/she not only identifies the products needed but also determines the purveyors a restaurant will utilize.

A **Medium, Independent** Operation usually seats 75 to 150 customers. With the increased size of medium, independent operations, the business is organized into departments such as kitchen, dining room, and beverage. The responsibility of purchasing lies with the department heads, the Dining Room Manager, Bar Manager, or the Executive Chef. The Department Head is responsible for the identification of the product needed and for placing orders with purveyors. The Chef is responsible for the identification and procurement of food items. The Beverage Manager must identify and procure beverage items. Each department head must identify the product/service needed within his/her department and then procure the products or services from the purveyor.

A **Large, Independent** Operation is a foodservice operation that seats more than 150 and often includes banquet facilities. Many hotel operations with multiple dining facilities, and single, high-volume restaurants, fall within this category. In this type of foodservice operation, a full time Purchasing Agent is usually employed. This person may have the title of Purchasing Agent or may hold a management specific title such as Food and Beverage Director, or Food and Beverage Controller. Within a large, independent foodservice operation, the decisions in the identification stage are still made by the department heads, while the procurement of the products and the task of dealing with purveyors is left to the full time Purchasing Agent.

The Multi-Unit Foodservice Operation

In **multi-unit operations**, the purchasing function is commonly directed from corporate headquarters. The individual stores are organized with managers and department heads, and most products are purchased through the regional central warehouse system. At times, the decision to purchase some products from local purveyors may be made by the store manager. If the decision is made to use local purveyors, the products purchased must still meet the standards of the corporate office. In most multi-unit foodservice operations, individual stores control the quantity of product to order, but the identification of the actual products needed and the setting of standards are determined by the corporate office.

"Who" should do the purchasing in the multi-unit operation depends upon the size of the foodservice operation. From this point on, the person having the responsibility and authority to perform the purchasing function will be known as the Purchasing Agent.

Identification of the Product Needed

The Purchasing Agent has the responsibility of identifying the quality and quantity of the products/services that need to be purchased to meet the standards of the foodservice operation. The Purchasing Agent decides on the products that are best for Standard Recipes, and those that can best meet the skill levels of employees.

There are many quality and quantity options of food and beverage products available for purchase. Products are available fresh, frozen (bulk or IQF), bottled, canned, in bulk quantities, or in individual PC (portion control) units. It is up to the Purchasing Agent to decide the form of product that best meets the foodservice operation's standards. This decision is based on the type of menu and the sales volume of the operation. Once the quality and quantity characteristics have been identified, the information is recorded on a specification form. A **Specification** is a detailed description of the product or service being purchased. It is a brief, yet specific, statement that describes the desired quality and quantity characteristics of the product or service. The Purchasing Agent must be certain that the specification is written explicitly to ensure the quality standards of the product. It is recommended that a business organize its specifications using headings identical to or similar to those listed in Figure 7.1.

Figure 7.1
Specification Card

SPECIFICATION CARD
Product Name: Green Beans
Intended Use: Three Bean Salad
Purchase Unit: 24 lb. case
Quantity/Packaging Standards Desired Edible Yield 88%
Quality Standards Fresh USDA Grade No. 1 Whole Bean: 2 sieve
Special Requirements:

SPECIFICATION CARD
Product Name: Shrimp
Intended Use: Shrimp Scampi
Purchase Unit: lb
Quantity/Packaging Standards: U-16/20
Quality Standards: fresh peeled and deveined
Special Requirements:

Exact Name of the Product. When creating a specification, it is important to be as precise as possible when naming the product needed. If you are purchasing lettuce, it is not enough to say "lettuce," due to the many different types of lettuce that are available. Instead, be specific as to the exact name of the lettuce product being purchased, using Green Leaf, Romaine, or Iceberg. When purchasing peppers, use Green, Yellow, or Red.

Intended Use or Menu Requirement. In addition to knowing the exact name of the product, it is important to know the intended use of the product. If a foodservice operation is offering a Shrimp Cocktail appetizer, and a Shrimp Scampi entrée; the Shrimp Cocktail appetizer might call for size U-10/12 shrimp (10 to 12 shrimp per pound), while the Shrimp Scampi entrée calls for size U-16 shrimp (16 shrimp per pound). On a very busy evening, if the operation runs out of the shrimp used in the Shrimp Cocktail appetizer, the chef simply has to leave the manager a memo to this effect. The manager refers to the specification listed for that particular menu item, and places the order. The specification sheet is a communication tool. In most situations, the Purchasing Agent knows the size of shrimp needed for each menu item, but for the novice or the trainee, this document is invaluable.

Purchase Unit. The **Purchase Unit** is the weight or size of the item to be purchased, stated in units of measure such as pound (of chicken), gallon (of 1% milk), or quart (of heavy cream). The purchase unit can also be stated in the size of the container in which the product comes: a #10 can of chopped tomatoes, a loaf of bread, or a 14 oz. bottle of ketchup. The Purchase Unit of a product is often a case. If the business is purchasing by the case, it is important to state the number and size of units within the case. When purchasing ketchup, for example, make sure that you specify if it is a case of twenty-four 14 oz. bottles, or one thousand 1 oz. P.C. (portion control) packets. Be specific as to the purchase unit to ensure that the product desired is ordered and received.

It is important when determining the size of the purchase unit that the Purchasing Agent takes into consideration the size of purchase unit that is most cost effective for the foodservice operation. The Purchase Unit selected often goes hand-in-hand with the intended use(s) of a product. The unit price of a product is usually less when the quantity of the purchase unit is larger. For example, a 3 gallon tub of ice cream costs the foodservice operation $25.00. The price per oz. of that 3 gallon tub is $0.07 per oz. The same ice cream purchased in a smaller quart unit costs $5.25 per qt., for a price per ounce of $0.16 per oz. The smaller the container, the higher the unit price. But be careful, if the use of the product is limited, a lower price does not necessarily guarantee a better buy for the restaurant. If the only use of ice cream is to serve it as a dollop on top of a piece of pecan pie, and the business only sells 8 pieces of pie every evening, then perhaps the better buy is a quart of ice cream. The 3 gallon drum could develop ice crystals long before its contents are depleted. A lower unit price is not always a good management decision. Once you decide upon a purchase unit, be certain to monitor large quantities of product that are left in walk-ins and reach-ins for long periods of time. It is good practice to evaluate the standard purchase units on a regular basis to avoid waste.

Quantity and Packaging Standards. Depending upon the type of product being purchased, it may be important to state weight, product size, portion size, edible yield, count requirements, and packaging standards. When the Purchasing Agent orders a case of greenhouse tomatoes, he/she must state how they are packed (5 × 6, or slab 100 count). It is also necessary that the Purchasing Agent consider how items are packaged: individually or in bulk. The more specific product details are, the greater the chance the purveyor will deliver products meeting the desired standards. Often a business will prefer a specific type of container: a 12 oz. bottle of Coors Lite° as compared to a 12 oz. can; or a paper/cardboard half gallon of Tropicana° Orange Juice in lieu of a plastic container. Packing decisions are important to quality and food costs. Does the business want to purchase 5 lb. tubs of Cole Slaw, or individual 4 oz. portion control size units of the same product? Is cheese purchased in 5 lb. blocks or sliced and individually wrapped? Remember that generally the closer a purchase unit is prepared to edible portion size, the higher the unit cost of the product.

Quality Standards. Quality standards are criteria used to indicate a level of "goodness" of a product or service. The most widely known quality standard is the grading system used by the United States Department of Agriculture. The USDA assigns government grades to well over one hundred different food products, based on visual testing.

The USDA also has certain recommendations of Edible Yield % for a variety of products (Appendix A). These recommendations give the Purchasing Agent a sound idea of what percent of the product being purchased is actually usable rather than waste. Edible Yield % was explained in Chapter 5 and will be important when determining how much to buy.

Another quality standard regularly used in the foodservice industry is that of Brand Names. Although Brand Names do not have to meet government guidelines, they do make a quality statement. When we hear Grey Poupon, or Perdue® Chicken, a guarantee of quality is definite. Knorr® sauces; Nabisco's Ritz Crackers; and Hobart® mixers "scream out" quality. Even though Brand Name items are usually more expensive, many foodservice operations believe that their guaranteed quality and consistency outweigh the additional expense.

Specific Product Information. If the purchasing agent fails to be precise concerning items within the categories previously mentioned, the area of specific product information needs to be expanded upon. Specific Product Information includes some or all of the information concerning a product.

Point of Origin. Knowing where a product comes from can also be important. Is it a Maine Lobster? Idaho Potato? Maryland Crab? If the origin of the product is important to the quality of the item being purchased, it should be stated. Point of Origin can also be very important in upholding Truth-in-Menu standards.

Preservation Method. Preservation Method refers to the state of the product when purchased. Is it fresh? Previously frozen? Frozen bulk? IQF (individually quick frozen)? Dried? Smoked? All of these preservation methods are important in maintaining product consistency within the menu. If the foodservice operation normally uses a smoked turkey breast for the preparation of a popular sandwich, and forgets to specify a smoked product when purchasing, the product served will be different.

Price Indicator. Prices of seasonal products rise and fall as the seasons change. Purchasing Agents regularly include the maximum price per unit that they are willing to spend for a product on the specification sheet. This price indicator reminds the purveyor to contact the Purchasing Agent prior to filling the purchase order if the prescribed price per unit is surpassed. Desired unit prices should not be stated on the specification, only the maximum unit price the foodservice operation is willing to pay.

When writing specifications, it is important to be exact in the description of the product to guarantee receipt of the item ordered. However, be careful not to overstate your requirements. Demanding a higher quality than actually needed will increase the cost of the product and may also complicate its acquisition. On the other hand, a lack of detail can leave the door wide open to the receipt of lower-end product quality. Writing specifications can be time consuming, but in the long run, specifications can save the business a great deal of time and money.

Although developing a specification system is a time consuming process, it is one that is basic to all cost controls within a foodservice operation. Specifications should be organized into a standardized form (Figure 7.1), and on file in multiple copies, so that individuals involved in the purchasing function have a copy available. The Purchasing Agent should have a copy to ensure that the proper product is being purchased, and the receiving clerk needs a copy to guarantee that the item received is indeed the product that was ordered. Potential purveyors also need to know the quality and quantity standards that the foodservice operation requires, especially when the food-service operation is using several purveyors, and those purveyors are in price competition.

As more foodservice operations become computerized, the traditional business documents are being replaced by computer programs. Instead of having a book of specifications, or a card file, businesses often store specifications in computer files so that any department can access them as needed.

Determining the Quantity of Purchase Units Needed

Determining how much to buy can often be a process of trial and error. Some Purchasing Agents find the task routine, while others find themselves constantly over or under purchasing. Experience and good record keeping are essential for success. The better a Purchasing Agent is at keeping records of product usage and purveyor delivery schedules, the better he/she is at determining the correct quantity to purchase. Foodservice operations must also take into consideration the time needed to perform the purchasing function, as well as the space required to store the products. Two methods that may be used to simplify the ordering task are: the Par Stock System and the Edible Portions per Purchase Unit System.

Par Stock System

The **Par Stock System** is a common approach that many foodservice operations use to determine the quantity of purchase units needed. The Par Stock system is based on past customer counts and product usage as well as purveyor delivery schedules and order procedures. There are two product levels in a Par Stock system.

The first level is known as the Maximum Par. The **Maximum Par** is the largest quantity of product that a property is able to have on hand, based on the storage space available, and the shelf-life of the product. Unfortunately, storage space (as discussed in Chapter 9), is often the last thing a restaurateur thinks of when looking for a building in which to operate a restaurant. While visualizing the front of the house and set-up of the equipment in the space identified as the kitchen, the entrepreneur often overlooks the amount of storage space available. The Maximum Par level cannot exceed the amount of storage space available. Even foodservice operations with plenty of storage space, find that they are at times unable to take advantage of quantity discounts because of the limited shelf-life, and/or expiration date of certain products. **Shelf-life** is the estimated amount or time that a product can be stored without spoiling.

The **Minimum Par** level is the smallest quantity of a product to have on hand based on purveyor lead time. **Lead time** is the time period that begins when the order is placed with the purveyor and ends when the order is received by the foodservice operation. Purchasing Agents must be familiar with their purveyor's lead times to ensure minimum par levels, and to guarantee the restaurant does not run out of a product before the new order can be delivered. If a foodservice operation runs out of a product (86'd), a **Stock Out** occurs. Although a Stock Out is not considered an actual dollar loss, it may result in a loss of sales due to customer dissatisfaction. If a stock out occurs, it is important that the manager handle the situation delicately to ensure that the customer returns. The minimum par level should be set high enough to guarantee an uninterrupted supply of products.

Purchasing Agents will often record the Maximum Par stock levels on the inventory order sheets used during the purchasing function. Posting the Maximum Par stock level on the order sheet alleviates the time-consuming process of determining how much product is needed. The

Purchasing Agent can take an inventory of what is on hand; record it on the order sheet; compare it to the Pars stated; and quickly determine how much to purchase (Figure 7.2). It is strongly recommended that par levels be evaluated at least on a seasonal basis because menu items change as seasons change. Evaluating par stock levels regularly, can prevent overstocking and waste.

Edible Portions per Purchase Unit

A second "How Much to Purchase" method is becoming more popular in the computerized foodservice industry. This method is presented by Charles Levinson in the book *Food and Beverage Operations: Cost Control and Systems Management* (Levinson 1988, Prentice Hall College Div.), and again by Feinstein & Stefanelli in their book *Purchasing: Selection and Procurement for the Hospitality Industry* (Feinstein & Stefanelli 2008, Wiley & Sons, Inc.). This mathematical process of determining the quantity of purchase units needed to meet production needs, analyzes each purchase unit to determine how many portions the purchase unit will yield. Although, it is highly unlikely that this method would be practical for purchasing all products, the process can be utilized to purchase major ingredients for Standard Recipes, special items needed for a catered event or banquet function, or simply for high cost ingredients that the Purchasing Agent wishes not to over purchase.

To ensure accuracy in the **Edible Portions per Purchase Unit** process, it is important that standard recipes are used, standard portion controls are maintained, and specification of food products are developed and followed. As with the Par Stock, this method depends on customer counts, product usage and delivery schedules, and the procedures of purveyors.

Figure 7.2

Inventory Order Sheets

Inventory Order Sheets

Food Category: SEAFOOD   Day/Date: Monday 6/30

Ingredient	On Hand	PAR	Order
Sole		60 lb.	
Scrod		50 lb.	
Lobsters, 1.25#		24 each	
Lump Crab		10 lb.	
Shrimp, 16/20		20 lb.	
Sea Scallops		6 lb.	
Tuna Loin		20 lb.	

The information required to execute the Edible Portion per Purchase Unit mathematical approach includes knowing: the Purchase Unit, the Standard Portion, the Edible Yield %, and the number of customers expected to be served. The Purchase Unit refers to the unit stated on the specification sheet that is used by the foodservice operation. A Standard Portion is the size of the portion that is stated on the Standard Recipe. The Standard Portion is normally stated in ounces. As explained in Chapter 5, an Edible Yield % may be determined by performing a yield test. Prescribed Edible Yields are also recommended by purveyors and governmental agencies such as the

US Department of Agriculture (Appendix A). The Edible Yield % identifies the amount of the purchased unit that is actually servable. The number of customers refers to the forecasted number of people expected to consume the products that are served. The number of customers can be determined by utilizing historical customer counts, or expected customers at a special event.

Banquet/Catering Approach. There are three steps involved in the Edible Portion per Purchase Unit method. Using this method to determine "How Much to Buy," chefs can calculate the quantities of purchase units needed to serve 250 covers. Use the following information to calculate how many units need to be purchased:

Item	Purchase Unit	Standard Portion	Edible Yield %
Leg of Lamb	1 lb.	6 oz.	43.8 %
Green Beans	24 lb.	3 oz.	91.7 %

Step A: As Purchased Portions per Purchase Unit. The first step is to estimate the number of portions derived from a purchase unit, when the purchase unit is assumed to be 100% usable. Formula:

Ounces in Purchase Unit	÷	Standard Portion	=	As Purchased Portions
Leg of Lamb (1 lb.) 16 oz.	÷	6 oz.	=	2.67 per lb.
Green Beans (24 lb.) 384 oz.	÷	3 oz.	=	128 per 24 lb.

As illustrated in this example, the As Purchased Portions derived tell us that a pound of Lamb will feed 2.67 people and a case of Green Beans will feed 128 people. Although it is rare that every ounce of a purchased product is usable, because most products have some waste, arriving at "As Purchased Portions" is a good first step in understanding how many portions each purchase unit actually yields. Many non-foodservice shoppers use this formula to determine how much to buy for a family dinner. Once the As Purchased Portions have been determined (assuming that the product is 100% edible), it is time to consider the Edible Yield % of products.

Step B: Edible Portions per Purchase Unit. The formula to determine the actual number of portions derived from a purchase unit is:

As Purchased Portions	×	Edible Yield %	=	Edible Portions
Leg of Lamb 2.67	×	43.8%	=	1.17 per lb.
Green Beans 128	×	91.7%	=	117.38 per 24 lb.

Using the formula above, it becomes clear that both the Leg of Lamb and the Green Beans are not 100% edible, and therefore, neither product will yield the number of As Purchased Portions previously calculated. Every purchase unit of Lamb (lb.) will feed 1.17 people and every case of green beans (24 lb.) will feed 117.38.

Step C: Quantity of Purchase Units. Knowing the number of covers each unit of purchase feeds, the number of units needed to be purchased to feed 250 customers can be determined. Formula:

Number of Covers	÷	Edible Portions	=	Quantity of Purchase Units
Leg of Lamb 250	÷	1.17	=	214 lb. (213.68)
Green Beans 250	÷	117.38	=	3–24 lb. cases (2.130)

The Purchasing Agent needs to order 214 lb. of Lamb and 3–25 lb. cases of Green Beans to feed 250 people. Always remember to round up to the next whole Purchase Unit to be certain that there is enough product to avoid a stock out, and to guarantee that there is a cushion in case any errors are made during preparation.

This mathematical approach should be used only as a guideline to determine the quantity of purchase units needed. The success of this process is dependent upon maintaining product specifications, proper preparation techniques, and portion control techniques. When performed correctly, the Edible Portion per Purchase Unit can be an effective control tool to reduce food cost dollars and waste. The more experienced Purchasing Agent or Executive Chef can easily determine the portions each purchase unit yields by simply performing the third step in the operation. By maintaining stated specifications of products and standard portion control, the number of edible portions achieved from each purchase unit should not change. Once this process is implemented, the only number that needs to be adjusted is the number of customers expected.

In a banquet or catering situation, this method can be utilized to substantially control food cost and to reduce waste. The number of covers forecasted may include a guaranteed percentage. Foodservice operations with banquet facilities will often plan for a 5% overage, to cover unplanned events such as a tray of food that falls to the floor, or a last minute guest increase. It is always beneficial to say "no problem," rather than to disappoint the host and the guests.

High Cost Product Approach. This mathematical approach can also be utilized in a full-service restaurant setting; however, it is unlikely that it would be the only method used to purchase all products because foodservice operations purchase hundreds of types of raw products to produce menu items. Determining each and every ingredient that a customer consumes would be impossible. The Edible Portion per Purchase Unit method is practical to specifically control the purchase of high cost items that are regularly used, such as: meats, seafood, poultry, and prepared desserts.

Example: A dinner menu has entrée offerings of: 2 steak dishes, 3 chicken dishes, 2 scallop dishes, and 3 shrimp dishes. Each of the steak entrées, chicken entrées, scallop entrées, and shrimp entrées offers the same quality and portion size as the other similar entrées within the same menu sub-classification. When using the high cost product approach in a full-service restaurant setting it is important to realize that every customer will not have the same menu item (unlike the banquet/catering approach). It is therefore important to include the Sales Mix of the menu offerings with the other necessary information.

Using the following information and the equations previously introduced, use the four step process to determine the number of pounds that must be purchased to feed a forecasted weekly customer count of 700 people.

Menu Item	Purchase Unit	Standard Portion	Edible Yield %	Sales Mix %
Steak	1 lb.	12 oz.	85%	20%
Chicken	1 lb.	8 oz.	88%	35%
Scallops	1 lb.	6 oz.	92%	18%
Shrimp	1 lb.	6 oz.	80%	27%

After the Purchase Unit, the Standard Portion and the Edible Yield % are determined, the sales mix must be examined. The Sales Mix percentage represents the popularity of one item as compared to that of the total items sold within a menu category. The Sales Mix % for steak is calculated by taking the number of steaks sold and dividing that number by the total number of entrées sold.

An example illustrating the calculation of a sales mix % is:

Number of Steaks Sold	÷	**Total Numbers of Entrées Sold**	=	**Sale Mix %**
Example: 20 steaks sold	÷	100 entrées sold	=	20% sales mix

A Sales Mix % is usually used to determine the popularity of a particular menu item within a menu classification and comparing it to other items within the same classification such as Appetizers with Appetizers, Entrées with Entrées, etc. The information needed to determine a Sales Mix % is discussed in detail in Chapter 11. When using the mathematical approach for high cost menu items in a full-service restaurant, calculate the As Purchased Portions (Step A), and then the Edible Portions achieved from each purchase unit (Step B). The first two steps of the *High Cost Approach* are the same as the first two steps of the *Banquet Approach*.

Step A Formula: As Purchased Portions per Purchase Unit. First, estimate the number of portions derived from a purchase unit, when the purchase unit is assumed to be 100% usable.

Ounces in Purchase Unit		÷	**Standard Portion**	=	**As Purchased Portions**
Steak	16 oz.	÷	12 oz.	=	1.33 per lb.
Chicken	16 oz.	÷	8 oz.	=	2 per lb.
Scallops	16 oz.	÷	6 oz.	=	2.67 per lb.
Shrimp	16 oz.	÷	6 oz.	=	2.67 per lb.

Step B Formula: Edible Portions per Purchase Unit. Next, determine the actual number of portions derived from a purchase unit.

As Purchase Portions		×	**Edible Yield %**	=	**Edible Portions**
Steak	1.33	×	85%	=	1.13 per lb.
Chicken	2	×	88%	=	1.76 per lb.
Scallops	2.67	×	92%	=	2.46 per lb.
Shrimp	2.67	×	80%	=	2.14 per lb.

Once the Edible Portion per Purchase Unit is determined, calculate the customers per menu item (Step C).

Step C-1 Formula: The Forecasted Number of Customers per Menu Item. The number of customers expected to order a particular menu item is based on the Sales Mix %. Unlike the Banquet Approach where every customer has each of the items on the menu, the High Cost Approach requires that the chef forecast the number of customers expected to order each menu item. Step C-1 calculates the number of customers expected to order a particular menu item.

Weekly Covers		×	**Sales Mix %**	=	**Customers per Menu Item**
Steak	700	×	20%	=	140 customers ordering steak
Chicken	700	×	35%	=	245 customers ordering chicken
Scallops	700	×	18%	=	126 customers ordering scallops
Shrimp	700	×	27%	=	189 customers ordering shrimp

Step C-2 Formula: Quantity of Purchase Units. Like the Banquet Approach, the last step is to calculate the number of purchase units needed to serve the forecasted number of customers for each of the menu items.

Customers per Menu Item		÷	**Edible Portions**	=	**Quantity of Purchase Units**
Steak	140	÷	1.13	=	124 lb. (123.89 lb.)
Chicken	245	÷	1.76	=	140 lb. (139.20 lb.)
Scallops	126	÷	2.46	=	52 lb. (51.22 lb.)
Shrimp	189	÷	2.14	=	89 lb. (88.32 lb.)

Remember that the amount indicated is but a purchasing guideline. Although this mathematical process appears to be time consuming, it is easily computerized. If the purchase units and specification information remain constant, the Edible Portion number derived from each purchase unit should not change. The only change incurred in both the banquet/catering and full-service restaurant, is the number of customers choosing each menu item. In both the banquet/catering approach and the high cost item approach of the full-service restaurant, the calculation that must be performed on a regular basis is the last step in determining the quantity of purchase units to be procured.

Procurement

Once a business identifies the product or service needed, it must develop specifications that describe the product or service and determine the quantity of units to be purchased. The product can then be ordered from an available and reliable purveyor. **Procurement** is the process in which the chef/manager selects the best purveyor and places an order for products as needed. The process to locate purveyors who offer the products described in the specifications can be a time consuming process, but one that is well worth the effort. It is the role of the Purchasing Agent to identify purveyors within the locale that offer the quality and quantity of products desired, a competitive price, and the delivery time and service needed. Selecting the appropriate purveyors reduces the amount of time needed for procurement.

The selection of purveyors should be made prior to picking up the phone to place an order. Authors Feinstein & Stefanelli, in *Purchasing: Selection and Procurement for the Hospitality Industry*, suggest a threefold process that includes an Initial Survey of possible purveyors; creating an Approved Supplier List; and lastly, choosing the best purveyor to meet the demands of your business.

Creating an Approved Purveyor List

The first step in the procurement process is to identify the different categories of products and services to be purchased by the foodservice operation. The exact names and purchase units of the products desired should be listed within the appropriate category. When speaking of food costs, the purchase categories would normally consist of: produce, meats, seafood, poultry, dairy, bread, and grocery. When looking at beverage costs, categories might include: beer, wine, alcohol, soft drinks, and bottled water. Within the overhead cost categories, the business may have items such as cleaning supplies, kitchen utensils, linen, paper/plastic, furniture, fixtures and equipment.

Once the categories of purchases have been stated, the process of identifying potential purveyors within each category begins. Potential purveyors can be found in the white pages of the phone book, in the yellow pages, and in trade journals. They may also be recommended by trade organizations or competitors. Find out which purveyors are available and what they can offer you. Purveyors may be within the restaurant's general vicinity, across town or the city, or even across state lines. The number of purveyors needed for each purchase category depends upon the size, location, and volume of the foodservice operation.

After compiling a list of potential purveyors, identify those that offer the quality of products and services required by the foodservice operation. Contact potential purveyors for an appointment to review and evaluate product quality and the availability of service they offer. Rather than randomly choosing purveyors, start by asking other foodservice operations, competitors, the Chamber of Commerce, or even the Better Business Bureau for suggestions. Try to identify and include at least three purveyors from every purchase category on the Approved Purveyor List. Once an Approved Purveyor List is identified, the foodservice operation can select the purveyors of choice.

Methods of Procurement

Just as the size of the foodservice operation dictates who has the responsibility and the authority to serve as the Purchasing Agent, so will the size of the foodservice operation determine how foodservice operations procure their products from purveyors.

Non-Competitive Procurement. In small, independent operations where the owner is the manager or chef who also performs the role of Purchasing Agent, there may not be adequate time to contact various purveyors on a daily or even weekly basis, to look for the best price. This size of business often uses the **non-competitive procurement** method and chooses a single purveyor per food category (produce, dairy, meats, grocery, etc.) from the previously prepared Approved Purveyor List. Small independent foodservice operations usually do not have enough business volume to get the "good deal" offered by quantity discounts. Small businesses often agree to purchase all their products from a single purveyor in a given category, as long as that purveyor is fair and reasonable in terms of price and service. Medium, Independent operations may also utilize this process.

It is important that small, independent operations prepare an Approved Purveyor List in case a purveyor does not have an item or the purveyor's original prices exceed the maximum price indicated by the operation. An Approved Purveyor List also allows the chef/ manager of a small, independent operation to occasionally check the prices of other purveyors to be certain the chosen purveyor is still the best choice.

One Stop Shopping. Another option for small- and medium-sized foodservice operations is One Stop Shopping. **One Stop Shopping** is a method of procurement used by a Purchasing Agent who purchases as many products as possible from a single purveyor. When a foodservice operation does not have time to compete for the best price and is trying to consolidate purchasing efforts, he/she may choose to buy as many products as possible from one purveyor. Purveyors such as Sysco in the northeast, distribute a large number of purchasing categories. They sell produce, meats, poultry, bread, grocery, dairy, and almost everything else a foodservice operation needs. Advantages of this method of procurement include the need for only one Purchase Order or one phone call, as well as receiving only one order. Disadvantages to the One Stop Shopping method of procurement include:

1. the availability of an alternative product in case the one normally ordered is unavailable.
2. a limited delivery schedule that may occur only once a week.
3. a very large and cumbersome delivery.
4. a steady growing price increase if the purveyor realizes that he is the only purveyor being used.

When choosing the One Stop Shopping method of procurement, be certain that the One Stop Purveyor has alternative products in case the normal product is not available. Also check prices with other purveyors on the Approved Purveyor List occasionally. As a business grows, both in the number of employees and in the sales volume, many more procurement options become available.

Competing for the Best Price. One of the main reasons to spend time creating an Approved Purveyor List is to get the best prices available. Purchasing Agents know that the purveyors listed on the Approved Purveyor List offer comparable product quality, quantity, and service.

The first step in finding the best prices is to develop a **Purveyor Bid Sheet** (Figure 7.3) for all purchase categories and to then list the products needed on the appropriate Purveyor Bid Sheet. Next, forward a copy of the specifications of all products listed on the Purveyor Bid Sheet to each purveyor listed on the Approved Supplier List. Once the specifications have been sent to each of the approved suppliers, the Purchasing Agent contacts the purveyor by phone or by computer, to get a price quote for each product listed. He/she then records the prices on the Purveyor Bid Sheet and selects the purveyor who offers the best prices.

Figure 7.3

Purveyor Bid Sheet

Purveyor Bid Sheet

Food Category   Seafood

Ingredient	Purchase Unit	Purveyor 1	Purveyor 2	Purveyor 3
Sole	lb	$7.25	$6.95	$6.75
Scrod	lb	$5.85	$6.25	$6.30
Lobsters, 1.25 lb.	each	$12.25	$11.67	$13.30
Lump Crab	lb	$14.25	$13.40	$13.50
Shrimp 16/20	lb	$9.95	$10.50	$10.30
Sea Scallops	lb	$12.50	$11.20	$11.95
Tuna Loin	lb	$14.25	$13.95	$14.50

Purveyor 1: Boston Fish Company
Purveyor 2: Sidney's Seafood
Purveyor 3: Quality Seafood

Standing Order. Many products, especially perishable items (bread and dairy), are needed on a regular basis (daily, weekly, etc.). Purveyors often offer foodservice operations the option of a Standing Order to accommodate this need. **Standing Orders** consist of a prescribed order that is received on a regular basis. Phone calls need not be made or purchase orders prepared. This automated process can be utilized within many categories including ordering flowers for dining room tables or side towels for staff. The quantity of products and the days of delivery may be set (for example, 100 side towels delivered every Monday and Thursday). The Standing Order may also be based on a Par Stock set by the foodservice operation. This par stock would be similar to the minimum and maximum par stock levels previously explained. The delivery person would know the maximum par stock levels of the items being delivered, would rotate stock, would remove post-dated product, and "max-out" the pars of the products needed. The Standing Order process can save the Purchasing Agent a lot of order time, although it is strongly recommended that total control not be given to the delivery person. On the day a Standing Order is to be delivered, be certain to inventory the products on hand and check that the invoice reflects what is actually needed.

Cash and Carry. Providing one's own delivery service is becoming more and more popular as large Cash and Carry operations expand to all regions of the country. These huge warehouses offer their members prices that are competitive with those of wholesale purveyors, although foodservice operations need to provide their own transportation of goods, and often their own bags and boxes. When searching for the best price, **Cash and Carry** is an option for the foodservice operator who has the time to use it. Other Cash and Carry options might include going to farmers' markets to pick and choose the freshest produce, or to the docks to purchase the catch of the day. When transporting cash and carry products that are going to be sold to customers, chefs must be certain to adhere to proper sanitation and food safety rules of handling, time, and temperature.

Contract Buying. In institutional foodservice, where menus are cyclical and customers are a captive market, food is often purchased on a contractual basis. The process of **Contract Buying** is similar to that of competing for the Best Price. Written specifications are forwarded to the purveyors listed on the Approved Purveyor List, and they are asked to place a bid for the contract. The purveyor then returns a written bid offering the requested products at a specific quantity, at a certain cost, and for a designated length of time. When all bids are returned, the Purchasing Agent chooses the bid approved and contracts to purchase the items needed. Contract buying is less frequently used in commercial operations because of customer preferences.

Stockless Purchasing. "When the buyer purchases a large amount of product, but arranges for the supplier to store it and deliver it as needed, the procedure is called **Stockless Purchasing**" (Feinstein & Stefanelli 2008, 272). Many purveyors offer this service to foodservice operations to encourage large quantity purchases. Stockless purchasing can be used to purchase paper goods such as placemats and napkins that have a printed logo. Businesses that use paper placemats and napkins rarely have enough storage space available to purchase these bulk items in a large quantity. When purchased in smaller numbers, the cost per unit increases, and when purchased in large numbers, the cost per unit decreases. It is much more cost effective for a business to purchase 200 cases of cocktail napkins up front than to place four separate orders of 50 cases throughout the year, because it costs the purveyor money to set the printing presses each time an order is placed. When purchasing a 200 case order, the presses have only to be set up once; less service, less charge.

Purveyors also offer Stockless Purchasing to foodservice operations because of the environmental conditions of storage areas, which may not be conducive to the storage needs of the products purchased. The area may be too damp, too hot, or too cold. Items that are often purchased using Stockless Purchasing include: match books, printed products with a logo, wine needed to fill the requirements of a new wine list, or perhaps a major staple food item such as salsa, which is used in many Tex-Mex chains. Tex-Mex chains might purchase huge quantities of salsa to get a quantity discount, store them in the purveyor's warehouse, and then have cases of the product delivered to the foodservice operation as needed. The size of the business operation and the amount of time the Purchasing Agent has to spend on procuring products will dictate the methods of procurement used.

Business Documents in Purchasing

The Specification Sheet, Inventory Sheet, and the Purveyor Bid Sheet are business documents used to assist the Purchasing Agent in documenting quality standards, amounts to be purchased, and prices offered by purveyors. These forms also help to control the in-house purchasing process. Once purchasing decisions have been made, a purchase order is prepared.

The Purchase Order

The **Purchase Order** is a formal document that informs the selected purveyor of what is ordered; how much is ordered; and the price that has been quoted for the items needed by the foodservice operation (Figure 7.4). The Purchase Order is also an in-house communication tool that informs departments, such as the Receiving Department and the Kitchen, of what was ordered and from whom. Purchase Orders are commonly prepared in triplicate: one for the purveyor, a second for the Receiving area, and the third for the business office.

The use of this document depends upon the size and the distribution of purchasing responsibility within a foodservice operation. The large restaurant, country club, or hotel should implement formal cost control documents that can be utilized by all departments, while smaller foodservice operations require less formal documents. Businesses that choose not to use formal Purchase Orders should still prepare an informal document that lists what was ordered and from whom. In a Small, Independent Operation (and often in the Medium, Independent Operation), where one person serves as both Purchasing Agent and Receiving Clerk, only pen and paper are needed to write down the items that have been ordered from each purveyor. Regardless of the size of the foodservice operation, a Purchase Order (formal or informal) is an important tool that should be utilized in the cycle of Cost Control.

Figure 7.4
Purchase Order

Purchase Order # 07-000-5234

University Inn
One Library Avenue
Collegetown   RI   ZIP 00000-0000

(401)555-8648

Purchase Order

Purveyor

Name	Quality Seafood
Address	50 Ocean Drive
City	Newport, RI 02840
Phone	(401) 555-FISH

Misc

Date	07/03/20XX
Requested Delivery:	07/05/20XX
Sales Rep:	H23
FOB	

Quantity Ordered	Unit	Description	Unit Price	TOTAL
30	lb.	Sole Fillet	$6.75	$ 202.50
15	lb.	Scrod Fillet	$6.30	$ 94.50
18	ea.	Lobsters, 1.25#	$13.30	$ 239.40
8	lb.	Lump Crab	$13.50	$ 108.00
16	lb.	Shrimp 16/20	$10.30	$ 164.80
10	lb.	Sea Scallops	$11.95	$ 119.50
18	lb.	Tuna Loin	$14.50	$ 261.00

	SubTotal	$ 1,189.70
	Shipping	

Payment

Select One...

Comments	delivery during regularly scheduled hours
Name	
CC #	
Expires	

Tax Rate(s)

TOTAL	$ 1,189.70

Office Use Only

Ordered by_____

There are many decisions to make within the purchasing function including **who** should make the buying decisions and perform the purchasing function. Once the business identifies who holds the responsibilities of Purchasing Agent, the **what** to buy, **where** to buy, **how** much to buy, and **when** to buy follow naturally.

Review Questions/Problems

1. Discuss why various people perform the role of Purchasing Agent in different-sized foodservice operations.

2. Research the products listed and write specifications using the guidelines provided in this chapter. A Specification form is provided on WebCom or Appendix F.

Granny Smith Apples	Sugar
Carrots	Whole Wheat Flour
Asparagus	Instant active yeast
Coffee	Unsweetened chocolate
Tenderloin	Heavy cream
Sole Fillet	Cornstarch
Balsamic vinegar	Granulated sugar

3. Explain how a par stock system is developed and what considerations must be thought through before setting par stock levels.

4. The Rotary Club is planning a pre-Thanksgiving Roasted Turkey banquet at The University Inn. The Inn manager has met with the Club president and has decided on the menu. Using the information provided, calculate the number of purchase units needed for each ingredient to prepare a Roasted Turkey dinner for 300 customers.

Ingredient	Purchase Unit	Portion Size	Edible Yield %
Turkey	1 lb.	6 oz.	40%
Mashed Potatoes	50 lb. bag	4 oz.	81%
Winter Squash	1 lb.	4 oz.	64%
Frozen Green Beans	2.5 lb.	4 oz.	98%
Wine	1.5 liters	6 oz.	98%

5. The University Inn bakeshop manager has received an order from one of its regular customers, Contemporary Caterers, for 60 asparagus, onion, ham, and cheddar cheese quiches. Using the information provided, calculate the number of purchase units needed for each ingredient to prepare the order?

Ingredient	Purchase Unit	Portion Size	Edible Yield %
Asparagus	1 lb.	6 oz.	53%
Onion	2 lb. bag	2 oz.	88%
Ham	1 lb.	5 oz.	65%
Cheddar Cheese	5 lb.	8 oz.	92%

6. The University Inn has performed a sales mix analysis for its menu and has determined the sales mix for the main ingredients of its entrées. The Inn has forecasted a customer count of 2,100 covers for the upcoming week. Using the information provided, calculate the number of **pounds** needed to produce the following menu items.

Item	Standard Portion	Edible Yield %	Sales Mix
Steak	10 oz.	75%	32%
Lamb Loin	6 oz.	40%	22%
Baked Ham	6 oz.	65%	28%
Veal Loin	5 oz.	75%	18%

7. The University Inn Bakeshop has a forecasted that it will sell a total of 300 loaves of bread (banana, cranberry, carrot, or zucchini) for the upcoming week. Using the information provided, calculate the number of **pounds** of each ingredient needed to produce the loaves of bread.

Item	Standard Portion	Edible Yield %	Sales Mix
Banana	oz.	65%	26%
Cranberry	oz.	95%	24%
Carrot	oz.	70%	15%
Zucchini	oz.	94%	35%

8. Explain the advantages and disadvantages of utilizing different methods of procurement for each style of independent operation and the multi-unit foodservice operation described in this chapter.

9. Explain the purpose of a purchase order.

10. Using the spreadsheet package of your professor's choice, develop a spreadsheet to calculate the number of Edible Portions derived from a Purchase Unit utilizing the Standard Portion and Edible Yield %.

11. Using the spreadsheet package of your professor's choice, develop a spreadsheet to prepare a purchase order document.

Receiving Controls

OBJECTIVES

Upon completion of this chapter, the student should be able to:

1. implement proper receiving controls within a foodservice operation.
2. follow the flow of goods through the receiving process.
3. prepare the business forms needed to provide the receiving information necessary for proper control of food, beverage, and supplies.
4. demonstrate the use and understand the purpose of the receiving log, receiving report form, and the purchase distribution journal.

KEY TERMS

Blind Receiving

Direct Purchase

Food Tag

Invoice

Invoice Stamp

Purchase Distribution Journal

Receiving Clerk

Receiving Log

Receiving Report Form

Storeroom Purchase

INTRODUCTION

Receiving is the process in which foodservice operators "check in" the goods delivered to the restaurant to ensure that these products meet the quality and quantity standards that have been determined in the purchasing function. During the purchasing function, products needed by the foodservice operation were identified and procured from the supplier offering the best price and service. An order was placed and the delivery made. The receiving process is the foodservice operator's first chance to take control of products and their costs by maximizing the efficiency of their use. The person responsible for the receiving function will be referred to as the **receiving clerk**. The person who serves as the receiving clerk varies depending on the size of the foodservice operation. Usually, it is only large foodservice operations with a formal storeroom process that have a full-time receiving clerk. In small and medium operations, this role is often performed by a chef, manager, department head, or trained employee.

Receiving tends to be one of the most ignored aspects of food and beverage cost control. Although every chef and manager realizes the importance of the receiving process, the function is sometimes taken too lightly. Foodservice operators often think that implementing a more thorough process of receiving goods "takes too much time." Most foodservice operators, if not all, could better control their costs by simply paying greater attention to the receiving controls they currently have in place. Occasionally, it is just a matter of taking more time to check in the goods, while at other times, a more efficient system is needed. William C. Schwartz, a former accountant for the National Restaurant Association, in his article "Eliminate Poor Receiving Habits," states that "nearly half an operation's variance (difference between actual and ideal food cost), is the result of poor receiving habits. To the average restaurant, this represents a whopping 2% of sales." Mr. Schwartz goes on to say that this 2% of sales would have been additional profit if it had not been spent to purchase food To put Mr. Schwartz's findings into dollar figures, a foodservice operation that brought in $2,000,000 in sales last year and unnecessarily spent 2% of that due to improper receiving practices, would have wasted $40,000 ($2,000,000 × 2%) more than necessary. The measures that follow can help foodservice managers to better control food and beverage costs and to ultimately generate increased profits. This chapter explains in detail how to properly receive goods and how goods flow through the receiving process.

Invoice Receiving: The Common Approach

An **invoice** is the bill prepared by the purveyor, which accompanies the delivery. It states what was ordered, the quantity, the unit price, the extensions, and total cost (Figure 8.1). The invoice is prepared in duplicate: a copy for the purveyor, and a copy for the foodservice operation. The invoice is often the only form used to check in products. The receiving clerk uses it initially to verify the quantity counts and the weight of the products delivered. The receiver will note a check mark when an item is delivered correctly or make a notation when not (see lobsters).

Figure 8.1

Invoice

Quality Seafood
50 Ocean Drive, Newport, RI 02840
(401)555-FISH

Invoice No. 00246-00

Invoice

Customer

Name: University Inn
Address: One Library Avenue
City: Collegetown   State RI   ZIP 00000-0000
Phone: (401)555-8648

Misc

Date: 07/03/201X
Order No.
Rep
FOB

Quantity			Description	Unit Price	TOTAL	
Ordered	Unit	Received				
30	lb.	✓	Sole Fillet	$6.75	$	202.50
15	lb.	✓	Scrod Fillet	$6.30	$	94.50
18	ea.	16	Lobsters, 1.25#	$13.30	$	239.40
8	lb.	✓	Lump Crab	$13.50	$	108.00
16	lb.	✓	Shrimp 16/20	$10.30	$	164.80
10	lb.	✓	Sea Scallops	$11.95	$	119.50
18	lb.	✓	Tuna Loin	$14.50	$	261.00
				SubTotal	$	1,189.70
				Shipping		
			Tax Rate(s)			
				TOTAL	$	1,189.70

Payment

Comments
Name
CC #
Expires

Terms: n/30

Office Use Only

Received by_____

Receiving is the foodservice operator's first chance to control products and costs once the products have arrived. Receiving Scenario #1: Typically, the products arrive at about 11:45 a.m. The shout of the word "delivery" echoes until it reaches the ears of the chef/manager. Ten minutes and two phone calls later, the chef/manager gets back to check in the order. The driver, frantically tapping his foot, gives the invoice to the chef/manager. The chef/manager quickly compares the invoice to the product delivery in front of him. He/she signs the invoice, and hurries into the kitchen to help with the lunch rush. The driver leaves. The goods sit in the receiving area (at the back door), until the lunch period is over. (Sound familiar?)

Invoice Receiving, as just described, is common at many foodservice operations and not a very effective cost control measure. How does the receiving clerk know which products were ordered if there were no purchase orders, no specifications, and no effort to check quality and quantity standards? Simple measures that can be taken to improve this process and to help ensure that Invoice Receiving is a useful cost control procedure.

Invoice Receiving: A Better Approach

Invoice Receiving can be an effective receiving control method if it is used correctly. The process should include the use of three purchasing documents: the specification, the purchase order, and the purveyor bid sheet (discussed in Chapter 7). When used in conjunction with additional purchase documents, tools, and techniques, invoice receiving can be a sound method of receiving goods.

We will now revisit the previous scenario, but this time implement the use of the three purchasing forms mentioned, as well as other tools and techniques to ensure quantity and quality standards.

Receiving Scenario 2: The goods arrive at 10:00 a.m. in the middle of the scheduled receiving hours. The receiving clerk, Tom the Prep Cook, sees the delivery driver open the back door. He stops his "prep" and meets the driver at the receiving door. Tom accepts the invoice from the driver and immediately begins checking in the goods as the first hand truck is emptied. While counting the items, he weighs products to ensure that the quantity stated on the invoice is exactly what has been delivered. He checks quality by opening boxes, dumping cases into wire baskets, and checking the temperature of refrigerated and frozen goods with a thermometer. To verify quality, he refers to the Specification for the product listed in the computer system (or in the specification file box close at hand). Once the delivery has been checked for quality and the stated quantities on the invoice have been confirmed, Tom compares the invoice to the Purchase Order. The Purveyor Bid Sheet is used if any questions concerning price arise. Once all the goods have been checked in, Tom brings the invoice to the chef/manager to sign. Tom hands the invoice back to the driver. The driver leaves, and Tom begins to put the goods away.

"Receiving Scenario #2" still utilizes the invoice as the initial document to receive goods, but this time, Tom the Prep Cook utilizes several other receiving techniques as well to ensure product standards. In reexamining Receiving Scenario #2 one step at a time, the purpose of each step can be clearly identified.

Receiving Hours. Established Receiving Hours are an effective tool to ensure that when deliveries are made, an employee has the time to properly check in the goods and to put them away immediately. Quality product standards are therefore maintained. Receiving Hours are agreed upon by the purveyor and the foodservice operation. Set Receiving Hours are beneficial not only to the foodservice operator, but also to the purveyor. An agreed upon delivery schedule reduces the time a driver has to wait around, which allows him to make more deliveries during the day.

Receiving Clerk. Notice that it is not the chef or manager who checks in the goods in Receiving Scenario #2. Chefs and Managers are too busy to devote a lot of time to the receiving function.

Receiving demands carefully monitoring products to ensure that quality and quantity standards are met. Proper training of another employee may better serve the process.

Invoice. The invoice is the initial document used to receive the goods. It is used to verify that the products delivered are exactly as stated on the invoice prepared by the purveyor. Although a product is listed on the invoice, this does not guarantee that the product has been delivered. The receiving clerk must have a document prepared by the restaurant stating what has been ordered to support the claim.

Tools. The scale is the most important tool in the receiving process because most products are purchased by weight. Even when products are purchased by the case, there are weight range standards that should be met. There is no possible way to guarantee that a business is receiving the quantity of products purchased by weight, unless the receiving clerk weighs the product. Many foodservice operations do not weigh products and rely totally on the honesty of their purveyors. Although this sounds wonderful, rest assured that the purveyors know exactly which accounts weigh products and which ones do not. This is not to say that purveyors are intentionally "out to get" foodservice operations, but unintentional errors do occur daily in the foodservice industry. Product specific equipment, such as the thermometer for refrigerated and frozen goods, is also essential to properly "check-in" products.

The Specification. The specification is a brief yet detailed description of the product or service being purchased. The specification should be available to the receiving clerk in case a question arises regarding whether or not a product meets a quality or quantity standard.

The Purchase Order. An invoice is a business form prepared by the purveyor, describing the order (units and costs) the foodservice operation has placed. A Purchase Order (whether formal or informal), is a document prepared by the Purchasing Agent, which lists exactly what has been ordered. Once the goods have been checked in, the Invoice items should be compared item by item with the Purchase Order list. Without a Purchase Order, the receiving clerk may unintentionally accept goods that should not be accepted. Failure to use a Purchase Order can contribute to the 2% excessive costs previously mentioned. Once accepted, these products are put away and perhaps never seen again until the monthly inventory. A formal Purchase Order, as described in Chapter 7, lists unit prices of the products ordered. This document can aid the receiving clerk if a price concern arises.

The Purveyor Bid Sheet. Sometimes the foodservice operation uses a piece of paper to record what was purchased and from whom, in lieu of a purchase order. In this case, a Purveyor Bid Sheet, as described in Chapter 8, can be used to confirm and check price information.

Signing the Invoice. Invoices are legal documents. When a foodservice operation opens an account with a purveyor, a signature card is signed by all management staff that have the authority to sign invoices. Once the invoice has been signed, the foodservice operation is legally obligated to pay the total due regardless of any errors. This is why it is extremely important that care is taken to thoroughly check orders.

Putting Goods Away Immediately. To get the maximum shelf life from products, it is important that products not remain out of their proper environment for any longer than absolutely necessary. In fact, many foodservice operations check in refrigerated and frozen goods in their own walk-ins at the time of delivery. Putting goods in their proper place also ensures that products do not "walk away." Products that are left out in the open or by the back door for long periods of time are often a temptation for thieves. Alleviate the temptation by putting goods away immediately.

Blind Receiving: The Best Approach

Another method of receiving that is used in the foodservice industry is known as **Blind Receiving**. This method is said to provide the best control for receiving goods. Although similar to Invoice Receiving, the invoice is not accepted from the driver until the goods have been checked for quality and quantity when using "blind receiving." As the goods are delivered, the receiving clerk carefully inspects the goods and checks that the products meet the specifications. The receiving clerk weighs products, checks temperatures, counts items, performs proper check-in techniques, and then records them on the receiving log.

The preparation of a **receiving log** helps the receiving clerk to more carefully inspect the products delivered. Not having the invoice in hand and not knowing what is supposed to be there, the receiving clerk takes more time to count and weigh products, and to check their quality. Once the receiving log is complete, the invoice is then accepted from the driver and compared to the receiving log to make adjustments as needed. After the receiving log has been compared to the invoice, the invoice is compared to the purchase order to guarantee that the products listed on the invoice were actually ordered by the foodservice operation. Both Invoice Receiving and Blind Receiving can be effective receiving techniques if the receiving clerk is properly trained and the foodservice operation allows adequate time for the process.

Other Business Forms in Receiving

Credit Memos. At times a product listed on the invoice is identified as not meeting the quality standards of the foodservice operation, or as one that had never been ordered. When these unwanted products appear (lobsters, Figure 8.1), the receiving clerk can request a credit memo from the purveyor's driver. A credit memo is a business form that adjusts the total of the invoice, by indicating on the memo the items that have been rejected and returned to the purveyor. The credit memo is prepared by the driver, usually in copy, and is attached to each copy of the invoice indicating the change to the invoice (Figure 8.2).

Figure 8.2

Request for Credit Memo

REQUEST FOR CREDIT MEMO				
Quality Seafood 50 Ocean Avenue Newport, RI 02840			Date 07/03/20XX Invoice No. 00246-00	
Quantity	**Unit**	**Item**	**Unit Price**	**Total**
2	ea.	Lobsters, 1.25#	$ 13.30	$ 26.60
Drivers Signature			Total	$ 26.60
Approved By:				

Pick Up Memos. At times, products that are not needed by the foodservice operation are mistakenly delivered and go unnoticed by both the receiving clerk and the management staff. Perhaps a case of twenty-four 10 oz. bottles of sparkling water was delivered rather than a case of twenty-four 10 oz. bottles of non-sparkling water. If the foodservice operation rarely gets a request for bottled sparkling water, the foodservice manager calls the purveyor to request a pick up. A Pick Up memo is then prepared by the purveyor to "pick-up" the product from the foodservice operation. When the driver brings the next order, he brings the Pick Up memo to collect the unwanted case, signs the memo and the driver returns the form to the purveyor so that the foodservice operation's account can be appropriately adjusted.

Figure 8.3
Invoice Stamps

INVOICE STAMP A

Received by:	Rick		Date	7/03/20XX
Unit Prices:	OK	Extensions:	OK	
Totals:	OK	Credit Memo:	$26.60	
Approved for Payment				
Check #		Date:		

Purchase Distribution Journal			
Acct #	50-325	Seafood	$1,163.10
Acct #			
Acct #			
Acct #			

INVOICE STAMP B

Received by:	Rick		Date	7/03/20XX
Unit Prices:	OK	Extensions:	OK	
Totals:	OK	Credit Memo:	$26.60	
Approved for Payment				
Check #		Date:		

Receiving Report Form	
Directs	$1,163.10
Stores	

The Flow of Costs

Once the goods have been received, the invoice is signed, and the goods put away, the bookkeeping function begins to track the flow of costs through the foodservice operation. This process begins at the receiving area where the invoice is stamped with a bookkeeping tool known as the Invoice Stamp (Figure 8.3). Traditionally, the Invoice Stamp was an inked rubber stamp, which consolidated all the invoice information into a given area, usually on the back of the invoice. Today, the Invoice Stamp can be unique to a business and can be specially ordered by a foodservice manager to include the information that the foodservice operation is interested in tracking. While an actual "stamp" is not required, the information that is consolidated into a specific area ensures that products and their costs are accurately tracked.

The Invoice Stamp usually identifies the date on which the goods were received and the individual who checked them in. By knowing who checked in the goods and who put them away, it is easy to confirm whether or not the product was actually delivered. Information concerning unit prices, extensions, and invoice totals are initialed to confirm accuracy. The verification of this information allows the bookkeeper to prepare the invoice for payment and to post the invoice to the current Accounts Payable file. When the invoice comes due, the manager pulls the actual invoice from the current Accounts Payable file, and initials the area Approved for Payment. The bookkeeper prepares the check, records the invoice number on the check, and transfers the date paid and the check number to the check number area on the Invoice Stamp. The recording of the invoice number on the check informs the purveyor of the actual invoice being paid. The check number is recorded on the invoice to document the number of the check used to pay the invoice and to support proof of payment. Most purveyors send a monthly Statement of Accounts to verify all transactions that have occurred between the purveyor and the foodservice operation. This statement helps both businesses to keep accurate records.

Other information included within the invoice stamp can be used to help track the types of products purchased or track where the products go after leaving the receiving area. Two effective tracking methods will be discussed. The information collected on Invoice Stamp A provides information to prepare The Purchase Distribution Journal, which is commonly used to track the money spent in the various areas of costs. The information collected on Invoice Stamp B provides information to prepare the Receiving Report Form that tracks the movement of goods from the receiving area to the storeroom or production.

The Purchase Distribution Journal

The **Purchase Distribution Journal** (Figure 8.4) assists the chef/manager to identify how much money is being spent in the different areas of cost. Foodservice operations may track not only food costs, but also the types of food categories such as produce, meats, seafood, poultry, dairy, and breads. Beverage Costs may be broken into liquor, wines, draught beer, bottled beer, and soft drinks. Overhead Costs might include paper/plastic supplies, linen, kitchen utensils, glassware, silverware, non-essentials, and cleaning supplies. Numbers are often used to classify various types of purchases on the foodservice operation's "Chart of Accounts." The chart of accounts is a system that assigns a number to each of the types of purchases. This system assists foodservice operations to classify costs accurately and consistently. A sample chart of accounts, recommended by the National Restaurant Association, can be found in Appendix C. As the goods are received, the receiving clerk identifies the account and records the purchase so that the bookkeeper can post the information to the Purchase Distribution Journal. Implementing a chart of accounts system,

Figure 8.4
Purchase Distribution Journal

PURCHASE DISTRIBUTION JOURNAL				Category:	Food		Month/Year:		July 20XX	
Date	Invoice #	Meats	Seafood	Poultry	Produce	Grocery	Dairy	Bakery	Other	Total
7/01	127645	$ 987.75		$ 198.56						$ 1,186.31
7/02	0635				$ 645.50					$ 645.50
7/03	00246		$ 1,163.10							$ 1,163.10
7/04	11135						$ 145.60			$ 145.60
7/05	246778-12					$ 998.34		$ 56.95		$ 1,055.29

and tracking the amount of money spent in each of the cost categories, can help management to identify the specifics of cost control.

Depending upon the number of purchase categories, the Purchase Distribution Journal may be broken down into several journals. One journal might identify food purchases, another beverage purchases, and yet a third for purchases in the Overhead Cost category. The Purchase Distribution Journal is usually prepared on a monthly basis. At the end of the month, a cost analysis can be prepared by totaling each of the purchasing categories and determining the percent of sales that each represents. In addition to knowing the percent of food sales spent to purchase food products, a business can also identify the exact percent that each category represents of total sales.

The information posted to the Purchase Distribution Journal can help foodservice managers to identify costs that are in or out of line. For example, it is March 6, and the foodservice operation has just received word from the accountant that the February food cost % reached an all-time high of 42%, which is six percentage points above what the operation considers to be normal. This figure tells the manager that much more money was spent to purchase the food items needed to produce food sales. The foodservice manager questions how the food cost % rose by 6%. If the foodservice operation regularly prepares a Purchase Distribution Journal, the foodservice operator can easily identify the category of purchases that were higher than usual during the month. Without the Purchase Distribution Journal the higher expenditures might never be identified. Even though it is too late to control last month's food cost, the foodservice manager, who has the Purchase Distribution Journal as an information tool, can now implement an additional control procedure to examine the excessive cost category.

The Receiving Report Form

Receiving Report Forms (Figure 8.5), are used in large foodservice operations that have a formal storeroom process, are used to track the movement of goods by classifying them into tracks/types. Products move from the receiving area into one of two areas; storage or production. A **Direct Purchase** goes directly into the production area when delivered and is assigned to the cost of sales when received. A **Storeroom Purchase** is taken to the storeroom to be stored until needed. The Storeroom Purchase is assigned to the cost of sales when requisitioned. The Receiving Report form helps the chef/manager to identify where the goods are kept so that they might be more efficiently controlled.

Figure 8.5

Receiving Report Form

RECEIVING REPORT FORM				Month/Year:		July 20XX				Page:	1
Date	Invoice #	Purveyor	Description	Food	Beverage	Other	$Directs	$Stores	General Info
7/01	127645	TJ	Meat/Poultry	$ 1,186.31				$ 1,186.31	
7/02	0635	CFV	Produce	$ 645.50			$ 645.50		
7/03	00246	QS	Seafood	$ 1,163.10			$ 1,163.10		
7/04	11135	KD	Dairy	$ 145.60			$ 145.60		
7/05	246778-12	STC	Grocery	$ 1,055.29			$ 56.95	$ 998.34	

Products classified as storeroom purchases that do not have a clearly designated purchase unit must be clearly identified before they are transferred. Examples include an "As Purchased" meat product, or an undressed fish. It is important that the cost, as well as the quantity of the product, is identified before putting it into the storeroom. Before this product is transferred to the storeroom, a food tag should be filled out and attached so that the storeroom clerk might accurately assign it to food cost when the product is requisitioned. The use of a **food tag** is also helpful in taking a monthly physical inventory (Figure 8.6). "Storage and Inventory Controls" are discussed in Chapter 9.

Figure 8.6
Food Tag

		Date	
TAG #	# 12435	Received	July 1, 20XX

Item	Leg of Lamb
Weight	8 lbs.
Total Cost	$32.25
Unit Cost	$4.03
Purveyor	TJ Meats
Date Issued	July 3, 20XX

		Date	
TAG #	# 12435	Received	July 1, 20XX

Item	Leg of Lamb
Weight	8 lbs.
Total Cost	$32.25
Unit Cost	$4.03
Purveyor	TJ Meats
Date Issued	July 3, 20XX

Both the Purchase Distribution Journal and the Receiving Report Form can help a business to identify costs and product movement throughout the foodservice operation. At the end of the month, new forms are started and the process of tracking product and costs continues.

Review Questions

1. Compare and contrast "Invoice Receiving" and "Blind Receiving." Why is Invoice Receiving more commonly used if Blind Receiving is said to have better control?

2. How can a foodservice operation improve its receiving techniques?

3. Explain how a manager might implement a Blind Receiving technique that would be effective and efficient within a foodservice operation.

4. Prepare a chart of accounts for a foodservice operation of your choice.

5. What is the difference between a "Direct Purchase" and a "Storeroom Purchase"? When is each assigned to daily food cost?

6. Using the computer program of your professor's choice, create a receiving report form that best meets the needs of your foodservice operation.

Chapter 9

Storage and Inventory Controls

© 2014, Baloncici, Shutterstock, Inc.

OBJECTIVES

Upon completion of this chapter, the student should be able to:

1. develop standards for proper storage controls.
2. perform and cost a physical inventory.
3. calculate the Cost of Sales.
4. maintain a perpetual inventory.
5. implement efficient and cost effective issuing controls.

KEY TERMS

Bin Card

FIFO

Inventory Turnover

Physical Inventory

Perpetual Inventory

Requisition

Transfer Memo

INTRODUCTION

Once products have been received, the products that did not go directly into production are moved to the storage area to be stored until needed. Maintaining proper storage control of these products is necessary to prevent spoilage and the theft of goods by both employees and non-employees. Control procedures of storage facilities vary from one foodservice operation to another depending upon the size of the foodservice operation. Larger foodservice operations usually employ a full-time storage clerk who is responsible for maintaining storage controls and for issuing products to production when needed. Smaller foodservice operations typically do not have a formal storeroom process or a full-time storage clerk. Managers at small properties have to develop standard operating procedures for the movement of products in and out of the storeroom. Regardless of the size of the foodservice operation and the person in charge of storage controls, many of the same standard storage control procedures must be implemented. The person responsible for storage controls will be referred to as the storage clerk.

Establishing Effective Storage Controls

There are several areas of concern that must be addressed when designing proper storage facilities and when implementing effective storage controls. Each of these areas of concern is discussed in detail with special attention given on how to efficiently and effectively maintain storage control.

The Size of the Storage Area.   The size of the storage area is usually smaller than what is desired by the foodservice operator. When foodservice operators first look at a facility, they commonly consider only the amount of room needed to store food and beverage items. Glassware, serviceware, paper supplies, cleaning supplies, extra furniture, fixtures, equipment, office supplies, and paper work from past years must also be stored somewhere. Recommendations made by professional organizations such as the Research Department of the National Restaurant Association state that as a rule of thumb, the space needed for all storage should be approximately five square feet per seat in the dining room.

Location.   Ideally, the storage facility should be located somewhere between the receiving and production areas to ease the flow of goods through the foodservice operation. When constructing a new building it may be easy to plan for space, but when moving to an existing building, the manager has to work at developing a secure and efficient flow of goods from wherever the storage space is located. Inconveniently located storage space makes daily operations more tedious and may increase the risk of theft and pilferage.

Theft and Pilferage.   Theft usually refers to the unauthorized removal of goods by a non-employee. Non-employees can be customers and/or delivery personnel. Pilferage is employee theft and is a serious threat to security and cost control within the foodservice industry. Employees are often caught removing products from restaurants for their personal use. Although employees may inadvertently take a piece of silverware or a side towel home in their aprons, these items rarely see their way back to the restaurant. Items that disappear unintentionally must also be replaced by the restaurant, which incurs additional costs to replace these items.

There must be storage controls in place to prevent both theft and pilferage. Camera technology is becoming more commonplace as a security control used to identify improper activity. In a formal storage facility there is usually a storage clerk in the storeroom during operational hours to control the products that enter and leave the storeroom. In facilities that do not have a formal storeroom and storeroom clerk, a simple lock and key method is commonly used. Storage facilities should be locked at all times and individuals should only be allowed to enter the storeroom when accompanied by authorized personnel. Unfortunately, this procedure can be a real headache for the kitchen, bar, or dining room that is unprepared for production. Proper planning of production (Chapter 10), helps to relieve this burden.

Storage Conditions.   To maintain quality products and to ensure their maximum shelf life, products must be stored at recommended temperatures and consumed prior to the end of their shelf-life. The shelf life of a product is the recommended amount of time a product will maintain its quality for use in production. Products must also be stored well out of the Temperature Danger Zone (41°F to 135°F, 5°C to 57°C) so that foodborne illnesses do not result. All perishable and non-perishable products have a recommended shelf life and recommended storage temperatures to maximize the useful life of the product, and to prevent foodborne illnesses. Storage temperature guidelines recommended by the Educational Foundation of the National Restaurant Association can be found in Figure 9.1

Proper storage temperatures are important and checking temperatures routinely is a necessity. Inspections at opening time, after lunch, and before closing should be done to guarantee that the equipment is maintaining its proper temperatures. This responsibility should be part of a kitchen employee's job description.

Storage Scenario #1: It is 10:00 p.m. and all but a few dinners have been prepared and served. The head line cook, Keith, informs the Manager On Duty (M.O.D.) that the temperature gauge in the main walk-in is running at about 45°F. The manager calls the Refrigeration Repair Service and leaves a message with the answering service. At almost midnight, when most of the kitchen employees are in the final stages of completing their job responsibilities and are almost ready to clock out, no call has yet been received from the refrigeration company. The M.O.D. decides to empty the walk-in and to assist Keith and the kitchen staff to find other space (reach-ins, bar coolers, keg coolers), to store the goods until the walk-in can be repaired. At 1:00 a.m., the refrigeration repair service calls to see if they can be of assistance. The M.O.D. asks them to arrive at 7.00 a.m. the next morning to repair the walk-in.

Figure 9.1
Temperatures

Temperature Danger Zone		41°F	to	135°F
Refrigeration Recommended Temperatures:	Meat and Poultry	32°F	to	40°F
	Fish	30°F	to	34°F
	Shellfish	35°F	to	45°F
	Eggs	38°F	to	40°F
	Dairy	38°F	to	40°F
	Fruits and Vegetables	41°F	to	45°F
Freezer Storage:		-10°F	to	0°F
Dry Storage		50°F	ideal	

In Storage Scenario #1, Keith performs his job responsibly. He knows what the temperature of the walk-in should be; he checks the temperature a number of times; and watches to be certain that the rise in temperature is not due to the regular opening and closing of the door. Once he realizes that there is a problem, he informs the manager.

Storage Scenario #1 continues . . . . Less than a week later, the temperature in the walk-in is again running high. It is Keith's night off. A different manager is on duty and the high temperature goes unnoticed. The next morning the opening manager is performing the opening inspection and identifies that the walk-in temperature reads 53°F. Thousands of dollars are lost because food that has been in the Temperature Danger Zone for too long a period of time has spoiled and cannot be safely used. See Figure 9.1 for recommended refrigeration temperatures.

Storage Equipment. Storage Equipment refers to shelving units, proper storage containers and moving equipment that makes the storage process easier and more efficient. Perishable items should be stored on slotted shelving units so that air may circulate among the products stored in refrigeration and freezer units. Non-perishable, canned, bottled, and dry goods should be stored on solid shelving. Some foodservice operations find that slotted shelving is less expensive than solid shelving and often use it for all products.

Storage Scenario #2: The bar manager receives a delivery of non-perishable food items (cases of canned juices, cocktail onions, Worcestershire sauce, cocktail olives, and a gallon of maraschino cherries), which are needed to produce and garnish beverages. The bartender who checks in the goods promptly transfers the products to the storage area to put them away. Everything in the dry storage area is placed in an orderly fashion on slotted five-shelf shelving units. The bartender opens a case of four 1 gallon glass jars of maraschino cherries and properly puts them away on the next to the top shelf of the shelving unit. As the bartender rotates the stock of maraschino cherries already on hand, one of the glass gallon jars crashes into another, cracking and spilling its contents on the shelf on which it was stored, and then drips through slotted shelves to the floor below.

Even though solid shelving is more expensive, it can help to save a great deal of time, energy, effort, and frustration. Foodservice operators who purchase slotted shelving units often use sheet pans for lining the slotted shelves to prevent catastrophes such as the one described in Storage Scenario #2. Solid shelving units are sturdier as well as more durable and practical.

Proper storage containers are also important. Products should not be stored in the container in which they have been purchased, unless the product has been purchased in its usable container (such as a 1/2 gallon of orange juice or a 14 oz. bottle of ketchup). Products should be stored in air tight, pest protected containers, to protect against contamination and foodborne illnesses. Cardboard cases and thick heavy paper bags do not provide protection from insects and rodents. In fact, roaches think of cardboard cases as condominiums and often travel to and from different establishments in the cardboard itself, rather than in the product. All food products should be removed from paper and cardboard containers before placed in storage.

Cleanliness.   In addition to storing products in proper storage containers, it is extremely important that the storage areas be kept clean so as not to attract rodents and insects. Storage areas must be broom swept daily and a regular pest control schedule should be implemented. Insects and rodents need not be seen to support the necessity of routine pest control maintenance. Once bugs are seen, chances are that many more (hundreds) have found a new home in cracks, walls, and equipment.

Storage Scenario #3: Richard has been recently hired as the Executive Chef of a brand new hotel in the southern region of the United States where the weather is warm and insects are plentiful. The brand new hotel does not yet have a pest problem, but Chef Richard schedules an appointment with the Head of Maintenance to discuss hiring a company to perform routine maintenance pest control for the new restaurant. Chef Richard knows the importance of routine maintenance even if a pest problem does not currently exist. The Head of Maintenance does not see the necessity of spending preventative monies. Chef Richard insists, but the Head of Maintenance denies the request. They spend almost two months debating the issue of Pest Control maintenance, and still the Head of Maintenance refuses to hire a service. Chef Richard goes to the General Manager of the Hotel to state his case. The General Manager hears his case, and tells Chef Richard that he will inform him of his decision by the end of the week.

Thursday night, as Chef Richard is performing the closing inspection of the kitchen, he sees a black mark on the hot water pipe running down the wall to the sink. He moves closer to get a better look. He finds about fifteen roaches gathered together absorbing the heat from the hot water pipe. Now there is a real problem. If he can see fifteen, there have to be more; but just how many more? Chef Richard continues to check all the warm areas in the kitchen looking for roaches. He finds them in the cappuccino machine, the motor of the cold water cooler, and in the baskets from which the bread is served to customers. They are everywhere. Chef Richard is frustrated that the foodservice operation went so quickly from being pest free to totally infested, because the infestation could have been prevented.

Storage Scenario #3 continues . . . The decision of the hotel's General Manager is to override that of the Head of Maintenance and to allow Chef Richard to hire a Pest Control Service. Chef Richard informs the General Manager of a need for the service and tells him of all the areas where he has now located roaches. Chef Richard calls several Pest Maintenance Control services to discuss the process of eliminating the pest problem.

Routine pest control maintenance is always important. The frequency of routine service may vary from region to region depending on the temperature and weather. Routine pest control maintenance is a sound measure to control contamination costs of products and to ensure that a business is not ruined by unwanted pests. Pests such as roaches, ants, rats, and mice are a serious problem. It is far easier to prevent a pest problem than to correct a pest problem. Even the best Pest Control services admit that one chemical application will not end the problem. At the first service, the fogging and spraying kills the roaches that have currently invaded the property, but as these roaches meet their death, they deliver egg sacks. A second chemical must be used to kill the eggs that have already built immunity to the first chemical used. Each egg sack is estimated to house anywhere from nine to twenty-five new roaches and the roach problem continues. Routine, preventative pest control service is a must.

Setting Up the Storage Areas. Adhering to the adage, "Every item has a place and every item in its place" is the best policy to describe setting up storage areas. All products in dry storage, walkins, and freezers should have a designated location, and these products should not be found anywhere but in that assigned spot. There is nothing more frustrating to a chef than not finding a product where it is supposed to be. An absence of product usually means that the product must have been used. The chef orders more. As the chef is putting away the new delivery, he finds four cases of the product that he was just looking for in a location other than where they should be. If this is a perishable product, chances are the foodservice operation will not be able to use and sell the entire product before it spoils. If this is a non-perishable product, it can be used, but it has already tied up money in inventory that could have been allocated somewhere else.

Well-organized storage facilities often use shelving labels to identify product location. Others have floor plans and shelving plans tacked to the wall or to the shelving units to indicate the product location so that products can be easily located for storage and distribution. Identifying a specific storage location for products allows for the advanced preparation of inventory sheets and a reduction in the amount of time needed to perform the monthly physical inventory.

FIFO (First In, First Out)

First In, First Out is the method of stock rotation that should be used to insure that products are used up before their shelf life expires. FIFO makes dollars and cents (and sense). If a product is purchased first, it should be used first. If this is common sense, why is it often a headache for most foodservice operators to convince employees to rotate stock properly? Stock rotation is a tedious, time consuming process because of the set-up of most storerooms. Storage areas must be "employee friendly" if managers expect that employees will rotate stock properly and efficiently.

There are two things that foodservice operators can do to make rotating stock "employee friendly." The first is to date products that do not already have expiration dates. The second is to organize the facility so that the actual process of stock rotation is easier for employees to perform. Figure 9.2 illustrates two methods of Storage Facility Set Up: one that encourages proper stock rotation and one that does not.

Poorly set up storage areas (Figure 9.2A) commonly have shelves that line the wall and make it very difficult to rotate stock. When the new stock needs to be put away, employees must remove the older product from the shelf and put the new product to the back. They must then return the older product in front of the new ones on the shelves. This process is tedious and time consuming. Storage Set Up, in Figure 9.2A, tempts the employee to improperly rotate stock. A more efficient storage set up (Figure 9.2B) provides free standing shelves where products can be removed from one side and stocked from the other side. This set up provides employees with a task that is less time consuming.

Figure 9.2
Storeroom Set Up

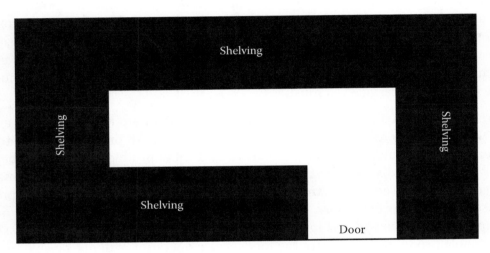

A

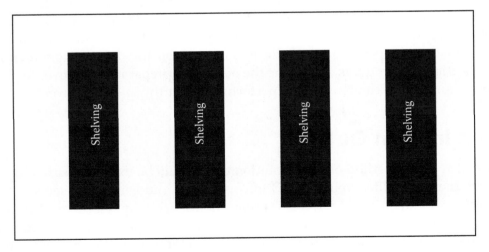

B

Establishing Standard Inventory Controls

Foodservice operations frequently use two types of inventories. One is the physical (periodic) inventory, which is an actual count of all food and beverage products on hand. The second is the perpetual inventory, which tracks the movement of food and beverage products on paper, rather than physically counting the products in storage. Both inventories are valid methods and complement one another in establishing inventory controls.

Physical Inventory

On the first morning of every month prior to any production, chefs and managers, often accompanied by a controller, count the food and beverage items in all the storage and production areas. This process is known as a Physical Inventory. A Physical Inventory is an actual count of all products on hand that will be used to produce sales. The two people taking the inventory go from storage area to storage area to count and record the products on hand. Although a physical inventory can be taken by one person, two people typically perform the inventory; one counts, and the other records the quantity on the inventory sheets. The presence of two individuals makes the process more efficient. A third individual may also participate as an observer to the process. The controller is a representative from the accounting office who provides oversight and additional control during the physical inventory.

The inventory sheets on which the physical inventory is taken should be prepared prior to taking the physical inventory (Figure 9.3). The preparation of inventory sheets ahead of time increases efficiency and reduces the time to perform the inventory. Inventory sheets should list the items by the location of the item rather than alphabetically. Taking a physical inventory, location by location, rack by rack, shelf by shelf, insures that nothing will be missed in the count. Although alphabetical preparation of inventory sheets appears organized, using them is totally unrealistic and chaotic.

A physical inventory is taken once a month so that it can be used to calculate the Monthly Cost and Cost % of Sales. The physical inventory closes the books on the previous month, and opens the books for the current month. Most chefs/managers look at a physical inventory as a check-up process. An explanation follows concerning how most foodservice managers place a dollar value on the physical inventory and how this figure is used to determine the monthly Cost of Sales.

Costing and Extending the Physical Inventory. Once the physical inventory is counted and recorded on the inventory sheets, the inventory is extended, totaled, and used to determine the monthly Cost of Sales. Because of the constant inventory turnover of food and beverage products, and the seasonal differences in prices, the most common method used to cost the physical inventory is the Latest Purchase Price method. This method is recommended by Laventhol and Harworth in the book they prepared for the National Restaurant Association (*Uniform System of Accounts for Restaurants,* 1990). The foodservice manager identifies the last price paid for each item from the invoices and then records it in the Unit Column of the Inventory Sheets. Knowing the quantity and unit costs of the items (multiply quantity × unit costs), the foodservice manager can then carefully extend and total the inventory. The Latest Purchase Price method is the most common one used for inventory values. When inventory needs to be replaced, the last price paid for a product is usually used because it is often still its market price. Although other methods of inventory costing may be chosen, research shows that the Latest Purchase Price is the most popular and the easiest to use. Computerized inventory spreadsheet programs that only require posting the quantity and price to the spreadsheet are also available. The computer uses these posted numbers and then quickly and accurately extends and totals the inventory. Once the total food inventory and the total beverage inventory have been determined, the Cost of Food Sales and the Cost of Beverages Sales can be reached.

Figure 9.3
Inventory Sheet

INVENTORY SHEET

Category:		Beverage/Bottled Beer		Location:	Beach Bar
QTY	UNIT	ITEM	COST	UNIT	EXTENSION
24	btl.	Coors, 12 oz.	$19.25	cs-24	$19.25
13	btl.	Coors Light, 12 oz.	$28.96	cs-24	$15.69
19	btl.	Budweiser, 12 oz.	$18.96	cs-24	$15.01
33	btl.	Miller High Life, 12 oz.	$14.50	cs-24	$19.94
12	btl.	Heineken, 12 oz.	$42.50	cs-24	$21.25
6	btl.	Michelob Ultra, 12 oz.	$14.50	cs-24	$3.63
8	btl.	O'doules, 12 oz.	$32.50	cs-24	$10.83
				Total:	$105.59

The Cost of Sales. The formulas to determine the Cost of Food Sales and the Cost of Beverages Sales are basically the same. Both are illustrated in Figure 9.4.

To calculate the Cost of Sales for the month of February, the opening inventory would be the total of the monthly physical inventory taken on February 1. The closing inventory would be the

Figure 9.4
Cost of Sales Formulas

Cost of Food Sales Formula	**Cost of Beverage Sales Formula**
Opening Food Inventory	Opening Beverage Inventory
+ Food Purchases	+ Beverage Purchases
= Total Food Available for Sale	= Total Beverage Available for Sale
Total Food Available for Sale	**Total Beverage Available for Sale**
- Closing Food Inventory	- Closing Beverage Inventory
= Cost of Food Sales	= Cost of Beverage Sales

total of the monthly physical inventory taken on March 1. When it is time to calculate the Cost of Sales for the month of March, the March 1 inventory becomes the opening inventory, and the total of the monthly physical inventory taken on April 1 serves as the closing inventory for March. The cost of the monthly physical inventory must be calculated to determine the Cost of Sales and to prepare the monthly Income Statement.

Perpetual Inventory

A **perpetual inventory** is a bookkeeping inventory that maintains a daily running balance of the quantity and costs of products on hand. It is very difficult to keep a perpetual inventory for the food items needed to run a foodservice operation because there are thousands of ingredients to track. A Perpetual Inventory is recommended for tracking high cost food items and for controlling beverage inventory.

Many foodservice operations control their beverage inventory using a perpetual inventory tool known as a **Bin Card**. The Beverage Bin Card (Figure 9.5) is used in conjunction with a Par Stock system at a bar. The Bin Card can be a physical card or can be set up as a computerized inventory system. As with the storage of food items, beverages should be assigned a permanent storage location. When beverage products are delivered and put into storage, the inventory on the Bin Card is increased. When beverages are requisitioned for use, the perpetual inventory is reduced and noted on the Bin Card. At any point in time, the manager can go to the liquor storage location to compare the bookkeeping perpetual inventory to the actual physical inventory of the products on hand. If the information on these two documents is not the same, an error (pilferage or unrecorded breakage) has occurred.

Inventory Turnover. **Inventory Turnover** refers to the number of times an inventory replaces itself on an annual basis. The inventory turnover rate is calculated separately for food and beverage products. To calculate the Food Inventory Turnover rate, use the following formula:

$$\text{Annual Cost of Food Sales} \div \text{Avg. Monthly Food Inventory} = \text{Food Inventory Turnover Rate}$$

A Beverage Inventory Turnover rate is calculated using this same formula but includes the Annual Cost of Beverage Sales and Average Beverage Inventory. The average inventory refers to the average monthly inventory for each product (total the twelve monthly inventories and divide the total by twelve). The Food Inventory Turnover Rate may occur on average 30 times per year (2–3 times per month), while the Beverage Inventory Turnover Rate is approximately 10 times per year (a little less than about once per month). What is thought to be a good Food or Beverage Inventory Rate for a business varies depending upon the amount of storage space available. The Inventory Turnover Rate is often used as an evaluation tool as well. An Inventory Turnover Rate that is high might indicate that a foodservice manager is spending too much time and energy purchasing and receiving goods. An Inventory Turnover rate that is lower than the recommended rate might indicate that the foodservice operation is storing too much product and tying up money in inventory that could be used elsewhere.

Figure 9.5

Bin Card

Product Name:		Mountain Spring Water		Unit:		case/24-11oz bottles	
DATE		STORAGE IN		STORAGE OUT		BALANCE ON HAND	
Month	Day	Units	Costs	Units	Cost	1 cs.	$16.00
April	01	15 cs.	$240.00			16 cs.	$256.00
April	08			4 cs.	$64.00	12 cs.	$192.00
April	16			6 cs.	$96.00	6 cs.	$96.00
April	23			4 cs.	$64.00	2 cs.	$32.00
April	30	14 cs.	$224.00			16.cs.	$256.00

Bin #   5200-0114

The Flow of Goods Continues

When goods are received they are identified as Direct Purchases or as Storeroom Purchases. Direct purchases go directly into production and storeroom purchases are placed in the storeroom to remain until needed for production. The Receiving Report Form (discussed in Chapter 8), identifies the products that enter the storeroom. The movement of stored products must then be tracked from inventory to production.

Issuing Food Products

A **Requisition** is a business form that lists and describes items removed from the storeroom. It is a request to remove the products from storage so that they may be used for production (Figure 9.6). The quantities requisitioned usually rely on the production forecasts (Chapter 10). The requisition is prepared by the chef/manager and filled by the storage clerk. Once the requisition is filled, the products are sent to the department that requested the products.

In foodservice operations where there are no formal storerooms, food requisitions are not utilized. Items are listed on paper and the chef/manager approves the products to be issued and escorts the employee to the storeroom to fill the requisition. When there is no formal storeroom process, it is extremely important that the storeroom facilities are always locked and that only authorized personnel have access to the keys.

Issuing Beverage Products

Although beverage products are usually issued using a beverage requisition, greater controls of alcoholic beverages should be maintained. Employees are more likely to pilfer a bottle of liquor or wine than a food item. To ensure that only the beverage products needed at the bar are requisitioned, beverage operations should use a beverage par stock system at each bar location. A beverage par stock system is similar to the par stock system previously discussed in Chapter 7, although this system is used to control in-process inventory rather than to control purchasing. In-process inventory can be viewed as par stock for production areas.

Figure 9.6
Storage Requisition

STOREROOM REQUISITION				SENT TO:	Beach Bar	
Qty.	Unit	Issued	Item	Unit	Cost	Total
2	cs.		Coors, 12 oz.	$19.25	cs-24	$38.50
3	cs.		Coors Light, 12 oz.	$28.96	cs-24	$86.88
2	cs.		Budweiser, 12 oz.	$18.96	cs-24	$37.92
2	cs.		Miller High Life, 12 oz.	$14.50	cs-24	$29.00
1	cs.		Heineken, 12 oz.	$42.50	cs-24	$42.50
1	cs.		Michelob Ultra, 12 oz.	$14.50	cs-24	$14.50
2	cs.		O'doules, 12 oz.	$32.50	cs-24	$65.00
2	cs.		Mountain Sparkling Water	$16.00	cs-24	$32.00
3	lt.		Rose's Lime Juice	$19.94	cs-12	$59.82
					Total:	$406.12

Requisitioned by: _____

File by: _____

To help control in-process inventories, it is a common practice to store the empty bottles of alcohol (spirits and wine) until the end of a shift when the closing bartender counts and records the bottles emptied on a Break Sheet. A Break Sheet illustrates the number and the kind of beverages that were consumed and emptied. The Break Sheet also identifies bottles that may have been removed legally from the restaurant and sent elsewhere (such as a guest room). The Break Sheet is used for all liquor and bottled wine, and may serve to help a full-service foodservice operation identify the beverage products that are most popular, and to analyze the par stock system at the bar. A completed Break Sheet is used to prepare a Beverage Requisition that lists the beverage items that are sent to the bar location. If the Par Stock at the bar is properly maintained and the Break Sheet properly prepared, the Par Stock at the bar should be filled to the maximum par stock level when the Beverage Requisition is filled. If not, a "hole" occurs (a product is not at the maximum par level), indicating that pilferage may have occurred. It is a good cost control practice to implement a Break Sheet to control beverage costs. The Break Sheet can be a formal document or simply a pad of paper that is used to record the bottles "broken" on an on-going, daily basis.

Transferring Products

Food and beverage products are often transferred from one department to another. The kitchen may requisition a case of oranges to prepare orange wedges for garnishes on dinner plates. The Bar may need six oranges to prepare slices of oranges to garnish a variety of beverages. Rather than preparing a requisition for oranges, the Bar may request them from the kitchen. To do this, a Food and Beverage Transfer document (Figure 9.7) must be filled out by the person doing the transferring. A Food and Beverage **Transfer Memo** identifies products that were once charged to one department, and assigns their cost to the department to which they are transferred.

There are many products that might be shared and used by both the kitchen and the bar departments. Just as oranges are needed by the bar and kitchen, so might wine be used to prepare a sauce. This sharing and transferring of products should be tracked so that each department is charged appropriately for the products that are used to produce sales. If an orange is used as a garnish on a beverage, the cost of the orange should be applied to beverage cost. If wine is used to prepare a sauce for a fillet of fish, the cost of the wine should be applied to food cost.

Figure 9.7

Food and Beverage Transfer

FOOD AND BEVERAGE TRANSFER					
Day/Date	Friday, April 5, 20XX				
Department From:		Kitchen	Department To:		Bar
Quantity	Unit	Item	Cost	Unit	Total
3	bun.	Celery	$54.00	cs-24	$6.75
40	ea.	Limes	$10.80	cs-54	$8.00
1	gal.	Marachino Cherries	$87.54	cs-6 gal.	$14.59
6	1/2 gal.	Orange Juice	$2.86	64 oz.	$17.16
				Total:	$46.50

Authorized by: _____

In a smaller business, where few formal documents are utilized, managers forego the Food and Beverage Transfer memo, and simply classify products as food costs or beverage costs. When transferring six oranges from the kitchen to the bar, in a small- or medium-size foodservice operation, a Food and Beverage Transfer memo may not be used. Instead, the total cost of oranges might just be assigned to food cost because the kitchen uses most of the oranges. To "wash out" the excess food cost, the cost of limes may be assigned to beverage cost, because the kitchen uses few limes and the bar uses most of them.

The preferred method of Storage and of Issuing documents selected is based on the size of the foodservice operation. The larger the business, the more formal and extensive the business documents used. All foodservice managers must be able to evaluate their storage and inventory control needs to implement the most cost effective systems possible.

Review Questions

1. Develop a flow chart illustrating the movement of food products from the receiving area to the production area. Which business forms would be needed to properly control the flow of food and to control costs?

2. Develop a flow chart illustrating the movement of beverage products from the receiving area to the production area. Which business forms would be needed to properly control the flow of beverages and to control their costs?

3. Using the Inventory Sheet found on WebCom or Appendix F, post the following information. Extend and total the inventory for items found in the beer cooler located at the Beach Bar of a small hotel.

Bottled Beer

Coors® 12 oz.	45 bottles	$20.25/cs–24
Coors Lite® 12 oz.	32 bottles	$29.80/cs–24
Budweiser® 12 oz.	15 bottles	$19.25/cs–24
Miller High Life® 12 oz.	22 bottles	$15.10/cs–24
Heineken® 12 oz.	14 bottles	$43.30/cs–24
Beck's® 12 oz.	16 bottles	$39.60/cs–24

4. Using the information below, calculate the Cost of Food Sales and the Cost of Food Sales % for the months of April, May and June.

Food Inventory		Food Sales		Food Purchases	
April 1	$12,450	April	$255,600	April	$82,325
May 1	$11,620	May	$221,800	May	$75,250
June 1	$12,740	June	$283,200	June	$92,760
July 1	$11,420	July	$303,250	July	$90,800

5. Using the following information, calculate the Cost of Beverages Sales and the Cost of Beverages Sales % for the months of July, August and September.

Beverage Inventory		Beverage Sales		Beverage Purchases	
April 1	$5,500	April	$130,500	April	$23,500
May 1	$6,200	May	$142,250	May	$25,350
June 1	$5,400	June	$135,230	June	$24,400
July 1	$6,100	July	$129,200	July	$23,870

6. Using the spreadsheet of your professor's choice, develop an inventory spreadsheet that a foodservice manager might use to arrive at total inventory.

Chapter 10

Daily Production Controls

© 2014, Oleksiy Mark, Shutterstock, Inc.

OBJECTIVES

Upon completion of this chapter, the student should be able to:

1. utilize proper methods of portion control to maintain consistency and to control the costs of both food and beverage items.
2. plan food production using past sales history to forecast production.
3. prepare and use a Production Forecast Report.
4. reconcile production reports with sales reports.
5. calculate Daily Food and Beverage Cost Reports to determine daily cost percents.

KEY TERMS

In House Promotion	Presentation	Steward Sales
In-Process Inventories	Production	
Preparation	Production Forecast Report	

INTRODUCTION

As the cost control cycle continues, the products move to the production stage. **Production** is the step at which food and beverage products and production areas are made ready for service to the customer. Production includes **preparation** and **presentation**. During the preparation phase, food and beverage items are "prepped," as are the production areas. The presentation phase encompasses the transfer of food from the production areas to where the customer is served. Cost control measures must be implemented in both the preparation and presentation phases to attain the goals of production. The goals of production can be viewed as consistency, customer satisfaction, and cost control. Control areas will be identified and control procedures explained to show how goals of production are met. Once the control measures have been explained, daily production and sales activities will be analyzed. Production Analysis is a process in which the chef/manager determines how well costs are controlled through the production process by determining Daily Cost percents.

Food Production Controls

Food cost control standards must be adhered to in order to maintain a consistent product and to reach the goal of profit desired by a foodservice operation. As discussed in Chapter 4, standards are the foundation to cost effective and consistent production results. Using standard recipes with portion controls, and producing consistent yields allows chefs/managers to accurately forecast production needs. The areas discussed next must be carefully examined and developed to ensure profitability.

Forecasting Food Production

Products that arrive to the production area are requisitioned from the storeroom. They arrive directly from the receiving area or are transferred from one department to another. In Chapter 9, we discussed how products are removed from the storage areas through the use of a requisition, and how these products are transferred and accounted for from one department to another. Chapter 8 showed how direct purchases found their way to the production area. But how does the chef/manager determine the amount of product needed?

The Production Forecast Report

Once the standard recipe and portion control measures are developed, the process of production can begin. The Production phase, as described in the introduction, begins when the menu items are actually produced. Before the production process occurs, the chef/manager must determine the need for production and must prepare a Production Forecast Report. The **Production Forecast Report** is a document used in the preparation stage of production to help the chef/manager make an educated guess about the number of customers expected during a given meal period. It also predicts the menu items that those customers will order, and the quantity of each item to prepare for production. This forecast is determined by using a past sales history of customers served and menu items sold (Figure 10.1).

The number of customers previously served can be tracked using a variety of procedures, including guest checks, hostess seating control sheets, and register readings. Once tracked, the number of customers served on a given day, often starts to show a consistent pattern. The number of customers projected should also take into consideration the number of reservations made, holidays and special events, or activities that might take place near the location of the restaurant. Business experience over a period of time helps chefs/managers to predict accurate guest numbers. Once forecasted, the number of customers expected should be posted to the production forecast report.

The process used to track and count individual menu items will be explained in Chapter 11. Once counted, the number of individual menu items is compared to the number of total items sold within the same menu category, and a popularity percentage is determined. This popularity percentage is known as a Sales Mix. A Sales Mix percentage illustrates how popular a menu item is as compared to other menu items within the same menu category. The Sales Mix can be used to help forecast the menu items that customers are most likely to choose.

Sales Mixes fall into regular patterns as do customers counts. The more familiar chefs/managers become with customer preferences, the better they are at forecasting the production needs of the foodservice operation. The Sales Mix percent of the items can be posted to the Forecast Production Sheet to help determine the number of portions of each menu item to be prepared.

Figure 10.1
Production Forecast Report

MENU ITEM	SALES MIX %	FORECASTED COVERS: 200 FORECASTED PRODUCTION	ADDITIONAL PREP	TOTAL FORECAST	PRODUCT ON HAND	NEEDED PREP	DAY/DATE Friday, April 5, 20XX TOTAL AVAILABLE	AMT L-O TIME R-0	ERRORS	KITCHEN SOLD
Baked Stuffed Sole	20%	40	0	40	2	38	40	2	0	38
Broiled Scrod	22%	44	0	44	6	38	44	4	1	39
Lobster	12%	24	10	34	0	34	34	2	0	32
Shrimp Scampi	15%	30	0	30	0	30	30	9:30PM	0	30
Baked Scallops	18%	36	0	36	4	32	36	8	0	28
Grilled Tuna Steak	13%	26	0	26	5	21	26	8:30PM	0	26
TOTALS	100%	200	10	210			210	16	1	193

Additional Prep:
Reason for Error: Special Reservation for 10, all ordering lobsters
Foodserver ordered Scrod should have been Sole

Once the Sales Mix is posted to the Production Forecast Report, the forecasted number of customers (covers) is multiplied by the Sales Mix % of each menu item. The result of this process is the number of portions to be prepped to meet production needs or Forecasted Preparation. Formula:

Total Forecasted Covers	×	**Sales Mix %**	=	**Forecasted Preparation**
PBR Baked Stuffed Sole: 200	×	20%	=	40 portions

The forecasted preparation should be adjusted by the chef/manager if there are any special events or excessive reservations for a particular evening, and an adjustment should be posted to the Additional Preparation Column. The reason for an additional preparation of menu items should also be stated on the production sheet. The Additional Preparation Column should be added to the Forecasted Preparation to arrive at the Total Forecast Column.

Once the Total Forecast has been determined, an inventory of unused product from the previous meal should be taken and recorded in the Number On Hand Column. The difference between the Total Forecast Column and the Number On Hand Column gives the number of portions that need to be prepped for the upcoming meal period. Formula:

Total Forecasted Preparation	–	**Product On Hand**	=	**Preparation Needed**
Baked Stuffed Sole: 40 portions	–	2	=	38 portions

The Product On Hand Column should then be added to the Preparation Needed Column and the total of both posted in the Total Available for Service column. The Total Available for Service column informs the manager of how many portions of each product are available for sale prior to service. The Total Available for Service column can be verified by comparing the recorded number available to an actual count of product available for sale prior to the meal's production phase.

The final step in preparing the Production Forecast Report occurs at the completion of service. Once the dining period has ended, a closing inventory of product is taken. The amount of the product remaining or depleted is recorded in the appropriate column. The amount left over is used as the amount "on hand" for the next meal's production needs. Items that "run out" are recorded as zero and the time that the item sold out is noted to assist the chef/manager with future forecasts. If the time were not recorded, it would not be known if the kitchen regularly exhausted the supply of product at 7:30 p.m., or at 9:45 p.m., just before the kitchen closed. The time at which the product runs out is a useful tool to maintain the Sales Mix. An accurate sales mix is an effective forecasting tool.

Accounting for the errors that are made during the production phase is important. The number and kind of production error should be posted to the Error column on the Production Forecast Report to track the food items used during production. The difference between the Total Available for Service and the Amount Left Over/Time Ran Out Column (including errors made during production), determines the number posted to the Kitchen Sold column. The Kitchen Sold column informs the chef/manager of the number of each menu item that left the kitchen, and should have produced a sale.

Production and Sales Reconciliation

Daily production results are often compared to daily sales results to ensure that all menu items leaving the kitchen are accounted for through sales. Some foodservice operations compare all menu items produced to menu items sold, while others perform the reconciliation for only high food cost menu items such as seafood and beef products. A close watch should be kept to guarantee that charges are recorded for all products leaving the production areas. With increased cash register computerization and the use of Price Look Ups (PLUs), the sales information needed to perform the reconciliation can be quickly accessed through a cash register reading. The reading can then be compared to the Production Forecast Report for accuracy before day's end. If there is a discrepancy, it is the chef's/manager's responsibility to discover the reason. An overdone entrée that is returned and not recorded on the error card, or an appetizer that is ordered but never charged for on the guest check, might explain the reasons for a discrepancy.

Using the Production Forecast Report and the Production Sales Reconciliation can help the chef/manager to control the cost of production. The Production Forecast Report can assist the chef to determine what must be requisitioned from the storage areas and the purchasing needs to meet the production forecasts. The Production Forecast Report also helps the kitchen to identify the number of products available for sale prior to and after the production process. The Production and Sales Reconciliation confirms that the items that have left the production area have been sold and paid for (Figure 10.2). Standard Procedures to support the reconciliation are discussed in "Standard Ordering Procedures."

Figure 10.2
Production/Sales Reconciliation Report

MENU ITEM	KITCHEN SOLD	RECORDED SALES	ERROR CARD	DIFFERENCE	REASON
Baked Stuffed Sole	38	38	0	0	
Broiled Scrod	39	38	1	1	Foodserver mis-order
Lobster	32	32	0	0	
Shrimp Scampi	30	30	0	0	
Baked Scallops	28	28	0	0	
Grilled Tuna Steak	26	26	0	0	
TOTALS	193	192	1		

In-Process Inventories

Many foodservice operations use an in-process inventory par stock system rather than customer counts, or sales mix and Production Forecast Reports, to ensure that the foodservice operation is prepared to meet production needs. In-process inventories reveal the amount of product available in production areas. Foodservice operations implementing the in-process inventory system have a maximum par for production each day. Rather than utilizing a Production Forecast Report, they implement an In-Process Inventory Preparation Sheet. The In-Process Inventory "Prep Sheet" is based on the sales history of the products themselves. The business develops a standard quantity (maximum par) daily to meet production needs. The preparation staff is informed of this par and prepares the number of menu items on the Prep Sheet. This method can be as effective as the Production Forecast Report as long as the procedures track the number of each menu item sold. It is also important when using the In-Process Inventory Par Stock System that the additional preparation of menu items is noted, so that the par stock level of that menu item might be changed to meet business needs. In-process inventory par levels should be evaluated on a regular basis.

The Flow of Goods

Once standards have been developed and production has been planned, the actual preparation begins and continues to the presentation stage. Goods are first ordered from the production areas.

Standard Ordering Procedures

Standard cost control policies for all foodservice operations should mandate that no food or beverage product may be prepared or removed from the kitchen or the bar unless accompanied by an order slip or ordered through a point of sale computer system. When the customer places the order with the server, the server generates the customer's order, which is placed with the kitchen or bar. To get the customers' orders to the production areas, paper guest checks or computerized point of sales systems may be used. In foodservice establishments that use hand prepared guest checks, the server records the customer's order on a heavy weight, two-piece, paper guest check, and physically walks to the kitchen to give the top "soft copy" dupe of the paper guest check to the expeditor to place the order with the kitchen. Paper, hand-written guest checks have a soft copy, no carbon required (NCR) "dupe," attached to the hard copy check, which transfers the customer order from the soft copy to the hard copy with one entry. The soft copy dupe is supplied to the kitchen while the hard copy of the order remains with the server as a record of what was ordered. In foodservice establishments that use point of sale computer systems to generate guest checks, the server enters the order into a computer terminal at the front of the house, and the order is sent electronically to the order station at the kitchen's front line which produces the "soft copy" dupe for tracking. Both the "soft copy" dupe of the handwritten guest check and the "paper tape" of the point of sale computer system inform the back of the house of the customer's order. The paper NCR guest check and the data entry into the point of sale system start the preparation of the guest check.

Whether the order is computer generated or delivered to the kitchen by a server, the soft copy dupe serves as payment for the products purchased from the kitchen by the server. The dupe represents cash. The dupe system is what the server normally uses to place orders with the kitchen and bar. The soft copy can be viewed as an I.O.U. permission slip that is used to order and to remove food and beverage products requested by customers from the production areas. The dupe or soft guest check process is a standard operating procedure, which guarantees that menu items have been properly recorded as sales. Even when a policy/standard exists stating that nothing is to leave a production area unless accounted for, foodservers occasionally make a request for a product without using a prepared soft copy check or inputting the order through the point of sale system. Requests of this type can lead to improper cost control because the sale was never recorded and the money may never be collected for the products consumed by the customer. The business also incurs additional costs and a loss of income. Granting requests for products that are not accompanied by a physical order slip should be avoided. The use of standard ordering procedures is important to both production and sales control.

Standard Order Pick-Up Procedures

Once the order has been placed electronically or with a soft copy guest check, a standard procedure must be implemented to inform the foodserver of when the order is ready for service. This can be done effectively using timing, server number lights, or foodserver pagers. It is sometimes the foodserver's responsibility to know the preparation times for all menu items. Once the order is placed, the foodserver must promptly return to the kitchen to pick up the order within the designated time period. This procedure can work well for trained kitchen and foodservice staff. The lighting system sometimes seen in dining rooms or near the kitchen door can also serve to inform the foodserver when an order is ready. The use of these lights is more common in casual businesses than in fine dining facilities. Pagers that vibrate are also worn by foodservers to inform them when meals are ready. When the order is ready, the expediter informs the foodserver by sending an electronic pulse that "buzzes" the foodserver. Many casual dining restaurants use this system. Once the dining experience has been completed, the foodserver prepares the guest check. The guest check is paid by the customer and the sales transaction is complete. The discussion of the flow of products, cash, and sales analysis continue in the Sales Control section of Chapter 11.

Determining Daily Cost %

When speaking of Food Cost %'s and Beverage Cost %'s, the chef/manager usually refers to the percent listed on the preceding month's Income Statement. These Food Cost percentages serve as historical data. Knowing the current month's daily food cost percentages and the daily beverage cost percentages is important to control costs on a daily basis. If cost percents are identified on a daily basis, chefs/managers can identify and correct any cost problem long before the end of the month.

Foodservice operations determine their Daily Food Cost % and Daily Beverage Cost % using the information that has been tracked through the cycle of cost control. The more information tracked through the cycle, the more accurate the daily food cost and beverage cost percentages. Daily Cost Percent Reports are prepared for a one-month time period. Once the month has ended, a new Daily Cost Percent report is started.

Determining Daily Cost %—A Simple Approach

The Simple Approach in determining a working daily cost percent is normally used by small foodservice operations that do not use business forms to track the movement of products and their costs through the cycle of cost control. Small foodservice operations rarely use business forms and track limited amounts of information. The daily Food Cost and Beverage Cost Percents of small operations commonly provide just a general trend of the Cost Percents. The only information needed to calculate the Daily Cost % using the Simple Approach is the information stated on the purveyor's invoice and the register reading that records daily sales. The total of a day's food invoices is posted to the Daily Purchases Column and the total of the day's food sales is posted to the Daily Sales Column.

Once the daily purchase and daily sales figures have been posted to the Daily Food Cost report, the Daily Food Cost percent is calculated.
Formula:

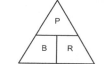

Daily Purchases	÷	**Daily Sales**	=	**Today's Daily Cost %**
Day 1: $1,222.32	÷	$6,325.89	=	19.3%

Because a business purchases a product on a given day, it does not mean that the product is used to produce sales on the same day. A purchase does not become a cost until it is used in production. The Daily Cost Percent as calculated in the Simple Approach is not really a Daily Food Cost Percent but rather a number that represents the percentage of Daily Purchases as compared to that same day's Daily Sales. Food Cost can never be higher than total purchases. The To-Date Food Cost Percent offers a more accurate picture of the Daily Food Cost Percent. To derive a To-Date Food Cost Percent, we must calculate the To-Date Purchases by totaling all the daily purchases made and posting them to the To-Date Purchases Column. The To-Date Sales Column must then be calculated by totaling all the Daily Sales figures during the month. Once the To-Date Purchases and To-Date Sales have been calculated, the To-Date Food Cost Percent is calculated:
Formula:

To-Date Purchases	÷	**To-Date Sales**	=	**To-Date Cost %**
Day 2: $4,577.07	÷	$13,308.55	=	34.4%

Because there are high purchase days and low sales days, and low purchase days and high sales days, it takes approximately seven to ten days for the Cost Percent achieved to illustrate a cost trend. Although the process of recording information is very simple it lacks the accuracy that most foodservice operations desire when calculating Daily Cost Percents. This method is really the only one that small foodservice operations can use because of the absence of tracking procedures for food and beverage items. The Simple Approach is better than nothing at all.

Figure 10.3
Daily Food Cost % Form—Simple Approach

DAY	DATE	DAILY PURCHASES	DAILY SALES	DAILY COST %	TO-DATE PURCHASES	TO-DATE SALES	TO-DATE COST%
M	4/1	$1,222.32	$6,325.89	19.3%	$1,222.32	$6,325.89	19.3%
T	4/2	$3,354.75	$6,982.66	48.0%	$4,577.07	$13,308.55	34.4%
W	4/3	$2,564.82	$5,823.40	44.0%	$7,141.89	$19,131.95	37.3%
R	4/4	$1,986.45	$6,456.23	30.8%	$9,128.34	$25,588.18	35.7%
F	4/5	$4,349.76	$8,320.15	52.3%	$13,478.10	$33,908.33	39.7%
S	4/6	$987.43	$9,208.44	10.7%	$14,465.53	$43,116.77	33.5%
S	4/7	$434.00	$7,325.21	5.9%	$14,899.53	$50,441.98	29.5%
M	4/8	$3,213.87	$6,504.32	49.4%	$18,113.40	$56,946.30	31.8%
T	4/9						
W	4/10						

Figure 10.3 shows food purchases and food sales, and calculates food cost percents. The Purchases divided by the Sales formula discussed above can also be utilized to derive the Daily Beverage Cost Percent and the To-Date Beverage Cost Percent. The process of tracking the invoices received from the purveyor and recording the daily sales are the same, except for the Daily Beverage Cost Percent. Foodservice operations are more likely to receive Beverage Purchases one or two days each week rather than every day. A general trend results in approximately seven to ten days.

Determining a Daily Cost %—An Accurate Approach

As the size and sales volume of foodservice operations increase, more business forms are implemented to track the movement and costs of food and beverage products. Medium and large operations heavily rely on business forms to determine the daily food cost percent and the daily beverage cost percent. The greater the amounts of information collected, the more accurate the working food cost percent. Knowing how to get the most accurate account of daily cost percents helps the foodservice operator to develop daily cost percent reports that meet the needs of the operation.

Daily Food Cost %—An Accurate Approach. In Figure 10.4 the column headings reflect the movement of food items required to derive an accurate working Daily Food Cost Percent. There are three steps in the Accurate Approach in determining the Daily Food Cost Percent.

Step 1: Determining the Daily Cost of Food Used. The Daily Cost of Food Used is the total cost of food for a day regardless of how it is used. To calculate the Cost of Food Used, the chef/manager must gather all the information concerning products sent to the kitchen to meet production needs. The following formula shows how to calculate the Cost of Food Used.

Step 1 Formula:

Requisitions	+	**Direct Purchases**	+	**Transfers To Kitchen**	=	**Cost of Food Used**
Day 1: $1,535.45	+	$576.23	+	$23.94	=	$2,135.62

Requisitions are the business forms that list and describe all items removed from the storeroom. Direct Purchases are those products, which when delivered, go directly into the production area. Transfers to the Kitchen are products transferred from other departments to be used in food production. Depending upon the setup of the foodservice operation, Transfers to the Kitchen may be listed in separate columns for different types of transfers, while those Transfers from the Bar to the Kitchen identify the liquor, beer, and wine needed for food production. Transfers from the Bakeshop include bread, rolls, and desserts. The Cost of Food Used informs the chef/manager of the amount of food sent to the kitchen during the day, but does not identify the quantity of these items actually used to produce sales. A food purchase does not become a food cost until it is used to produce food sales.

Step 2: Determining the Daily Cost of Food Sales. The Cost of Food Sales (Food Cost) refers to the amount of money spent to purchase the food items needed to produce daily food sales. To determine the Cost of Food Sales, subtract all food items that were not used to produce food sales from the Cost of Food Used.

Step 2 Formula:

Cost of Food Used	–	**(Transfers From the Kitchen)**	=	**Daily Cost of Food Sales**
	–	**(Employee Meals)**		
	–	**(In-House Promotion Expense)**		
Day 1: $2,135.62	–	(54.50 + 64.00 + 50.00)	=	$1,967.12

Figure 10.4
Daily Food Cost % Form—An Accurate Approach

DAY	DATE	REQS	DIRECT PURCHASE	TRANSFER TO KITCHEN	COST OF FOOD USED	TRANSFER FROM KITCHEN	EMPLOYEE MEALS	IHP	DAILY COST OF FOOD SALES	DAILY SALES	Month/Year		April 20XX	
											DAILY COST %	TO-DATE COST OF FOOD SOLD	TO-DATE SALES	TO-DATE COST %
M	4/1	$1,535.45	$576.23	$23.94	$2,135.62	$54.50	$64.00	$50.00	$1,967.12	$6,325.89	31.1%	$1,967.12	$6,325.89	31.1%
T	4/2	$1,789.32	$675.00	$32.67	$2,496.99	$56.00	$68.00	$33.00	$2,339.99	$6,982.66	33.5%	$4,307.11	$13,308.55	32.4%
W	4/3	$1,576.12	$555.78	$42.00	$2,173.90	$52.50	$68.00	$45.00	$2,008.40	$5,823.40	34.5%	$6,315.51	$19,131.95	33.0%
R	4/4	$1,765.76	$768.00	$23.69	$2,557.45	$49.75	$68.00	$48.00	$2,391.70	$6,456.23	37.0%	$8,707.21	$25,588.18	34.0%
F	4/5	$1,998.75	$825.30	$39.50	$2,863.55	$46.50	$80.00	$55.00	$2,682.05	$8,320.15	32.2%	$11,389.26	$33,908.33	33.6%
S	4/6	$2,675.40	$325.00	$45.00	$3,045.40	$51.50	$80.00	$48.00	$2,865.90	$9,208.44	31.1%	$14,255.16	$43,116.77	33.1%
S	4/7	$1,854.38	$255.90	$55.00	$2,165.28	$39.00	$64.00	$44.00	$2,018.28	$7,325.21	27.6%	$16,273.44	$50,441.98	32.3%
M	4/8	$1,495.75	$545.80	$26.75	$2,068.30	$45.00	$64.00	$38.00	$1,921.30	$6,504.32	29.5%	$18,194.74	$56,946.30	32.0%
T	4/9													
W	4/10													

Transfers from the Kitchen. Although the Transfers from the Kitchen include transfers to all and any department, this column most often represents food products that are sent to Bar Production areas to be used as garnishes. Even though the garnishes are food, they are not used to produce food sales and should be classified as beverage costs rather than food costs. Many of the Daily Food Cost forms used in larger hotels have separate "Transfers From" columns to identify the departments to which food is transferred, such as Room Service, Mini Bar, and To Go Items.

Other Transfers from the Kitchen might include steward sales and signing privileges of management staff. **Steward Sales** are those purchases that employees are allowed to make from the purveyors through the restaurant. The purchase of a Thanksgiving Day Turkey might be allowed as a steward sale. In this case, the product is purchased and included on the invoice of the food-service operation but is paid for by the employee. This cost must then be deducted from the Cost of Food Used.

Signing privileges of management staff when they dine at the foodservice establishment should also be subtracted from the Cost of Food Used. Management staff often has the benefit of dining at "no cost," although there is a cost to the business to serve the food even if a food sale has not occurred. When a benefit is provided for an employee, the value of the meal should be assigned to labor cost. What is important to remember when determining the daily Cost of Food Sold, is that only the products used to produce food sales are included in the Cost of Food Sold figure.

Employee Meals. Many foodservice operations provide employees with meals. Employers may provide employees with meals at no cost, at a partial cost, or at a full cost. Regardless of the option offered, a meal value must be assigned for every meal provided. When a meal is provided at no cost to an employee, the meal value is assigned to Labor Cost. The cost of the food used to prepare the meal is subtracted from the Cost of Food Used, which in turn is reflected in a reduction in daily food cost. A meal provided at a cost to both the employer and employee is assigned to Employee Meals (the portion paid by the employer), and to food cost (the portion paid by the employee).

In-House Promotions. **In-House Promotions** are internal advertising expenses related to food items that are given away to loyal customers. Chefs/managers often provide an appetizer "with the compliments of the chef," to thank customers for their patronage. The cost of the food used to produce the In House Promotion does not result in a food sale and is not included in the Cost of Food Sales. Another example of an In-House Promotion is food items that are prepared and sent to the bar to be used to promote beverage sales. Since these hors d'oeuvres are complimentary to the customer, they do not produce food sales. The hors d'oeuvres are also not used to produce a beverage product so they cannot be classified as a beverage cost. Promotional products are used to get customers to stay a little longer and to spend more money. Some costs can only be classified as a "cost of doing business" and are neither food nor beverage cost, but rather an internal advertising expense.

Step 3: Determining the Daily Food Cost %. Using the formula listed below, the foodservice manager is able to account for all products that are used to produce food sales. The process used in determining the Daily Food Cost percent is similar to that used in the Simple Approach to Determine a Daily Food Cost %. Simply replace the Daily Purchases (in the simple approach) by the Daily Cost of Food Sales figure.

Step 3 Formula A:

Daily Cost of Food Sales	÷	**Daily Sales**	=	**Daily Food Cost %**
Day 1: $1,967.12	÷	$6,325.89	=	31.1%

As accurate as the Daily Food Cost Percentage is, it does not take into consideration the In-Process Inventories. **In-Process Inventories** are products originally sent to the kitchen by requisitions, direct purchases, or transfers that are not used to produce daily food sales. The products left unused are "in process" and are intended to be used for the next day. It is for this reason that the To-Date Cost of Food Sales, the To-Date Sales, and the To-Date Food Cost % should still be utilized. Even though the Daily Food Cost % is fairly accurate, the To-Date Food Cost % becomes more and more accurate as the month progresses and the in-process inventories are used up. If a chef requisitions a fifty pound bag of flour, the chances are very good that the entire fifty pounds are not used to produce sales on a single day. The To-Date % Column accounts for in-process inventories.

The formula to calculate the To-Date Food Cost % in the Accurate Approach is as follows:

Step 3 Formula B:

To-Date Cost of Food Sales	÷	**To-Date Sales**	=	**To-Date Food Cost %**
Day 2: $4,307.11	÷	$13,308.55	=	32.4%

The Accurate Approach can be adjusted to meet the needs of any foodservice operation and is easily transferred to a computerized spreadsheet program to alleviate some of the time consuming mathematical procedures. Calculating a Daily Food Cost % is a useful tool in helping the chef/manager to identify how the foodservice operation is performing long before the month's end.

Calculating the Daily Beverage Cost %—An Accurate Approach

To determine the Daily Beverage Cost %, a foodservice operation may choose the Simple Approach previously explained, or a more accurate determination of the working Daily Beverage Cost %. An explanation of an Accurate Approach that better identifies a foodservice operation's beverage costs on a daily basis can be found in (Figure 10.5).

The Daily Beverage Cost % is calculated every day and is kept for a one-month time period. As in the accurate approach to determine the Daily Food Cost %, there are three steps in determining a fairly accurate Daily Beverage Cost %. The following items must be considered in calculating an Accurate Daily Beverage Cost Percentage.

Figure 10.5
Daily Beverage Cost % Form—An Accurate Approach

DAY	DATE	ISSUES	TRANSFER to BAR	ADDITIONS	COST OF BEVERAGE USED	TRANSFER FROM BAR	IHP	SIGNING PRIVILEGE	SUBTRACTIONS	DAILY COST OF BEV SALES	DAILY BEVERAGE SALES	DAILY BEVERAGE COST %	TO-DATE COST OF BEV SALES	TO-DATE BEVERAGE SALES	TO-DATE COST %
M	4/1	$517.54	$54.50	$0.00	$572.04	$23.94	$48.00	$30.00	$0.00	$470.10	$2,345.57	20.0%	$470.10	$2,345.57	20.0%
T	4/2	$444.56	$56.00	$0.00	$500.56	$32.67	$55.00	$0.00	$0.00	$412.89	$1,986.43	20.8%	$882.99	$4,332.00	20.4%
W	4/3	$375.45	$52.50	$0.00	$427.95	$42.00	$48.00	$0.00	$0.00	$337.95	$1,876.99	18.0%	$1,220.94	$6,208.99	19.7%
R	4/4	$576.78	$49.75	$0.00	$626.53	$23.69	$44.00	$45.00	$0.00	$513.84	$2,543.78	20.2%	$1,734.78	$8,752.77	19.8%
F	4/5	$627.89	$46.50	$0.00	$674.39	$39.50	$38.00	$66.00	$0.00	$530.89	$3,356.75	15.8%	$2,265.67	$12,109.52	18.7%
S	4/6	$706.75	$51.50	$0.00	$758.25	$45.00	$50.00	$76.00	$0.00	$587.25	$3,912.34	15.0%	$2,852.92	$16,021.86	17.8%
S	4/7	$577.68	$39.00	$0.00	$616.68	$55.00	$33.00	$25.00	$0.00	$503.68	$2,789.78	18.1%	$3,356.60	$18,811.64	17.8%
M	4/8	$578.00	$45.00	$20.00	$643.00	$26.75	$45.00	$25.00	$0.00	$546.25	$2,214.39	24.7%	$3,902.85	$21,026.03	18.6%
T	4/9														
W	4/10														

Month/Year — April 20XX

Step 1: Determining the Cost of Beverages Used. The first step is to identify all the areas from which alcohol is sent to the Beverage Production Area.
Formula:

Issues	+	**Transfers To Bar**	+	**Additions**	=	**Cost of Beverages Used**
Day 1: $517.54	+	$54.50	+	-0-	=	$572.04

Issues. "Issues" can be recorded on requisitions coming from liquor storage, wine storage, bottled beer storage, keg beer storage, and food storage areas that are used to provide beverages. Food Issues from storage might include mixes such as juices, sodas, milk, cream products, containers of non-perishable garnish products (maraschino cherries, olives, cocktail onions, frozen strawberries, whipped cream, cinnamon sticks), and any other product used to prepare a beverage item.

Transfers to the Bar. Transfers to the Bar most often reflect food items that have been transferred from the kitchen to the bar to produce a beverage. Rather than preparing a Food Requisition for six oranges, the bar can transfer the six oranges from the kitchen and transfer their cost using a Transfer Memo.

Additions. Foodservice operations utilize an Addition Column for items that are neither issues nor transfers, but which need to be included in the Cost of Beverages Used. These items might be fresh strawberries purchased from a farmers' market to be used as a garnish, or a purchase sent directly to the beverage production area when delivered. All products sent to Beverage Production must be accounted for and included in the Cost of Beverages Used.

Step 2: Cost of Beverages Sales. To arrive at the Cost of Beverages Sold, take the Cost of Beverages Used and subtract any beverage products sent to beverage production and not used to produce a beverage sale.
Formula:

Cost of Beverages Used	–	**(Transfers From the Bar)** **(In-House Promotions)** **(Signing Privileges) (Subtractions)**	=	**Cost of Beverage Sales**
$572.04	–	($23.94 + $48.00 + $30.00)	=	$470.10

Transfers from the Bar. These items can be noted as Transfers from the Bar to other departments. This column most often represents alcoholic beverage items that are used in cooking.

In-House Promotions. The In-House Promotions column identifies the beverage items that are given away "with compliments of the manager." The product given away should not be included in the Cost of Beverage Sales because it is not used to produce a Beverage Sale. Instead, the cost should be documented as an internal advertising expense.

Signing Privileges. Management staff will sometimes have the privilege of signing for a beverage item at no cost. When this occurs and a beverage sale is not incurred, the cost must not be included in the Cost of Beverage Sold. The signing privilege is considered to be an employee benefit and should be accounted for as a labor cost.

Subtractions. This column is used to record any other costs that should not be included as a Cost of Beverage Sold. Some foodservice operations include errors within this column, even though the error should be included in the Cost of Beverage Sold. A production error will increase the beverage cost.

Step 3: Calculating the Daily Beverage Cost %. Step 3 should be performed using the same procedure as that used previously in Step 3 of Determining the Daily Food Cost percent. "Daily Beverage Cost %" is calculated as follows:

Formula:

Daily Cost of Beverage Sales	÷	**Daily Beverage Sales**	=	**Daily Beverage Cost %**
Day 1: $470.10	÷	$2,345.57	=	20.0%

A running total of the Cost of Beverages Sold is posted to the To-Date Cost of Beverages Sold column. The total Beverage Sales are then posted to the To-Date Beverage Sales column. Lastly, the To-Date Cost of Beverages Sold is divided by the To-Date Beverage Sales to determine a To-Date Beverage Cost %.

Formula:

To Date Cost of Beverage Sales	÷	**To Date Beverage Sales**	=	**To Date Beverage Cost %**
Day 2: $882.29	÷	$4,332.00	=	20.4%

As the month progresses, the in-process inventories are realized and accounted for in the To-Date Beverage Cost Percent. This formula can be used by managers to calculate a fairly accurate working Beverage Cost % on a daily basis. Some foodservice operations track not only total Beverage Sales but individual totals for liquor sales, wine sales, beer sales, and non-alcoholic beverage sales. These foodservice operations commonly develop a Daily Beverage Cost Percent form for each type of beverage product served.

Knowing the working daily food cost and beverage cost percents can be a useful tool in assisting chefs/managers to control cost and to identify product usage. Implementing such a tool can prevent an outrageous surprise of high costs at the end of the month.

Review Questions

1. Using the following information and the Daily Cost—Simple Approach Sheet on WebCom or Appendix F, calculate the Daily Cost % and the To-Date Cost %.

Date	Day	Today's Purchases	Today's Sales
Aug. 1	W	$4,263.70	$12,182.75
Aug. 2	T	$3,451.23	$12,485.08
Aug. 3	F	$4,543.55	$13,345.20
Aug. 4	S	$5,612.33	$14,255.10
Aug. 5	S	$4,998.56	$13,867.35
Aug. 6	M	$3,277.68	$12,320.56

2. Given the following numbers and the information provided on the Accurate Approach Food Cost form on WebCom or Appendix F, calculate the Daily Food Cost % and the To-Date Food Cost %

Date/Day	Aug 1/W	Aug 2/R	Aug 3/F	Aug 4/S
Requisitions	$1,245.35	$1,678.34	$1,898.33	$2,003.55
Direct Purchases	$555.60	$447.54	$789.86	$334.50
Transfers to Kitchen	$65.80	$55.43	$33.56	$22.50
Transfers from Kitchen	$32.50	$44.20	$32.45	$25.66
Employee Meals	$36.50	$40.50	$44.00	$42.00
IHP	$19.50	$22.00	$25.00	$23.50
Daily Sales	$5,557.10	$5,927.45	$9,035.55	$7,091.84

3. Using the following information and the Daily Beverage Cost % form on WebCom or Appendix F, calculate the Daily Beverage Cost % and the To-Date Beverage Cost %.

Date/Day	Aug 1/W	Aug 2/R	Aug 3/F	Aug 4/S
Issues	$657.30	$585.22	$778.90	$823.44
Transfer to Bar	$44.50	$33.75	$55.75	$46.80
Additions	$0.00	$0.00	$25.00	$0.00
Transfers from Bar	$22.50	$28.95	$27.56	$32.00
IHP	$45.00	$33.50	$28.50	$42.50
Signing Privileges	$35.00	$22.25	$44.50	$38.50
Subtractions	$0.00	$0.00	$0.00	$40.00
Beverage Sales	$3,328.55	$2,428.47	$4,698.33	$4,206.85

4. Using the spreadsheet program of your professor's choice, develop a spreadsheet to determine the Daily Food Cost % and the To-Date Food Cost % for a medium-sized foodservice operation.

5. Using the spreadsheet program of your professor's choice, develop a spreadsheet to determine the Daily Beverage Cost % and the To-Date Beverage Cost %.

3 Sales and Labor Analysis

Chapter 11

Sales Controls and Analysis

© 2014, Karuka, Shutterstock, Inc.

OBJECTIVES

Upon completion of this chapter, the student should be able to:

1. implement proper guest check controls to meet business needs.
2. follow the flow of sales from the guest check to the income statement.
3. calculate Sales Mix from sales history reports.
4. calculate the Break-Even Point of Sales.
5. complete a Menu Engineering worksheet.

KEY TERMS

Actual Sales	Cover	Sales
Average Sale per Cover	Menu Engineering	Sales Journal
Break-even	Potential Sales	Sales Mix
Contribution to Sales	Register Reading	Turnover Rate

INTRODUCTION

Sales are the revenues that foodservice operations generate by selling goods and services to customers. Sales refer to the total dollar amount spent by customers to purchase products (food and beverage) and services when dining in a foodservice establishment. The collection and tracking of the sales dollars (payments received) is a part of the sales control information needed by managers to make sound business decisions. To be successful and to forecast future sales, managers also need to track the number of customers served and the menu items chosen by the customers so that proper purchasing and scheduling might be implemented.

"Sales Control" is a system set up to maintain the flow of sales money derived from the products and services sold to customers. It is a tracking system used to identify the number of people served during a given meal period, and a tool for determining how well menu items are selling. Information gathered through this system is then used to prepare a sales analysis that identifies and analyzes current sales and to forecast future sales.

It is important to refer to the cycle of cost control to see how sales affect the amount of product that must be purchased and produced, and the number of employees that must be scheduled. Sales have an effect on every step of the cost control cycle and sales tracking systems provide information that can help to control the costs of operating a business.

The Flow of Sales

Where do "Sales" begin? **Potential Sales** begin when a manager creates a menu because the menu is a merchandising tool that promotes sales. Potential Sales can be forecasted by setting the selling prices of menu items (Chapter 5). To keep track of **Actual Sales**, the process begins when the customer places an order with the foodserver. When a party of four enters the establishment, they are greeted by the host/hostess and escorted to their table. The customers are presented menus, and soon after, a foodserver approaches the table and introduces himself/herself. The foodserver asks if the guests would like to order something refreshing to drink. The customers request a liter bottle of sparkling water. The foodserver records the order to memory or writes the order on an order pad (informal guest check). *Voilà!* The process of recording actual sales has begun. While the flow of recorded sales information varies slightly from one foodservice system to another, the basic flow of recorded sales is as follows:

Guest Check → Cash Register → Cashier's Report → Daily Sales Report → Monthly Sales Journal → Annual Sales Journal

Regardless of the sales control system that restaurants use, they will follow a somewhat common model to track sales. These areas of sales control will be discussed in the appropriate sequence.

Guest Check Preparation

Regardless of the type of guest check preparation a foodservice operation chooses as its standard operational procedure (computer-generated or hand-prepared), the information recorded is the same. As more and more foodservice operations become computerized, fewer are using hand-prepared guest checks. Front of the house Point of Sale Cash Register systems are often the first computer systems in which foodservice operations invest. Point of Sale computerization of guest checks and sales controls alleviate much of the tedious summation of day-to-day sales activities that were at one time compiled from hand-prepared guest checks. Computer generated guest checks also provide managers with a sense of control, because servers have fewer input and addition errors. While most properties choose to computerize sales control, some independent foodservice operations still find hand-prepared guest checks and sales control their method of choice. Businesses that stay with hand-prepared checks sometimes do so because of the expense of the Point of Sales system, while others believe that the hand-prepared checks better "fit" the concept of their foodservice operation. Appendix D provides control tools for using non-computer generated/hand-prepared guest checks and sales control analysis.

In Point of Sales systems, every foodserver has a server number and each table in the dining room an assigned table number. When a dining party is seated, the server uses his/her server number to open a guest check for the table assigned and records the number of covers seated at the table. The guest check for that table is now ready to generate an order. Upon receiving the order from the customer, the server moves to the order terminal to formally input the order. This order is then transmitted to the order station terminal in the kitchen or a paper "dupe" is generated and physically walked to the kitchen. As the customers continue to add additional items such as beverages or desserts, the foodserver adds these to the appropriate guest check using the server and table numbers. When the customer requests the check, the foodserver goes to the order terminal, prints the guest check for the specified table, presents it, and collects payment. Point of Sale systems provide sales control that is often not realized with hand-prepared guest check systems. At the completion of a server's shift, the sales system can identify whether a guest check has been started within the system and has not been recorded as paid.

Cash Register and Cashiering Controls

Whether the cash register is part of a Point of Sales system or not, most foodservice operations utilize cash registers to record sales transactions and store payments received for sales transactions. Cash registers vary only in the amount of information that they are able to record. A cashiering control system must also be implemented to confirm that the sales recorded are equal to the payments collected.

Recording Sales Transactions. The total dollar amount brought in through the sale of products and services sold to customers is known as Sales. Cash Registers are able to keep track of different types of sales. The two most common classifications of sales that foodservice operations track are Food Sales and Beverage Sales. "Food Sales" are defined as the total dollar amount of money brought in through the sale of food items, and "Beverage Sales" refer to the total dollar amount of money brought in through the sale of beverage items. In addition to these two categories, restaurants may also have additional sales categories that are placed under the headings of "Other Income." "To-Go Food," "Merchandise," "Catering," or "Gift Certificates." Hotel operations might also include sales categories for each of the foodservice operations in the hotel (fine-dining, casual, beach bar), as well as for "Room Service" and "Banquet" sales. In addition to the classifications of sales, foodservice operations track food and beverage sales by meal period to determine exactly how much each meal period contributes to the overall daily sales. The number of categories and meal period sales a business chooses to track depends on the depth of analysis desired. Separating sales into categories can also provide information for developing and monitoring marketing efforts. The tracking and collection of sales taxes (state and/or local) often accompanies sales collection. Foodservice operations are responsible for collecting and recording sales taxes, and for posting to a separate liability account until payment is required.

Point of Sale (POS) Cash Registers also record sales information other than sales dollar amounts. The POS system can track customers and their menu selections. Computerized cash register systems can record the number of people served as the guest check is opened, and track menu selections that are tracked utilizing a PLU (Price Look Up) numerical code. In the PLU system every food and beverage item is assigned a numerical code that the cash register tallies when the register reading is taken. The computerized cash register system has greatly reduced the amount of time and energy needed to gather valuable sales information.

A Place Holder for Payments. Cash registers hold the payments from sales transactions. When guest checks are paid, payments (cash, credit card vouchers, checks, gift certificates) are collected and kept in the cash register until Cash Out. Cash Out is a process performed by a cashier to prove that the amount of sales recorded is equal to the total payments received. The foodservice operation decides on the methods of payment that are acceptable. The size of the customer base often dictates the types of payments allowed. The larger the customer base, the more extensive the methods of payments. Businesses that accept "cash-only" may restrict their market share because many people elect not to carry cash. Foodservice operators must also realize that credit card transactions involve a service charge from the credit card company. Foodservice operations that accept credit cards as payment usually accept the fact that credit cards are a necessary cost of doing business. The fee paid to the credit card companies is recorded as an operating expense.

Regardless of the forms of payment accepted, a business must develop standard procedures concerning payment. Circling credit card expiration dates to ensure that the credit card is current; requiring a signature on the guest checks as well as on the credit card voucher; and asking for a valid picture ID when accepting checks are all sound practices. Customers sometimes think that these controls are ridiculous; however, most appreciate this special attention when their credit cards or checks are lost or stolen.

When money received as payment is removed from the cash drawer, Paid-Out Receipt slips are placed in the drawer to document the money taken during the sales period. The Paid-Out Receipts account for money removed during a business shift to pay credit card tips, COD invoices, etc. Paid-Out Receipts are just as important as cash because they represent cash that was once part of the original bank or the proceeds of a sales transaction. If a Paid-Out Receipt is lost, the cash drawer will be short of money.

Cashier Control Methods. At the end of the day when the service period has ended, the manager takes a register reading. A **register reading** is a print out of sales activity that can be viewed as a spreadsheet of information. This reading provides the details of the sales revenue generated; the number of customers served; and the total number of every menu item that has been sold during the day. The register reading is compared to payments collected to guarantee that the monies for all sales have been collected. It is the server's responsibility to make sure that the sales transaction is completed and the guest check is paid.

In restaurants that use Point of Sale computer cash register systems, one of two cashiering methods is commonly used. One method involves the customer or the server taking the guest check to a cashier to present payment. The cashier accepts payment; provides the necessary change or prepares credit card documents; and inputs the information into the cash register system to record that the guest check is paid. An employee serving as the cashier at a cashier station is required to implement this method. At the end of a meal period, it is often the cashier's responsibility to prepare a Cashier's Report to summarize the type of payments received. Once the sales activity for the meal period is complete, a register reading is performed. Although register readings are used routinely to tally total daily sales activity (z reading), businesses often take a register reading for every meal period (x reading), and then total the meal period sales activity to arrive at a daily sales figure. As part of the Cashier's Check-out procedure, the Cashier's Report and the register reading are compared to prove cash. "Proving cash" refers to the process of confirming that the sales recorded are equal to the payments collected for the meal period. If there is an overage or a shortage, there has been an error in either recording sales or handling payment.

The second cashiering method involves each foodserver acting as his/her own cashier. When the customer pays the guest check, the server accepts payment and provides the necessary change or prepares the credit card documents. The foodserver then inputs the information into the cash register system that records the guest check as paid. At the end of the service period, the foodserver prepares a *Foodserver Checkout* before turning over all payments collected to management. Each foodserver must also request an individual foodserver's *register reading* from a manager at the end of the meal period, which provides the foodserver's total sales information. At this time, any "open" guest checks (started but not paid) are also identified. The foodserver then prepares a cashiers report for his/her own sales transactions. The foodserver totals the payments received and compares these to his/her register reading. At the end of the reconciliation process, the foodserver's register reading, cashier report, and payments collected are turned in to management for confirmation. The closing manager prepares a Cashier Summary Report to total all sales and payments collected from each foodserver for a meal period. Both systems have benefits and costs and foodservice operations choose the method that best tracks their flow of sales.

Daily Sales Report. Information from the Cashier's Report (or Cashier Summary Report) is then tallied and posted to a Daily Sales Report. The Daily Sales Report provides the foodservice manager with an overall picture of the total amount of sales recorded and payments received for a given day. Once the daily sales information has been proven or adjusted as needed, the daily sales information is posted to the Daily Sales and Cash Receipt Journal.

Daily Sales and Cash Receipts Journal. The **Daily Sales and Cash Receipts Journal** (Figure 11.1) is a one month compilation of daily sales and payments received. This journal is a spreadsheet used to record daily sales totals by category (food, beverage) and the types of payments collected (cash, checks, credit cards) throughout a month. The sales totals of each category in the Sales Journal are then utilized to prepare the monthly income statement. Many Point of Sale computer systems automatically transfer sales totals and payment types to a Sales Journal once the daily sales and payment information have been reconciled.

Figure 11.1
Sales and Cash Receipts Journal

SALES JOURNAL												Month:	March 20XX	
SALES RECORDED								PAYMENTS COLLECTED						
Date	Food Sales	Beverage Sales	Other Sales	Total Sales	Sales Tax Collected	Tips Charged	Total Recorded	Cash	Checks	MC/V	AMX	O-CC	Gift Certificate	Other Payments	Total Collected
3/1	$11,535.25	$3,453.76	$0.00	$14,989.01	$749.45	$988.50	$16,726.96	$8,706.95	$400.00	$5,783.22	$1,636.79		$200.00		$16,726.96
3/2	$11,624.05	$2,549.33	$25.00	$14,198.38	$709.92	$875.60	$15,783.90	$7,938.41	$650.00	$4,992.55	$1,987.94	$140.00		$75.00	$15,783.90

The Annual Sales Journal. The Annual Sales Journal is made up of the monthly sales totals for each of the Sales Categories. The total of the Annual Sales Journal is used in preparing the Annual Income Statement (Chapter 6).

Once the foodservice operator has gathered all the sales information and prepared the sales journal, this information is used to compare the daily, weekly, or monthly total of sales in each category. The annual sales journal shows increases and decreases of sales activities in particular categories of sales that the foodservice manager tracks. This analysis can help a business to identify increases in sales that may have resulted from additional marketing, and to forecast for the upcoming season.

All cash register systems have a minimum capability of providing a food sales total, a beverage sales total, and a tally of sales tax. In addition, most Point of Sale cash register systems print out the total number of customers served (covers), the average each customer spent, the number of each menu items sold (sales mix), and a summary of how the items sold contributed to total sales (percent contribution to sales).

Tracking Customers and Their Choices

The number of customers served and their food and beverage choices can be tracked by a computerized Point of Sales cash register system. Often times, all the information can be retrieved from a register reading. Once the sale period has ended and the sales information is gathered, the collected information may be used to analyze how well the foodservice operation is doing. Knowing the number of customers (covers) who visit the establishment, the amount of money each customer is spending, and the menu items customers are selecting, is integral to analyze current sales, to make future sales forecasts, and to estimate current and potential profit derived from current and future sales.

Covers

A **cover** refers to a person served by the restaurant during a given meal period. Keeping track of how many people are served at breakfast, lunch, and dinner can help the chef to better plan production, and assist the manager to accurately schedule personnel for those meals. Covers can be tracked using a Point of Sale cash register system that is generated when the foodserver enters the number of people to be served when opening a guest check, or at the front door by the host/hostess keeping a *Seating Control Sheet* (a master list of people seated at each table throughout the given meal period). An example and explanation of a Seating Control Sheet can be found in Appendix D.

Turnover Rate

Turnover rate refers to the average number of times guests have occupied all the seats in the dining room during a given meal period. The formula for calculating the turnover rate is:

Covers Served	÷	**Number of Dining Seats**	=	**Turnover Rate**
250	÷	100	=	2.5 (250%)

If a restaurant serves 250 people and has 100 seats in its dining room, the turnover rate is 2.5 or 250%. The average turnover rate depends upon the type of restaurant operation. A fine dining restaurant may only have an average turnover of 1.5, while a fast-paced, family pub might have an average turnover of 4.0. The turnover rate is normally calculated using only the number of customers served in the dining room(s) (it does not include bar, lounge, or takeout food traffic).

Average Sales per Cover

An estimate of the amount of money that each customer is expected to spend is a sound forecasting tool for the foodservice manager. The **Average Sales per Cover** (also known Guest Check Average), is the average amount spent by each person entering the restaurant. The formula for determining the Average Sales per Cover is:

	Total Sales	÷	**# Covers Served**	=	**Average Sale per Cover**
Example:	$9,200	÷	250	=	$36.80

If a restaurant brings in $9,200 in sales, serving 250 covers, the Average Sale per Cover is $36.80. The Average Sales per Cover formula is often used to help foodservice operations to forecast the amount of money a foodservice operation may generate in sales. If a restaurant has an Average Sale per Cover of $36.80, and knows that it normally serves 400 customers on Saturday night, the foodservice manager can forecast the expected sales and budget.
Formula:

Average Sale per Cover	×	**Forecasted Covers**	=	**Forecasted Sales**
$36.80	×	400 covers	=	$14,720

An Average Sales per Cover is usually prepared for the whole restaurant, as well as for each sales person (foodserver, bartender). If a foodserver is responsible for $1,200 in sales and has served 35 customers, the Individual Average Sale per Cover is calculated as follows:

Server Total Sales	÷	**Server # Covers Served**	=	**Server Average Sale per Cover**
$1,200	÷	35	=	$34.29

The Server Average Sales per Cover is often used by foodservice operators to identify the best salespeople. The greater the individual sales, the larger the profit the business makes. Restaurants often reward their best salespeople with preferred shifts and good sections.

While the information needed to determine the information as calculated above is often achieved by taking a register reading, it is also important that managers not place all control in the hands of the foodservers. A host/hostess should also track the number of covers served on a Seating Control Sheet (explained in Appendix D). The Seating Control Sheet usually offers the most accurate customer count, because foodservers may intentionally or unintentionally misrepresent the number of customers served to make their individual sales efforts look more impressive. For example, if a foursome is seated in a section and two of the people order appetizers, and the other two order entrées, the foodserver might only record two covers. This misrepresentation skews both the overall Average Sales per Cover and the Server Average Sales per Cover. The number of covers served and the Average Sales per Cover are important in predicting future sales totals.

Sales Mix

The **sales mix** (or Popularity Index), refers to the percentage of customers who order a particular menu item. The sales mix percentage is normally calculated per food category. The quantity of each type of appetizer, entrée, and dessert sold is compared to the total quantity sold in each respective category. To calculate a sales mix, take the number of each item sold and divide it by the total items sold in each category.

Formula:

	Number of Each Entrée Sold		÷	**Total Entrée Sold**	=	**Sales Mix**
Entrée:	Stuffed Shrimp	60	÷	250	=	24.0%
	Steak au Poivre	44	÷	250	=	17.6%
	Grilled Chicken	66	÷	250	=	26.4%
	Fillet of Sole	80	÷	250	=	32.0%
	Total Entrées	250			=	100.0%

Just as the Average Sales per Cover can help forecast the potential sales, the sales mix can help to determine how many customers will order a particular menu item. Foodservice operators who calculate sales mix percentages on a routine basis see patterns concerning the items ordered and the time periods during which they are requested. The Sales Mix should be maintained on a daily basis because percentages change daily. Menu items often develop a pattern of popularity on certain days of the week because a 17.6% sales mix for Steak au Poivre on a Tuesday night might increase to 30% on a Saturday night. Knowing the specific sales mix percentages of menu items can help in forecasting production during a given meal period. The following examples include the sales mix percentages for the entrées previously determined to forecast production needs.

Production Forecast

Formula:

Entrées	**Expected Covers**	×	**Sales Mix %**	=	**Amount to Prep**
Stuffed Shrimp	220	×	24% (.24)	=	53 (52.8)
Steak au Poivre	220	×	17.6% (.176)	=	39 (38.7)
Grilled Chicken	220	×	26.4% (.264)	=	58
Fillet of Sole	220	×	32% (.32)	=	70
Total Entrées				=	220

If foodservice operators accurately forecast the menu items that need to be produced, they can more accurately predict the products that must be purchased to meet production needs.

Contribution to Sales %

The Contribution to Sales percentage represents each menu item's contribution to total sales. Contribution to Sales % looks at the entire menu and the sale of each and every menu item. The Sales Mix % compares the number of each item sold, while the Contribution to Sales % analyzes the dollar value that each menu item contributes to sales. Food items are compared to Total Food Sales and beverage items are compared to Total Beverage Sales. The formula to calculate the Contribution to Sales percent is:

Total Sales $ of Each Menu Item Sold	÷	Total Sales	=	Contribution to Sales %
$364.00	÷	$4,000.00	=	9.1%

Sales Analysis

There are many ways of performing a Menu and Sales Analysis. Some methods are simple while others are more complex. Two types of analysis will be discussed: Break-Even Analysis and Menu Engineering. Break-Even Analysis is a procedure used to determine the amount of sales needed before realizing a profit. "Menu Engineering," developed and presented by Michael L. Kasavana and Donald I. Smith in their book *Menu Engineering—A Practical Guide to Menu Analysis* (1990, Hospitality Pub.), is a unique and fun way to analyze menu items by classifying the items as Stars, Plowhorses, Puzzles, and Dogs.

The Break-Even Point of Sales

Break-Even is the point at which the sales dollar brought in, is equal to the costs expended to produce those sales. (Labor Cost $ + Overhead Cost $ + Cost of Sales $ = Break-Even Sales $). The Break-Even point of sales may be used to assist foodservice operators in deciding the days of the week or times of the year to stay open or close. There is no profit at the Break-Even point of sales.

Calculating the Break-Even Point of Sales. The Break-Even Point of Sales can be determined annually, quarterly, monthly, weekly, or on a daily basis. Most foodservice operations operate on a weekly cycle. A weekly Break-Even point allows the foodservice operation to determine the sales dollars and to analyze whether a profit has been made. A Weekly evaluation allows time to implement control measures that might be needed. When Calculating the Break-Even Point of Sales, both Labor Costs and Overhead Costs are classified as fixed costs. Fixed costs are those that are not expected to increase or decrease as sales fluctuate.

A Labor Cost dollar can be determined by compiling payroll journals, payroll taxes, and benefits paid from the weekly payroll ledger. A weekly Overhead Cost can be determined by knowing the annual overhead cost and dividing that figure by 52 (weeks). The cost of sales is a variable cost that fluctuates in direct relation to the increases and decreases in sales. As sales increase, the variable cost increases; as sales decrease, the variable cost decreases. Because actual sales are not yet known, foodservice operators use the Cost of Sales %. Even though variable costs rise and fall as do sales, the variable cost % should remain fairly constant if proper standards of control are implemented.

Setting Up the Formula. The formula to solve for the Break-Even Point of Sales is:

[(Labor Cost $ + Overhead Cost $) ÷ (1 – Cost of Sales %)] = Break-Even Sales

A simple way to arrive at the Break-Even Point of Sales is to utilize a tool that is similar to the Simplified Profit and Loss Statement. Remember that Cost of Sales (Food and Beverage) is a variable cost and Labor Costs and Overhead Costs within the Break-Even Formula are fixed costs.

Break-Even Sales	$ _____	_____ %
Variable Cost	$ _____	_____ % Variable Cost %
Fixed Cost	$ _____	_____ % Fixed Cost %

Application of the Formula. Using the following information, calculate the Break-Even Point of Sales for the University Inn.

The University Inn has an estimated Weekly Labor Cost of $12,700 and an estimated weekly Overhead Cost of $6,800. The restaurant maintains a 35% Cost of Sales. What is the Break-Even Point of Sales?

Post the information given to the Break-Even Chart: Fixed Costs (Labor Cost and Overhead Cost), total $19,500, and Cost of Sales %, which is the Variable Cost %.

Break-Even Sales	$ _____	_____ %
Variable Cost	$ _____	__35__ % Variable Cost %
Fixed Cost	$ __19,500__	_____ % Fixed Cost %

If Sales are always 100% and the variable cost % is 35%, the fixed cost can be determined as 65% (100%–35%).

Break-Even Sales	$ _____	__100__ %
Variable Cost	$ _____	__35__ % Variable Cost %
Fixed Cost	$ __19,500__	__65__ % Fixed Cost %

If the fixed cost is $19,500 and this amount is 65% of the Break-Even Point of Sales, calculate the Break-Even Point of Sales by dividing the Fixed Cost by the Fixed Cost %.
Formula:

Fixed Cost	÷	**Fixed Cost %**	=	**Break-Even Point of Sales**
$19,500	÷	65% (.65)	=	$30,000

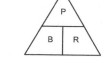

Now that the Break-Even Point of Sales is calculated as $30,000, the foodservice operator knows how much he/she needs to generate in sales per week to cover operating expenses. If the foodservice operator knows that the business needs to bring in $30,000 in sales to Break-Even, and wants to maintain a 35% Cost of Sales, what would the Cost of Sales budget be?

Break-Even Sales	$ __30,000__	__100__ %
Variable Cost	$ _____	__35__ % Variable Cost %
Fixed Cost	$ __19,500__	__65__ % Fixed Cost %

The formula to determine the Cost of Sales at Break-Even is:

Break-Even Point of Sales	×	**Variable Cost %**	=	**Variable Cost % Break-Even**
$30,000	×	35%	=	$10,500

The Variable Cost $ at the Break-Even Point tells the foodservice operator the amount of money available to purchase food and beverage items needed to produce sales. To prove the forecasted break-even point of sales, post the variable cost to the Break-Even Chart. By adding the forecasted fixed cost of $19,500 to the forecasted variable cost of $10,500, we arrive at the forecasted break-even sales amount of $30,000. This is the dollar amount in sales that a business must generate to cover all of its costs. Once all costs have been paid and a profit is generated, the break-even point is established.

Break-Even Sales	$ 30,000	100 %	
Variable Cost	$ 10,500	35 % Variable Cost %	
Fixed Cost	$ 19,500	65 % Fixed Cost %	

This information is useful when trying to control food and beverage costs. The Break-Even Point can be used to determine the estimated weekly profit, known as Break-Even Analysis.

Break-Even Analysis. The Break-Even Point of Sales can be compared to actual weekly sales and may be used to determine whether or not a profit has been made. Using the information from the previous example, we know that the University Inn must bring in $30,000 per week to Break-Even. If the foodservice operation brings in $35,000 worth of actual sales in a given week, what is the University Inn's profit?

The first step in the Break-Even Analysis is determining the difference between the Actual Sales and the Break-Even Sales. The difference is called Additional Sales.
Formula:

Actual Sales	–	**Break-Even Point of Sales**	=	**Additional Sales**
$35,000	–	$30,000	=	$5000

The University Inn has sales of $5,000 more than the dollar amount needed to Break-Even (Additional Sales). Because this figure does not represent a clear profit, if sales rose by $5,000, how much was spent to purchase the goods that were sold?
Formula:

Additional Sales	×	**Cost of Sales %**	=	**Additional Variable Cost**
$5,000	×	35% (.35)	=	$1,750

If the University Inn spent an additional $1,750 to purchase the goods sold, and the Labor and Overhead Costs are fixed, the University Inn realized a potential profit of $3,250.
Formula:

Additional Sales	–	**Additional Variable Cost**	=	**Potential Profit**
$5,000	–	$1,750	=	$3,250

The University Inn can expect an approximate profit of $3,250 for the week.

Break-Even Covers. Thus far, the Break-Even Point of Sales has been referred to as a specific dollar amount needed to cover expenses. The Break-Even Point of Sales may also be based on the average sale per cover. Break-Even Covers are defined as the number of persons that must be served (covers) to achieve the Break-Even Point of Sales. Using the information already provided for the University Inn, and the average sale per cover of $36.80, the formula to determine the number of covers needed to Break-Even is:
Formula:

[Fixed Cost $	÷	**(Average Sale per Cover**	×	**Fixed Cost %)]**	=	**Break-Even Covers**
[$19,500	÷	($36.80	×	65%)]	=	815 Covers

Knowing the number of customers needed to Break-Even can help a foodservice operator to realize when profit making begins. If a foodservice operation customarily brings in 250 customers per day, take the 815 Break-Even customer figure and divide it by the 250 customers per day to arrive at an approximate four-day period (3.26 days) for the business to Break-Even. Knowing the foodservice operation's Break-Even Point of Sales, and the number of customers served to reach the Break-Even point, is useful information for a foodservice operator. For a new business, forecasted costs must be used rather than actual data. The more attention to detail in tracking the sales and cost information needed, the more reliable the Break-Even point.

Menu Engineering

Menu Engineering was developed by Michael L. Kasavana and Donald I. Smith in *Menu Engineering: A Practical Guide to Menu Analysis* (1990, Hospitality Pub.). This process analyzes the popularity and contribution margin of each menu item, and classifies the items as "Stars," "Plowhorses," "Puzzles," and "Dogs." The following definitions help to clarify the Menu Engineering classifications.

Stars	High popularity, high contribution margin items
Plowhorses	High popularity, low contribution margin items
Puzzles	Low popularity, high contribution margin items
Dogs	Low popularity, low contribution margin items

The popularity of a menu item can be determined by tracking the number of each item sold. To determine the contribution margin of each menu item the foodservice operator must know the selling price and the food cost of each item.

To use the Menu Engineering process, the foodservice manager must have the following information available about the items in the analysis: the number of each menu item sold, the selling price of each menu item, and the food cost of each menu item. Menu Engineering is explained in Figure 11.2. Each column is labeled with a letter and thoroughly explained column by column.

Figure 11.2
Menu Engineering

Menu Engineering

Food Category: APPETIZERS   Time Period/Dates: MARCH 20XX

A	B	C	D	E	F	G	H	I	J	K	L	M
Menu Item	# Sold	Sales Mix%	Selling Price	Food Cost	Contrib. Margin	Total Sales	Total Costs	Total CM	CM %	Sales Mix Category	CM Category	Item Classification
Chicken Wings	143	14.7%	$8.50	$2.55	$5.95	$1,215.50	$364.65	$850.85	15.7%	High	High	STAR
Mozzarella	103	10.6%	$6.95	$2.25	$4.70	$715.85	$231.75	$484.10	8.9%	High	Low	PLOWHORSE
California Rolls	69	7.1%	$7.50	$1.88	$5.62	$517.50	$129.72	$387.78	7.2%	Low	Low	DOG
Florentine Bruchetta	171	17.6%	$7.95	$2.07	$5.88	$1,359.45	$353.97	$1,005.48	18.6%	High	High	STAR
Calamari	200	20.6%	$6.25	$1.25	$5.00	$1,250.00	$250.00	$1,000.00	18.5%	High	Low	PLOWHORSE
Shrimp	57	5.9%	$9.50	$4.28	$5.22	$541.50	$243.96	$297.54	5.5%	Low	Low	DOG
Nachos	171	17.6%	$7.95	$1.99	$5.96	$1,359.45	$340.29	$1,019.16	18.8%	High	High	STAR
Quesadilla	57	5.9%	$7.95	$1.50	$6.45	$453.15	$85.50	$367.65	6.8%	Low	High	PUZZLE
		0.0%			$0.00	$0.00	$0.00	$0.00	0.0%			
		0.0%			$0.00	$0.00	$0.00	$0.00	0.0%			
		0.0%			$0.00	$0.00	$0.00	$0.00	0.0%			
		0.0%			$0.00	$0.00	$0.00	$0.00	0.0%			
		0.0%			$0.00	$0.00	$0.00	$0.00	0.0%			
TOTALS	971	100.0%				$7,412.40	$1,999.84	$5,412.56	100.0%			
Desired Sales Mix % =		8.75%			$5.57	= Average Contribution Margin				Potential Food Cost % =		26.98%

Column A. Column A is prepared by simply listing the menu items of the sales category analyzed. Menu Engineering is used to analyze menu items within the same menu classification.

Column B. Column B presents the number of times each item within a category has been sold during a stated time period. The total of Column B represents the total number of items sold within the category being analyzed.

Column C. Column C asks for the Sales Mix %. The formula to solve for this is:

Number of Each Item	÷	**Total Items Sold**	=	**Sales Mix %**
Chicken Wings: 143	÷	971	=	14.7%

The percentages in this column should add up to 100%.

Column D. The Selling Price of each menu item is posted in Column D.

Column E. Column E includes the Food Cost of each Menu Item. The Menu Item's Food Cost must include all food costs incurred in serving the customer. As discussed in Chapter 5, a Standard Portion Cost of a menu item is often the same as a Standard Plate cost. The food cost may include garnishes, bread and rolls, and accompaniments to the entrée ordered.

Column F. The Contribution Margin is calculated by subtracting the Menu Item's Food Cost from the Menu Item's Selling Price. The Contribution Margin informs the business of how much each menu item contributes to other costs and profits (Col. D—Col. E = Col. F).
Formula:

Menu Selling Price	–	**Food Cost**	=	**Contributing Margin**
Chicken Wings: $8.50	–	$2.55	=	$5.95

Column G. Total Sales is calculated by multiplying the number of each menu item sold by the menu item's selling price (Col. B × Col. D = Col. G).
Formula:

Total Number Sold	×	**Menu Selling Price**	=	**Total Sales**
Chicken Wings: 143	×	$8.50	=	$1,215.50

Column H. The Total Food Cost is calculated by multiplying the number of each menu item sold by the menu item's food cost (Col. B × Col. E = Col. H).
Formula:

Total Number Sold	×	**Food Cost**	=	**Total Food Cost**
Chicken Wings: 143	×	$2.55	=	$364.65

Column I. The Total Contribution Margin (CM) is calculated by multiplying the number of each menu item sold by the menu item's contribution margin (Col. B × Col. F = Col. I).
Formula:

Total Number Sold	×	**Contribution Margin**	=	**Total Contribution Margin**
Chicken Wings: 143	×	$5.95	=	$850.85

The amount solved for in Column I can be confirmed by subtracting the Total Food Cost from the Total Sales for each menu item.

Column J. The Contribution Margin % illustrates the percentage of the total contribution margin represented by each menu item. To solve for the Contribution Margin %, divide each menu item's Total Contribution Margin by the Total of Column I.

Formula:

Menu Item Total CM	÷	Total CM	=	Contribution Margin
Chicken Wings: $850.85	÷	$5,412.56	=	15.7%

Column K. Column K is the Sales Mix Category. Menu items listed here fall into a high or a low category based on popularity. The formula used to determine whether a menu item is high or low has two steps:

Formula:

Step One:	100%	÷	Number of Menu Items Being Analyzed	=	Expected Sales Mix %
Step One:	100%	÷	8 Menu Items	=	12.5% Expected Sales Mix

If the menu items analyzed are all selling at the same rate, each menu item has the same Sales Mix %. In Figure 11.7, we are analyzing eight appetizers. If the foodservice manager expects to sell appetizers at the same rate, a Sales Mix % of 12.5% is expected for each menu item. When analyzing ten items, each menu item has a 10% Expected Sales Mix (100% ÷ 10 menu items = 10%). If analyzing fifteen items, each menu item has a 6.67% Expected Sales Mix (100% ÷ 15 menu items = 6.67%), and so on. The first step in assigning a category a high or low designation is to solve for the Expected Sales Mix percent.

Formula:

Step Two:	Expected Sales Mix	×	70%	=	Desired Sales Mix %
Step Two:	12.5%	×	70%	=	8.75%

The Desired Sales Mix % is used by foodservice operators to identify whether or not a menu item is popular and carries its own weight. The 70% "hurdle rate" is developed to identify whether or not a menu item maintains the popularity standard as developed by Kasavana and Smith. If the Sales Mix % of a menu item is less than the Desired Sales Mix %, the menu item is considered LOW in the Sales Mix Category (Column K). If the Sales Mix % of a menu item is equal to, or greater than, the Desired Sales Mix %, the menu item is considered HIGH in the Sales Mix Category (Column K).

Column L. The Contribution Margin Category is assigned to Column L. The first step is to determine the Average Contribution Margin by taking the Total Contribution Margin (Column I), and dividing it by the total number of menu items sold (Column B). Using the example in Figure 11.2, the Average Contribution Margin is calculated in the following way:

Total Contribution Margin	÷	Total Menu Items Sold	=	Average Contribution Margin
Example: $5,412.56	÷	971	=	$5.57

If the Contribution Margin of each menu item (Column F) is lower than the Average Contribution Margin ($5.57), the menu item is considered LOW. If the Contribution Margin of each menu item is higher than the Average Contribution Margin ($5.57), the menu item is considered HIGH.

Column M. The Menu Item Classification column is assigned by using the results posted to Column K (Sales Mix Category) and Column L (Contribution Margin Category). Each menu item qualifies for one of the four classifications already mentioned: "Stars," "Plowhorses," "Puzzles," and "Dogs."

Sales Mix Category	Contribution Margin Category	Classification
High	High	Star
High	Low	Plowhorse
Low	High	Puzzle
Low	Low	Dog

Valuable pieces of information such as the Potential Food Cost % can also be obtained from the Menu Engineering worksheet. The Potential Food Cost % is calculated by taking the total of Column H (Food Cost), and dividing it by Column G (Food Sales) to provide the chef/manager with an estimated food cost percent for the menu category being analyzed. The following equation shows how the Potential Food Cost % is calculated in Figure 11.2.
Formula:

Total Food Cost	÷	**Total Food Sales**	=	**Potential Food Cost %**
$1,999.84	÷	$7,412.40	=	26.98%

Decision Making Based on Menu Classification

Once the classification of the menu item has been identified, pricing, content, design, and positioning decisions must be made. Recommendations to be considered when making decisions concerning each of these categories include a careful analysis of how these categories are defined.

Stars. Stars are high in both popularity and contribution margin. The menu items that are classified as stars are not only selling well but are contributing considerably to the profit of the business. Many times, stars are the restaurants "signature items." When examining the menu items classified as stars, note the following:

1. locate *stars* in a highly visible area of the menu
2. raise the *star's* menu price slightly so that the contribution margin will increase without affecting the item's popularity, or . . .
3. just leave the *stars* alone. If they're *stars*, they are already a hit.

Plowhorses. Plowhorses are high in popularity, but low in contribution margin. A Plowhorse contributes to the overall profits of a business, but does not singularly contribute much. The popularity of the item allows the operation to sell a lot of these items, although the dollar contribution per item is limited. Plowhorses should be kept on the menu, but a foodserver must try to increase the contribution margin by selling additional items to the customer. When evaluating Plowhorses, consider:

1. increasing the price. But be careful! Although the first instinct is to increase the selling price of the product, remember that customers are often sensitive to price increases. It may be possible to increase the price, but only enough to cover increased food costs that affect the menu item.
2. not reducing the quality or quantity standards of the *plowhorse* menu item. Instead, replace the items that accompany the *plowhorse* menu items with lower cost products to reduce the overall food cost of the menu item.
3. relocating the menu item to allow for the more popular and higher contribution margin menu items to be in the profile areas.

Puzzles. Puzzles are items that contribute well individually to the contribution margin, but are not very popular. Decision guidelines for puzzles include:

1. relocating the menu item to a high profile area on the menu or including it in a high merchandising campaign. Possibly renaming the *puzzle* may be enough to market the item.
2. removing the menu item. If the *puzzle* is very low in popularity, labor intensive, or made of highly perishable product, remove it. At times the *puzzle* is kept on the menu to keep the "regular" customer happy.
3. decreasing the menu item's selling price. Maybe the only reason that the menu item is a *puzzle* and not a *star* is because it is overpriced.

Dogs. A Dog is a menu item that is unpopular and does not contribute to the profit of the business. The following recommendations should be considered for the Dog:

1. remove the item from the menu; especially if the *dog* has no ingredients similar to those of other menu items.
2. raise the *dog's* price so that the item has the potential of becoming a *puzzle*. This may seem puzzling because "who would pay for a higher priced *dog*?"
3. keep the *dogs* on the menu, because their sales are often accompanied by other profitable sales.

Menu Engineering is a tool used to help identify how well menu items are selling. Menu Engineering helps a foodservice operator to identify the popularity of a menu item and its contribution to the profits of the business. Sales Control and Analysis are important in the cycle of cost control because it is within this step that recommendations are made for menu improvements.

Review Questions

1. Describe three ways to track covers. Which method has the most control? Explain why.

2. Calculate the Turnover Rates for the following and identify the type of foodservice operation (Fine Dining, Family, or Quick Service) that would typically have each of these Turnover Rates.

	Covers Served	Dining Room Seats
a.	100	100
b.	50	25
c.	360	80
d.	250	50
e.	300	55

3. Calculate the Average Sale per Cover using the information provided. What type of foodservice operation would typically have a similar Average Sale per Cover?

	Total Sales	Covers
a.	$8,500	200
b.	$1,250	45
c.	$7,800	325
d.	$11,340	180
e.	$11,440	300

4. Calculate the Sales Mix % for the following Desserts:

	Menu Item	Number Sold
a.	Chocolate Heaven	15
b.	Chocolate Chip Pie	22
c.	Deep Dish Apple Pie	8
d.	Mile High Lemon Meringue Pie	18
e.	Strawberry Ladyfinger Torte	12

5. Using the Sales Mix % results from question 4, forecast the number of each dessert needed for Saturday night's forecasted 160 covers.

6. The following are sales totals from each menu category on a menu. Determine the Contribution to Sales % for each category.

a.	Appetizers	$ 550.75
b.	Soups	$ 375.00
c.	Salads	$ 325.25
d.	Entrées	$1,578.50
e.	Desserts	$ 675.25

7. Using the following information, calculate the weekly Break-Even Point of Sales and the Cost of Sales $ at the Break-Even Point.

	Labor Cost	Overhead Cost	Cost of Sales %
a.	$ 8,200	$5,800	38%
b.	$ 4,600	$3,500	40%
c.	$ 11,800	$7,400	32%
d.	$12,200	$9,500	35%

8. Using the Break-Even Point of Sales calculated in question 7 and the Final Sales figures below, calculate Additional Sales, Additional Cost of Sales $, and Estimated Profit.

	Final Sales
a.	$25,000
b.	$16,000
c.	$33,500
d.	$36,550

9. Using the information given below, determine the number of covers needed to reach the Break-Even Point of Sales.

	Labor Cost	Overhead Cost	Cost of Sales %	Average Sale per Cover
a.	$ 9,500	$ 6,800	35%	$30.50
b.	$14,300	$ 8,900	38%	$32.00
c.	$ 7,500	$ 5,850	30%	$23.75
d.	$11,500	$ 8,000	30%	$40.00
e.	$15,300	$11,200	32%	$55.00

10a. Post the following information to the Menu Engineering worksheet found on WebCom or Appendix F, and solve by identifying each menu item as a Star, Plowhorse, Puzzle, or Dog.

Menu Item	Number Sold	Menu Price	Food Cost
Steak Oscar	32	$29.50	$11.21
Veal Marsala	18	$24.95	$ 9.98
Baked Stuffed Sole	22	$26.95	$ 7.54
Broiled Salmon	48	$25.50	$ 7.40
Rosemary Chicken	28	$22.25	$ 5.56

10b. Based on these findings, what recommendations would you make concerning each menu item?

11a. Post the following information to the Menu Engineering worksheet on WebCom or Appendix F or on WebCom and solve by identifying each menu item as a Star, Plowhorse, Puzzle, or Dog.

Menu Item	Number Sold	Menu Price	Food Cost
Strawberry Shortcake	52	$9.50	$3.21
Pumpkin Cheesecake	18	$8.25	$4.00
Chocolate Heaven	32	$8.95	$3.50
Peanut Butter Volcano	44	$7.95	$3.65
Banana Split Royal	65	$8.50	$2.40
Golden Raisin Carrot Cake	22	$7.25	$3.18

11b. Based on your findings, what recommendations would you make concerning each menu item?

12. Using the spreadsheet program of your professor's choice, develop a Menu Engineering Spreadsheet.

Chapter 12

Labor Cost Controls and Analysis

© 2014, Karuka, Shutterstock, Inc.

OBJECTIVES

Upon completion of this chapter, the student should be able to:

1. explain the three components of labor cost: wages, salary, and benefits.
2. prepare a work schedule utilizing the three methods of irregular, split, and swing.
3. calculate the departmental labor cost.
4. utilize the requirements of the Fair Labor Standards Act.
5. explain the law concerning TIP declaration.
6. calculate taxable income, determine withholdings for Federal Income Tax, Social Security, Medicare, and determine net pay.
7. calculate the employer's total labor cost.

KEY TERMS

Benefits	I-9	Organizational Chart
Departmental Labor Cost	Indirectly Tipped Employees	Salary
Direct Income	Irregular Scheduling	Split Shift
Directly Tipped Employees	Job Analysis	Swing Shift
Exempt Employees	Job Description	W-2
Federal Income Tax	Job Specification	W-4
FICA	Labor Cost Control	Wage
FLSA	Meal Credit	
FUTA	Non-Exempt Employees	

INTRODUCTION

Labor Cost can be defined as the total amount spent to pay the wages, salaries, and benefits of employees. A wage is an hourly rate of pay, while a "Salary" is a fixed amount of income based on the job performed rather than the amount of time needed to perform the job. In addition to wages and salaries, employers must make contributions known as benefits, on behalf of the employee. All businesses must provide benefits that are dictated by federal law (often referred to as payroll taxes), although some employers voluntarily offer additional benefits. The labor cost of a foodservice operation includes all benefits offered to employees whether voluntary or not.

Labor Cost percent is that percent of sales that is spent to pay wages, salaries, and benefits. This cost can be as high, if not higher than, the Cost of Sales %. Labor Cost % can range from 15–40%, depending upon the type of foodservice operation. Knowing what is involved in the foodservice operation's labor cost dollar is important because it is the first step to labor cost control. **Labor Cost Control** refers to controlling the dollars a foodservice operation is spending on labor without jeopardizing the quality of the product and service. The true purpose of labor cost control is not merely to reduce labor cost dollars, but rather to get the most of every labor cost dollar spent.

Both the employer and the employee benefit by knowing the labor laws, which dictate paying employees fairly at a minimum legally established rate. Foodservice operations must pay their employees properly and fairly to avoid devastating consequences.

Labor Cost: What Is It?

Labor cost is the cost of paying employees' wages, salaries, and benefits. Each of these areas will be examined to show what a chef/manager might do to get the most out of a labor cost dollar.

Wages

A **wage** is a pay rate that is based on an hourly time period. The employee receives an hourly wage for each hour he/she works. Gross pay is normally calculated by multiplying the total hours worked by the hourly rate. There are standards that must be met by employers when paying employees' wages. The Fair Labor Standards Act (**FLSA**), written in 1938, implemented the first Federal Minimum Wage and also determined a fair work week of 40 hours. The Federal Minimum Wage is the least amount an employer may pay an employee for one hour of work. Effective July 2009, the Federal Minimum Wage is $7.25 per hour. Employers must pay their employees at least $7.25 per hour for every hour worked under the fair work week of 40 hours. (*At the time of printing, the federal government had just started a discussion to increase the Federal Minimum Wage.*) Please refer to the US Department of Labor's website at: http://www.dol.gov/whd/minimumwage.htm to determine the current federal minimum wage. The federal minimum wage is the least amount paid to employees in every state within the United States of America with the exception of those states where the State Minimum Wage is higher than the Federal Minimum Wage. If a state has a higher State Minimum Wage than the Federal Minimum Wage the employer must abide by the state law. Please refer to http://www.dol.gov/esa/minwage/america.htm for the individual states' federal minimum wages.

Other exceptions to the Federal Minimum Wage law are also given in the FLSA. For example, there are special rules for hiring full-time students under the age of 18, including the option of paying them a reduced minimum wage and restricting their work hours. The current federal law concerning the full-time student wage rate states that individuals under the age of 18 may not be paid less than 85% of the current minimum wage. Most states also have additional special guidelines for employees under eighteen.

Another exception to the FLSA applies to employees who customarily receive gratuities (TIPS: to ensure prompt service), as part of their income. An employee who customarily receives gratuities, directly or indirectly, must claim the money received through TIPS as part of their gross earnings. A directly tipped employee is one who receives gratuities directly from the customer. An indirectly tipped employee is one who usually receives a portion of the gratuities earned by other directly tipped employees. If an employee normally receives at least $30.00 per month in gratuities, the employer is allowed to take a TIP credit per hour to pay the tipped employee. Currently, employers may pay tipped employees $2.13 per hour as long as the tipped employee's wages plus the amount of tips earned equal or exceed the minimum wage. If not, the employer is required to make up the difference. Some states have implemented their own TIP credit policy. If the state's tip credit policy is more beneficial to the employee, it supersedes the Federal regulation. The Tips earned by employees must be declared as income. Federal guidelines concerning TIP declaration are discussed later in this chapter.

In addition to the Federal Minimum Wage, the Fair Labor Standards Act has also declared a fair work week of 40 hours. The implementation of the 40-hour-work week also defined overtime laws. Federal law as it relates to overtime pay is 1.5 times the hourly rate of pay for all hours worked over 40 per week. Some states, and even some companies, have their own overtime rules such as time and a half for every hour after eight hours per day. If a state or company has its own overtime rules and procedures, the employer must again use the overtime policy that is most beneficial to the employee. Employees who normally receive wages for work performed are considered **non-exempt**

employees. They are not exempt from federal and state wage and hour laws as described in the Fair Labor Standards Act. All current laws regarding the payment of hourly wage employees can be found at the US Department of Labor's website at: http://www.dol.gov.

Salary

A **salary** is a fixed amount of income based on the job performed rather than the amount of time needed to perform the job. To receive a salary and to be exempt from the provisions of the FLSA, employees must be executives, professionals, administrative or sales persons, and must also fulfill certain prescribed requirements. All FLSA exemptions state that for an employee to qualify for a salary, an employee must be paid a minimum of $455 per week ($23,660 annually). The *executive* exemption specifically mentions that the salaried worker must manage two or more full-time employees, and have the authority to influence management decisions regarding the wage earners. In addition to a salary of at least $455 per week, the *professional* exemption requires advanced knowledge and includes work that requires discretion and judgment. Further information regarding all FLSA exemptions can be found at the US Department of Labor website: http://www.dol.gov.

Based on the information provided, can a line cook be (legally) paid a salary? Yes, as long as the cook earns at least $455 per week and the position fulfills the requirements of one of the exemptions. In addition to working behind the line, the cook may have the professional expertise that is required by the professional exemption, may perform other management functions at least 60% of the time, or have full responsibility over at least two full-time employees. Depending upon the type of exemption, this individual may qualify as a salaried employee within the foodservice industry.

Wage earners often find themselves offered a salary for "a job well done." They look to this as a reward for being a true member of the team and accept a weekly salary of $650 (which sounds rather appealing for a 40-hour work week). Unfortunately, they actually work 55 to 60 hours per week and do not receive overtime pay. Some employers knowingly try to take advantage of employees in this way. Others do it unknowingly because of their ignorance of the law. The Department of Labor was created to provide information and assistance to both the employer and the employee to avoid both of these situations. There is a Federal Department of Labor, in addition to Departments of Labor in many states. These bureaus exist to ensure that employees are paid fairly and correctly. Employees who normally receive a salary for work performed are considered **exempt employees** who need not adhere to federal and state wage and hour laws as described in the Fair Labor Standards Act.

Benefits and Federal Taxes

The **benefits** that are part of the employer's labor costs include those items and services that are provided an employee at no cost to the employee. Benefits might include health insurance, paid vacations, sick days, employee meals, uniforms, holiday pay, and bonuses (all of which are strictly voluntary on the part of the employer). Federally mandated benefits, usually qualified as employer payroll taxes, are benefits that employers must contribute, and provide at no cost to the employee. Workman's Compensation, which is an insurance paid by the employer to protect an employee who might be injured on the job, is a mandated benefit. Workman's Compensation rates vary according to a foodservice establishment's safety record. In addition to workman's compensation, there are two other federal labor laws that effect labor cost.

FICA (Federal Insurance Contribution Act) is a payroll tax that is contributed to by both the employee and the employer. The Federal Insurance Contribution Act includes two types of benefits: Social Security, which is a retirement supplement for workers who qualify, and Medicare, which is health care for those who are of retirement age. FICA taxes are based on both the employee's income and TIPS earned. In 2014, employers must withhold 6.2% of an employee's earnings up to a taxable wage base of $117,000 for Social Security purposes. A taxable wage base is the annual amount of income that is subject to social security taxes. Employers must also withhold 1.45% annually on income and tips earned by employees for Medicare. There is no taxable wage base for Medicare withholdings. Medicare withholdings are based on all income earned annually. Refer to the Social Security Administration website at http://www.ssa.gov for updates and additional information.

At this point a question may arise concerning why money coming out of the employee's paycheck is considered part of the employer's labor cost dollar. Every penny withheld from the employee's paycheck must be matched by the employer. Employees currently contribute a total of 7.65% (6.2% to Social Security and 1.45% to Medicare) of their income to FICA and employers match this 7.65% contribution in addition to the wages and salaries paid. The 7.65% contributed by the employer is considered as a labor cost.

FUTA (Federal Unemployment Tax Act) is solely an employer contribution. Employers must contribute 6.2% of an employee's first $7,000 of annual income and tips to unemployment. Although considered a tax, this contribution is a benefit for the worker who is laid off due to a lack of work caused by a seasonal demand or by the reorganization of a company's work force. Many states also have their own unemployment programs for which employers are provided a credit toward their federal tax payments. Due to a high labor turnover in the foodservice industry, FUTA can be a very costly benefit for foodservice employers. Labor turnover rate refers to the number of times staff members are replaced annually. For example, if a restaurant normally employs 60 people, but throughout the year has 150 employees who have filled those 60 positions, the labor turnover rate is 2.5.

Formula:

Total # Employees	÷	**# Needed Employees**	=	**Labor Turnover Rate**
Example: 150	÷	60	=	2.5 (250%)

The National Restaurant Association estimates the average labor turnover rate for the foodservice industry at 300%. This percentage is much higher than that of other types of businesses. Why is the labor turnover rate so high in the foodservice industry? The answer to this question can be debated for hours. Reasons vary, but some conclude that the foodservice industry attracts employees who "are only working until they can find a different job," possibly in their area of study. Others conclude that so many employers fail to implement a good training program and employees get "fed up" with not knowing their job, and leave to find another. Employers respond by asking why they should spend money training these employees when they are just going to leave anyway. The debate is endless.

So, how does a high labor turnover rate effect the FUTA contributions of an employer? At the beginning of every year, as well as each time a new employee is hired, foodservice employers must contribute 6.2% of the employee's gross income to FUTA, and continue to contribute this amount throughout the course of the year until the employee has earned $7,000. FUTA is not withheld from an employee's pay but is paid by the employer in addition to the employee's gross income. A foodservice operation with a low turnover rate might well finish contributing its annual FUTA contributions by mid-year because most of its workers will have earned $7,000 by then. A foodservice operation with a high turnover rate on the other hand, might be paying FUTA contributions throughout the year since every employee who leaves must be replaced. FUTA taxes paid for the new employee begin anew and are paid until the new employee earns $7,000 or until the end of the year, whichever comes first. As seen in the example provided, an employer's labor cost dollar does not just include the wages and salaries that are paid the employee, many other expenses are also incurred. The example that follows shows how FICA and FUTA taxes affect the total labor cost.

Example. It's the second week in February and the University Inn's wages and salaries for the weekly payroll total $14,000. In addition to that $14,000, the employer must also pay an additional 6.2% to Social Security, 1.45% to Medicare, and 6.2% to FUTA. How much in additional labor costs would have to be expended for these three contributions?

Wages and Salaries		Payroll Taxes		Employer Contribution
$ 14,000	×	6.2% Social Security	=	$ 868
	×	1.45% Medicare	=	$ 203
	×	6.2% FUTA	=	$ 868

Weekly Total:	$ 14,000	+	$ 1,939	=	$ 15,939
Half Year Total:	$364,000	+	$ 50,414	=	$ 414,414
Yearly Total:	$728,000	+	$100,828	=	$828,828

By including the three contributions listed above, the employer is paying an additional 13.85% (or in this case an additional $1,939 per week, which is $100,000 per year), over and beyond the wages and salaries paid to the employees. When an employer also offers health and dental plans, bonuses, vacations, sick days, holiday pay, employee parties, uniforms, etc., (voluntary contributions), in addition to wages and salaries, the total monies paid an employee are quite substantial.

The many voluntary benefits that may be provided to the employee, at the expense of the employer, are becoming increasingly available to foodservice employees. The federal government has guidelines concerning voluntary benefits. The most common voluntary benefit, and the only one that will be discussed in this chapter, is the employee meal. As previously stated, employee meals should not be included in food cost but rather in labor cost. There are several options for employers who offer employee meals. The federal government allows employers to reduce the cash wages paid an employee in an amount equal to the actual cost of the meal to the foodservice operation. Many states also have provisions for meal credits. Foodservice operations should contact the Department of Labor in the state where their operation is located for information.

Employee Meals. Employers have the option to provide meals to employees at a cost, at no cost, or at a discount. Employee meals may be provided through employee dining services. A single offering may be prepared each day, or the choice of a variety of menu items might be made available. Meals provided the employee at no charge should not be considered a part of the employee's gross income if they are furnished on premises and are for the convenience of the employer. The employer does not pay FICA or FUTA taxes on the value of meals provided to employees.

To calculate the value of employee meals, the employer must simply assign a fair food cost value to the food provided. This value is then transferred from food cost to labor cost. Employers sometimes offer employees a discounted meal price (such as 50% off the menu selling price). The money paid by the employee remains as a food cost because it is producing a sale. Food provided an employee at no cost is assigned to labor cost. Another method used by employers allows each employee a set dollar amount for the purchase of meals. An employee might be allowed to order anything on the menu that is under a $10.00 sales price. The value of the food cost is then based on the working food cost, and is assigned to labor cost. Any time an employee orders an item that costs more than $10.00, he/she is responsible to pay the difference. If an employer provides employees meals on a regular basis, he/she may charge a reasonable amount for these meals or deduct a **meal credit** from the employee's wages and salaries.

Remember that only tip credits and meal credits can be deducted from employees who are paid a minimum wage, and that Federal law states that shortages and breakages may only be deducted from employees who earn more than minimum wage. Many states have implemented laws that disallow such deductions. Both federal and state laws and regulations should be examined prior to paying wages, salaries, mandatory taxes, voluntary benefits, etc.

Hiring the Right Employee

Before any hiring takes place, it is important that foodservice operators know exactly for what and for who they are looking. In preparing to hire employees, the first thing that needs to be done is to chart out the structure of the foodservice operation by using an organizational chart. An **organizational chart** identifies the various levels of authority and responsibility within the foodservice operation. Employees need to know and understand the chain of command. Figure 12.1 illustrates the organizational chart of a medium-sized foodservice operation.

The Organizational Chart divides the foodservice operation into departments. Foodservice operations often analyze their weekly payroll based on the percent that each department represents of the total labor cost. This percentage is known as the Departmental Labor Cost percent. The number of departments within a foodservice operation depends upon the number of employees and the size of the foodservice operation. The **Departmental Labor Cost** identifies the amount of money spent within each department and the percent of the total labor cost that each department represents. If at the end of a week, the labor cost is determined to be higher than customary, the departmental labor cost % can help to identify the department that exceeded the usual amount. Once the organizational chart has been established, the following steps should be followed to assist foodservice operators in hiring and training efficient and effective personnel.

Job Analysis

A **Job Analysis** is the first step that should be taken to understand a job. It is the process of actually observing a job while it is being performed; interviewing current employees who are performing the job; and perhaps doing the job to really understand what it entails. The job analysis should be prepared by the chef/manager prior to preparing a job description.

Job Description

The **Job Description** is a detailed list of all the duties and responsibilities that must be performed to complete a given job. Job descriptions are needed for every job within the foodservice operation. Access to job descriptions before, during, and after a shift provides employees the opportunity to check their own work. Job Descriptions are great training tools for new employees and can assist seasoned employees as well.

Job Specification

Once an employer lists what needs to be done to complete a job, he/she must also identify the skills and personality traits needed to properly perform that job. A **Job Specification** is a list of skills and personality traits necessary for a particular job. During the interviewing process, the chef/manager can ask questions based on the job specification to assess whether the individual being interviewed possesses the skills needed. A job specification usually identifies three types of skills: technical skills, interpersonal skills, and comprehensive skills.

Figure 12.1
Organizational Chart

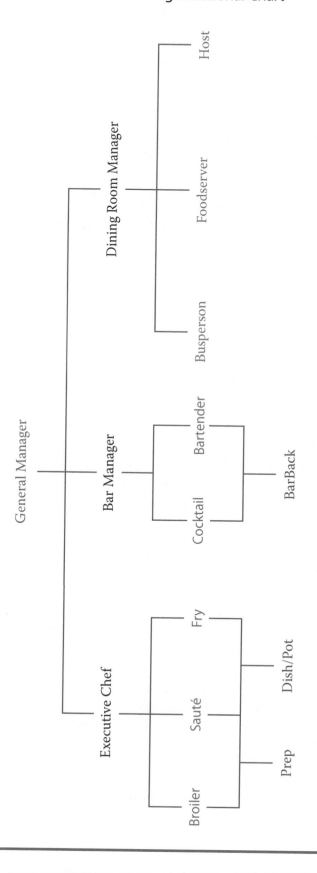

Technical skills are those that refer to job knowledge, (knowing how to perform a job). If the chef/manager is developing a job specification for a broiler cook, the technical skills needed would include the ability to identify meat products and knowledge of appropriate internal cooking temperatures.

Interpersonal skills refer to the human relation skills that are necessary to perform a job. The Broiler Cook, who will also serve as an expediter, needs good communication skills (the ability to give directions and orders), organizational skills, and time management skills. The skills needed to perform a particular job should be well explained to a prospective hire. It is much easier to train someone who already has some knowledge of the job at hand.

Comprehensive skills refer to an overall understanding of how each job relates to every other function within the foodservice operation. This third skill is most important when an individual climbs up the ranks on the organizational chart.

Once the job has been analyzed and described and the skills needed have been identified, the chef/manager should develop and keep interview questions on file. When a position becomes available, the chef/manager can easily pull the questions from the interview file for use. Employing an established set of questions for all interviews allows for a more equitable evaluation of potential employees.

The New Hire

Upon hire, a new employee must fill out two federal forms, the I-9 and the W-4 prior to performing any work function. It is the law that employers keep these forms on file for each and every employee. Severe penalties may be imposed if an employer fails to comply.

Immigration Reform Control Act (IRCA)

The Employment Eligibility Verification (I-9) form is used to verify employment eligibility in the United States of America. Employers must retain these forms so that they are available for inspection by officers of the Immigration and Naturalization Service and the Department of Labor. The I-9 form documents the identity and employment eligibility of an employee. Employees do not have to be United State citizens to be employed, but non-citizens must complete proper procedures as stated by the IRCA to have employment status. The I-9 form must be held for three years after the employee is hired, or one year after the employee leaves the foodservice operation, whichever is later (Figure 12.2).

Employees Withholding Allowance Certificate

The W-4, as it is more commonly known, must be filled out to inform the employer of the employee's marital status and of the number of dependents he/she is claiming. Federal Income Tax withholdings are based on gross income, marital status, and the number of dependents claimed. Employees may be "exempt" from Federal Income Tax withholding if they do not have any income tax liability in the preceding year and do not expect any in the current year. Employees who claim an exempt status on their W-4 must file a new W-4 every year of employment by February 15 to claim this exemption. These individuals must still contribute to Social Security and Medicare. If an employee has not filed an Employee's Withholding Allowance Certificate with the employer by the end of the first payroll period, the employer may withhold tax dollars as if the employee were claiming a single status with no withholding allowances (Figure 12.3 on page 181).

Figure 12.2
I-9

OMB No. 1615-0047; Expires 06/30/09

Department of Homeland Security
U.S. Citizenship and Immigration Services

**Form I-9, Employment
Eligibility Verification**

Please read instructions carefully before completing this form. The instructions must be available during completion of this form.

ANTI-DISCRIMINATION NOTICE: It is illegal to discriminate against work eligible individuals. Employers CANNOT specify which document(s) they will accept from an employee. The refusal to hire an individual because the documents have a future expiration date may also constitute illegal discrimination.

Section 1. Employee Information and Verification. To be completed and signed by employee at the time employment begins.

Print Name: Last	First	Middle Initial	Maiden Name

Address *(Street Name and Number)* | Apt. # | Date of Birth *(month/day/year)*

City | State | Zip Code | Social Security #

I am aware that federal law provides for imprisonment and/or fines for false statements or use of false documents in connection with the completion of this form.

I attest, under penalty of perjury, that I am (check one of the following):
☐ A citizen or national of the United States
☐ A lawful permanent resident (Alien #) A _____
☐ An alien authorized to work until _____
(Alien # or Admission #) _____

Employee's Signature | Date *(month/day/year)*

Preparer and/or Translator Certification. *(To be completed and signed if Section 1 is prepared by a person other than the employee.) I attest, under penalty of perjury, that I have assisted in the completion of this form and that to the best of my knowledge the information is true and correct.*

Preparer's/Translator's Signature | Print Name

Address *(Street Name and Number, City, State, Zip Code)* | Date *(month/day/year)*

Section 2. Employer Review and Verification. To be completed and signed by employer. Examine one document from List A OR examine one document from List B and one from List C, as listed on the reverse of this form, and record the title, number and expiration date, if any, of the document(s).

	List A	OR	List B	AND	List C
Document title:					
Issuing authority:					
Document #:					
Expiration Date *(if any)*:					
Document #:					
Expiration Date *(if any)*:					

CERTIFICATION - I attest, under penalty of perjury, that I have examined the document(s) presented by the above-named employee, that the above-listed document(s) appear to be genuine and to relate to the employee named, that the employee began employment on *(month/day/year)* _____ **and that to the best of my knowledge the employee is eligible to work in the United States. (State employment agencies may omit the date the employee began employment.)**

Signature of Employer or Authorized Representative | Print Name | Title

Business or Organization Name and Address *(Street Name and Number, City, State, Zip Code)* | Date *(month/day/year)*

Section 3. Updating and Reverification. To be completed and signed by employer.

A. New Name *(if applicable)*	B. Date of Rehire *(month/day/year) (if applicable)*

C. If employee's previous grant of work authorization has expired, provide the information below for the document that establishes current employment eligibility.

Document Title: _____ | Document #: _____ | Expiration Date (if any): _____

I attest, under penalty of perjury, that to the best of my knowledge, this employee is eligible to work in the United States, and if the employee presented document(s), the document(s) I have examined appear to be genuine and to relate to the individual.

Signature of Employer or Authorized Representative | Date *(month/day/year)*

Form I-9 (Rev. 06/05/07) N

Continued

Figure 12.2 —*Continued*

LISTS OF ACCEPTABLE DOCUMENTS

LIST A	LIST B		LIST C
Documents that Establish Both Identity and Employment Eligibility	Documents that Establish Identity		Documents that Establish Employment Eligibility
OR		**AND**	
1. U.S. Passport (unexpired or expired)	1. Driver's license or ID card issued by a state or outlying possession of the United States provided it contains a photograph or information such as name, date of birth, gender, height, eye color and address		1. U.S. Social Security card issued by the Social Security Administration *(other than a card stating it is not valid for employment)*
2. Permanent Resident Card or Alien Registration Receipt Card (Form I-551)	2. ID card issued by federal, state or local government agencies or entities, provided it contains a photograph or information such as name, date of birth, gender, height, eye color and address		2. Certification of Birth Abroad issued by the Department of State *(Form FS-545 or Form DS-1350)*
3. An unexpired foreign passport with a temporary I-551 stamp	3. School ID card with a photograph		3. Original or certified copy of a birth certificate issued by a state, county, municipal authority or outlying possession of the United States bearing an official seal
4. An unexpired Employment Authorization Document that contains a photograph (Form I-766, I-688, I-688A, I-688B)	4. Voter's registration card		4. Native American tribal document
	5. U.S. Military card or draft record		5. U.S. Citizen ID Card *(Form I-197)*
5. An unexpired foreign passport with an unexpired Arrival-Departure Record, Form I-94, bearing the same name as the passport and containing an endorsement of the alien's nonimmigrant status, if that status authorizes the alien to work for the employer	6. Military dependent's ID card		6. ID Card for use of Resident Citizen in the United States *(Form I-179)*
	7. U.S. Coast Guard Merchant Mariner Card		
	8. Native American tribal document		7. Unexpired employment authorization document issued by DHS *(other than those listed under List A)*
	9. Driver's license issued by a Canadian government authority		
	For persons under age 18 who are unable to present a document listed above:		
	10. School record or report card		
	11. Clinic, doctor or hospital record		
	12. Day-care or nursery school record		

Illustrations of many of these documents appear in Part 8 of the Handbook for Employers (M-274)

Figure 12.3
W-4

Form **W-4** Department of the Treasury Internal Revenue Service	**Employee's Withholding Allowance Certificate** ▶ **For Privacy Act and Paperwork Reduction Act Notice, see reverse.**	OMB No. 1545-0010

1 Type or print your first name and middle initial	Last name	2 Your social security number

Home address (number and street or rural route)

3 ☐ Single ☐ Married ☐ Married, but withhold at higher Single rate.
Note: *If married, but legally separated, or spouse is a nonresident alien, check the Single box.*

City or town, state, and ZIP code

4 If your last name differs from that on your social security card, check here and call 1-800-772-1213 for a new card . . . . . . ▶ ☐

5 Total number of allowances you are claiming (from line G above or from the worksheets on page 2 if they apply) . **5**
6 Additional amount, if any, you want withheld from each paycheck . . . . **6** $
7 I claim exemption from withholding for 1997, and I certify that I meet **BOTH** of the following conditions for exemption:
 • Last year I had a right to a refund of **ALL** Federal income tax withheld because I had **NO** tax liability; **AND**
 • This year I expect a refund of **ALL** Federal income tax withheld because I expect to have **NO** tax liability.
 If you meet both conditions, enter "EXEMPT" here . . . . ▶ **7**

Under penalties of perjury, I certify that I am entitled to the number of withholding allowances claimed on this certificate or entitled to claim exempt status.

Employee's signature ▶

Date ▶ , 19

8 Employer's name and address (Employer: Complete 8 and 10 only if sending to the IRS)	9 Office code (optional)	10 Employer identification number

Cat. No. 10220Q

Tip Declaration

All tips received by employees are considered taxable income and are subject to Federal Income Tax, Social Security, and Medicare withholdings. If employees are involved in some type of tip splitting, they need only declare their share of the tips earned. There are two types of tipped employees: directly and indirectly tipped. **Directly tipped** employees are those who receive gratuities directly from the customer. **Indirectly tipped** employees are those who receive gratuities from the directly tipped employee. It is the responsibility of all employees who receive tips to report 100% of their share of tips earned to their employer. Federal guidelines regarding how and when to report tips are explained below.

Employee Responsibilities to TIP Declaration

Employees who earn less than $20 in TIPS per month while working for an employer, may choose not to report those tips to the employer, but must include the tips earned on their federal income tax return. Employees who receive more than $20 in TIPS per month while working for any one employer, must report the tips to the employer so that the appropriate taxes are withheld. It is the employee's responsibility to keep a daily record of all TIPS earned and to identify tips received as cash or credit card receipts from customers or other employees. Employees must maintain records of all TIPS distributed to other employees through tip sharing, as well as the name of the person to whom the shared tips were distributed, and the daily amount distributed. Use of the Internal Revenue Service (IRS) Form 4070-A, Employee's Daily Record of Tips, is recommended. Employee tip tracking responsibilities must be conveyed to all employees who receive tips. Information concerning federal regulations in declaring tips should also be provided to the employee. Tip declarations to employers ensure that proper withholdings are taken from the employee's pay.

Employer Responsibilities to TIP Declaration

In large foodservice operations (operations that employ 10 employees per day), and where tipping is customary, employers must develop a system to ensure that at least 8% of the business' food and beverage sales are declared as earned income by tipped employees. At the end of every year, employers at large foodservice operations must file an IRS Form 8027 to report the foodservice operation's food and beverage sales and the total employee tips (cash and charge), declared to the employer. By filing IRS Form 8027, the employer is able to identify whether or not the 8% of food and beverage sales have been met (through the declaration of tips). If the tips reported are greater than the required 8%, the employer guarantees that the tips received by the employees have been accurately recorded. If the tips reported to the employer do not meet the required 8% of food and beverage sales, the employer must assign additional amounts of income as tips to directly tipped employees. Employers may allocate tips based on gross receipts, hours worked, or upon good faith. (Figure 12.4)

To alleviate the process of tip allocation at year's end, employers should implement a system throughout the year to monitor employee tip declaration. A common method used to monitor tip declaration is known as the Gross Sales Method. To use the Gross Sales Method, employers must require that directly tipped employees record their daily gross sales on the same form on which they declare TIPS. The employer can then compare the tips declared by the employee to the 8% of each employee's gross sales. Indirectly tipped employees must be instructed to declare 100% of all tips earned. Although it is not the employer's responsibility to declare tips for employees, monitoring the tips throughout the year prevents the allocation of tips at the end of the year.

Pre-Payroll Preparation

Most foodservice operations pay their employees on a weekly or biweekly basis. Salaried employees receive a standard weekly compensation, while hourly wage earners are paid based on the number of hours they work. Before payroll preparation, the chef/manager must devise a schedule to inform wage earners of their work schedule. Employers must also implement a system to track the number of hours actually worked by each employee.

Schedule Preparation

The schedule preparation discussion that follows is based on a payroll that is prepared on a weekly basis. Schedules for the hourly wage earners are traditionally prepared weekly by the manager or department head. Foodservice operations differ from other businesses because of the constant progression of peak and non-peak work periods that they experience. Peak periods can be seasonal, weekly, or even daily. Daily peak periods are the hours when a foodservice operation provides customer service. Daily non-peak periods refer to the hours in between meals when preparation takes place. It is uncommon that a full staff is needed during non-peak periods, and managers must be creative in scheduling employees during these hours to control labor costs. Figure 12.5 illustrates the three scheduling methods that may be employed.

It is rare that chefs/managers need a full staff for the entire 7:00 a.m. to 3:00 p.m., and 3:00 p.m. to 11:00 p.m. time periods. A full staff is usually only required during the peak periods within those times. Chefs/managers try to maximize the efficiency of their labor cost dollar and their work force by using an employee scheduling technique that effectively handles non-peak and peak periods. By scheduling different start and finish times for almost every employee, the maximum number of staff needed during the day is present during the foodservice operation's peak periods. Irregular scheduling allows employees to work a scheduled eight-hour shift.

Figure 12.4

IRS Form 8027

Form **8027**

Department of the Treasury
Internal Revenue Service

**Employer's Annual Information Return of
Tip Income and Allocated Tips**

▶ **See separate instructions.**

OMB No. 1545-0714

┌ Name of establishment

Number and street (see instructions)

└ City or town, state, and ZIP code

Employer identification number

**Type of establishment (check
only one box)**

☐ **1** Evening meals only

☐ **2** Evening and other
meals

☐ **3** Meals other than
evening meals

☐ **4** Alcoholic beverages

Employer's name (same name as on Form 941)

Establishment number
(see instructions)

Number and street (P.O. box, if applicable)

Apt. or suite no.

City, state, and ZIP code (if a foreign address, see instructions)

Does this establishment accept credit
cards, debit cards, or other charges?

☐ Yes (lines 1 and 2 **must** be completed)
☐ No

Check **if:** Amended Return ☐
Final Return ☐

Attributed Tip Income Program (ATIP). See Revenue Procedure 2006-30 . . . . ▶ ☐

1	Total charged tips for calendar year	**1**
2	Total charge receipts showing charged tips (see instructions)	**2**
3	Total amount of service charges of less than 10% paid as wages to employees	**3**
4a	Total tips reported by indirectly tipped employees	**4a**
b	Total tips reported by directly tipped employees	**4b**

Note. Complete the **Employer's Optional Worksheet for Tipped Employees** on page 6
of the instructions to determine potential unreported tips of your employees.

c	Total tips reported (add lines 4a and 4b)	**4c**
5	Gross receipts from food or beverage operations (not less than line 2—see instructions) .	**5**
6	Multiply line 5 by 8% (.08) or the lower rate shown here ▶_____ granted by the IRS.
(Attach a copy of the IRS determination letter to this return.)	**6**

Note. If you have allocated tips using other than the calendar year (semimonthly, biweekly,
quarterly, etc.), mark an "**X**" on line 6 and enter the amount of allocated tips from your
records on line 7.

7 Allocation of tips. If line 6 is more than line 4c, enter the excess here **7**

▶ This amount must be allocated as tips to tipped employees working in this establishment.
Check the box below that shows the method used for the allocation. (Show the portion, if
any, attributable to each employee in box 8 of the employee's Form W-2.)

a Allocation based on hours-worked method (see instructions for restriction) . . .   ☐
Note. If you marked the checkbox in line 7a, enter the average number of employee hours
worked per business day during the payroll period. (see instructions) _____
b Allocation based on gross receipts method . . . .   ☐

c Allocation based on good-faith agreement (Attach a copy of the agreement.) . . .   ☐

8 Enter the total number of directly tipped employees at this establishment during 2008 ▶

Under penalties of perjury, I declare that I have examined this return, including accompanying schedules and statements, and to the best of my knowledge and belief,
it is true, correct, and complete.

Signature ▶   Title ▶   Date ▶

For Privacy Act and Paperwork Reduction Act Notice, see page 6 of the separate instructions.   Cat. No. 49989U   Form **8027** (2008)

Another scheduling method known as the **Swing Shift** is illustrated in Figure 12.5. The swing shift is an eight-hour shift during which an employee actually works two peak periods rather than one. A **Split Shift** occurs when an employee works an eight-hour shift, but the eight hours are scheduled in two four-hour blocks, with a lengthy break in between the two blocks. This type of shift assists managers in scheduling full staff during peak meal periods. The split shift is often welcomed by front of the house employees who work the lunch peak period, go home, and then return to work during the dinner peak period. This schedule is much like one where an employee works two days in one and receives gratuities for both meal periods worked. Working parents may find this shift attractive because it allows them to meet their children at the school bus and to better balance family commitments. Some employees dread this type of shift because the hours between the two short shifts do not allow enough time for one to actually get home, relax, and then return to work. Split shifts should not be regularly used unless requested by an employee. Once the weekly schedule is prepared informing employees of days on and off, the work schedule can be used as a basis for payroll preparation.

Monitoring Wage Earners Hours

Traditionally, foodservice operations use time cards with either a time clock or a management signing technique to control and record the actual hours employees work. Employees arrive on schedule, find their time card in the time card rack, and punch the time clock that records the time they start work. At the end of the work shift, employees pull their card from the rack and punch out. Some of the more sophisticated time clock systems do not allow employees to clock in more than five minutes ahead, or five minutes after the scheduled time without the approval of management. Time clocks are easy to use, but unfortunately, they do not provide the control that many foodservice operations desire.

Although the use of time cards with a management signing process ensures that the manager is aware of the employee's exact arrival and departure times, the process can become bothersome to a busy manager. Many foodservice operations employ both techniques to guarantee time accuracy and management knowledge and control.

Hours worked by employees are now often tracked through a point of sale computerized cash register system. The employee punches a code or slides an ID card through the register system to "clock in" and "clock out." The code or ID card prevents employees from improperly clocking other employees in and out. The computer cash register system is an investment for foodservice operations that can be used in a number of ways including the tracking of wage earners hours. This computerized system also allows managers to program the weekly schedule into the computer.

Payroll Preparation

When the pay period ends, the manager gathers and totals the hours clocked on the time cards or takes a register print out of hourly wage earner activity. It is a good control method to compare the hours worked by each employee to their posted work schedule to identify any problems. Discrepancies can occur because of an unauthorized schedule change; a dedicated employee who replaces a sick employee, or a not so sincere employee who agrees to let the last person out punch everyone else out. Chefs/managers must develop systems to ensure that excessive labor costs do not occur because of employee dishonesty.

In industry today, it is rare that foodservice operations prepare their own payroll. Even the foodservice operation that employs a full-time bookkeeper rarely prepares payroll because it is

Figure 12.5
Weekly Scheduling Strategies

Kitchen Schedule							
	Meals Served: Lunch and Dinner				Week Ending: April 1		
Employee Name	Monday	Tuesday	Wednesday	Thursday	Friday	Saturday	Sunday
Sally Sous Chef	3–11	3–11	3–11	off	off	3–11	3–11
Larry Line Chef	9–5	9–5	3–11	3–11	3–11	off	off
Lucy Line Chef	off	off	9–5	9–5	3–11	3–11	3–11
Luke Line Chef	10–6	10–6	12–8	12–8	off	9–5	off
Laura Line Chef	3–11	3–11	off	off	9–5	10–2/6–10	3–11
Leon Line Chef	12–8	12–8	off	3–11	9–5	off	12–8
Lou Line Chef	off	off	10–6	9–5	10–2/6–10	3–11	9–5
Totals	2–1–2	2–1–2	2–1–2	2–1–2	3–3	3–3	2–1–2

such a time consuming procedure. It is imperative that payroll is accurately prepared to guarantee that employees are paid properly and on time. Poor morale can result when employees are not paid on time.

The amount of payroll preparation activity that most foodservice operations perform is limited to simply totaling and checking the hours worked by wage earners. The hours are then posted to payroll sheets prepared by a payroll company. Foodservice operators also post the tips declared by each employee so that the employee can be taxed appropriately. When a foodservice operation sets up a payroll account with a payroll preparation company, all the hourly wage and W-4 information is provided to the company so that the payroll can be easily processed. At the end of the year and as part of the payroll company's employment agreement, the payroll company prepares all the payroll tax documents needed (**W-2**, Wage and Tax Statements, etc.). The cost of the payroll service varies depending upon the number of employees on staff. It is important to first research a payroll company's price and the services it provides.

As more foodservice operations become computerized, payroll preparation programs are being implemented into these operations. If a foodservice operation prepares its own payroll, the person preparing the payroll should be well versed in payroll and labor laws. It is usually a good idea to leave payroll preparation to the experts, and it is well worth the cost charged by a payroll preparation company to prevent payment and tax withholding errors.

Calculating Gross Pay and Taxable Income

Whether the foodservice prepares its own payroll or hires a payroll preparation company, it is important that the payroll is calculated correctly and that the difference between the employee's gross pay and net pay is understood. Gross income is the total dollar amount that an employee earns before any payroll taxes and benefits are withheld. It is the amount on which most payroll taxes and benefits are calculated. Net income is the actual dollar amount the employee receives after payroll taxes and benefits have been withheld. Most businesses have two checking accounts; one for accounts payable to pay invoices, etc., and a second solely for payroll. When the foodservice operator deposits money into its payroll account, the dollar amount deposited should be equal to the gross pay plus any other taxes the employer contributes (such as FICA, as previously explained). By depositing the appropriate amount of money, the foodservice operator guarantees that all payroll checks will clear and that there are adequate funds to cover payroll taxes when they come due.

The following payroll sample information is for four employees of the University Inn. Using the prescribed numbers, we will calculate the weekly net pay for the four employees in Figure 12.6.

Employee	Marital Status	W-4 Allowances	Hourly Wage	Weekly Salary
Mary Manager	S	1	—————	$800.00
Larry Line Cook	M	3	$12.00	—————
William Waiter	M	2	$ 2.50	—————
Bette Busperson	S	EXEMPT	$ 7.25	—————

The week ended April 1, and the hours were totaled and compared with the weekly schedule. The totals are as follow:

Employee	Hours Worked	Regular Hours	Overtime Hours	Tips Declared
Mary Manager	Salary	—————	—————	—————
Larry Line Cook	44	40	4	—————
William Waiter	38	38	-0-	$350.00
Bette Busperson	15	15	-0-	$ 50.00

Figure 12.6
Payroll Ledger

Employee	MS	WA	Hours Worked		Wage Rate		Total Wages	Weekly Salary	Total Paid by Employer	Tips Declared	Wage/Hour Total	Deductions				Net Pay
			Reg	O-T	Reg	O-T						FICA	Medicare	Federal Tax Withheld	Total Deductions	
Mary Manager	S	1				$0.00	$0.00	$800.00	$800.00		$800.00	$49.60	$11.60	$138.00	$199.20	$600.80
Larry Line Cook	M	3	40	4	$12.00	$18.00	$552.00		$552.00		$552.00	$34.22	$8.00	$42.00	$84.23	$467.77
William Waiter	M	2	38		$2.50	$3.75	$95.00		$95.00	$350.00	$445.00	$27.59	$6.45	$33.00	$67.04	$27.96
Bette Busperson	S	Ex	15		$7.25	$10.88	$108.75		$108.75	$50.00	$158.75	$9.84	$2.30	$0.00	$12.14	$96.61

To calculate the gross pay for hourly wage earners, multiply regular hours worked by the hourly wage, and then multiply the overtime hours worked by the overtime wage. Add both totals. To calculate the gross pay for salaried personnel, simply transfer the stated weekly salary to the gross pay column.

Taxable Income for non-tipped employees is found in the gross pay column. Taxable income for all tipped employees is a combination of gross pay and tips declared. Remember that Federal Income Tax, Social Security, and Medicare are based on **direct income** (wages, salaries, and tips declared).

Determining Payroll Deductions and Net Pay

To calculate the amount of **Federal Income Tax** to withhold for each employee, use Appendix E, Federal Income Tax Tables. The withholdings, the taxable income, marital status, and the number of withholding allowances claimed must be known to calculate the tax. Marital status and the number of withholding allowances claimed are taken from the W-4 filed by the employee. To read the Federal Income Tax tables, first identify the filing status of the individual. There are separate charts for single and married employees. Next, look down the left hand column until the taxable income amount determined falls between the ranges of "at least"–"but less than." The last step in reading the Federal Income Tax Tables is to travel across the top line of the chart that reads "And the number of withholdings allowances claimed is." Stop at the number claimed. With one hand, travel vertically down the number of withholding allowances claimed, and with the other hand, travel horizontally across the "at least" "but less than" line. The amount of taxes to be withheld is found where the line and column intersect. Post this Federal Income Tax figure to the appropriate column on the payroll ledger. Many states also have a State Income Tax that must be withheld from the employee's gross income. Every state has a different system and a State Income Tax authority should be contacted before preparing payroll.

Another tax that must be calculated and withheld is the Social Security tax. Social Security taxes are 6.2% of taxable income, and must be taken weekly until an employee has earned the taxable wage base. Medicare taxes are 1.45% of taxable income and are taken throughout the year because there is no taxable wage base for Medicare. Multiply each percentage by the taxable income column and post the tax to the appropriate column on the payroll ledger. Total the three deductions and post this total to the Total Deductions column. Subtract the Total Deductions from the Gross Pay column to determine the Net Pay.

The gross income paid to the four employees in the example illustrates the wages and salaries of the four employees. In addition to the Gross Income that must be deposited into the foodservice operation's payroll account to cover the employees' net pay and the employees' contributions to Federal and FICA taxes, employers must also deposit a 6.2% contribution to Social Security, a 1.45% to Medicare, and an additional 6.2% for FUTA so that these taxes might be paid when due. Knowledge of payroll calculation and labor laws is very important to control costs. This chapter concentrates on just a few of the payroll taxes/benefits that must be paid by employers. Much of the information needed to prepare payroll is published annually by the Internal Revenue Service and is available to all interested. Managers should refer to Publication 15 and Circular E (the Employers Tax Guide) for current information concerning taxes that must be withheld.

Review Questions

1. Explain the federal law regarding:
   Federal Minimum Wage
   Overtime Wage
   TIP Credit
   Meal Credit
   Minimum Wage for those under 18 years of age
   Social Security
   Medicare
   FUTA

2. Name and explain the purpose of the two documents kept in every employee's file.

3. Explain the employee's and employer's responsibilities regarding TIP declaration.

4. Explain in detail the three scheduling methods discussed within this chapter.

5. Using the payroll ledger work sheet provided in Appendix F (or WebCom), and the following information, calculate the net pay for the employees listed. How much money must be deposited in the payroll account to cover all the payroll taxes discussed in this chapter?

Employee	Marital Status	W-4 Allowances	Hourly Wage	Weekly Salary
Mike Manager	M	3	—————	$550.00
Lucy Line Cook	S	1	$14.25	—————
Wanda Waiter	S	1	$ 2.58	—————
Bob Busperson	S	EXEMPT	$ 7.25	—————

Employee	Marital Status	Regular Hours	Overtime Hours	Tips Declared
Mike Manager	Salary	—————	—————	—————
Lucy Line Cook	40	40	-0-	—————
Wanda Waiter	45	40	5	$450.00
Bob Busperson	35	35	-0-	$ 75.00

6. Using the spread sheet program of your professor's choice, set up a payroll ledger to calculate the payroll illustrated above.

Appendices

Appendix A

Measurement, Equivalents, and Edible Yields

The following information is taken from the *Food Buying Guide for Child Nutrition Programs*. (http://www.fns.usda.gov/tn/foodbuying-guide-child-nutrition-programs). It is prepared by the Nutritional and Technical Services Division and the Human Nutrition Information Service of the United States Department of Agriculture and the National Marine Fisheries Service of the United States Department of Commerce. The purpose of the information provided here is to help the student determine measurement equivalents. Edible yields are included so that the student can use this information in costing and purchasing procedures in foodservice operations.

I. Measurement Equivalents
Metric Equivalents

US Weight	=	Metric	Metric	=	US Fluid Ounces
1 oz.	=	28 grams	1.75 liters	=	59.2 ounces
1 lb.	=	454 grams	1.5 liters	=	50.7 ounces
2.2 lbs.	=	1 kg	1.0 liters	=	33.8 ounces
1.05 quarts	=	1 liter	750 milliliters	=	25.4 ounces

Volume Equivalents

3 tsps.	=	1 Tbsp.	1 peck	=	8 quarts
2 Tbsps.	=	1 fl. oz.	1 bushel	=	4 pecks
8 fl. oz.	=	1 c.	2 pts.	=	1qt.
2 c.	=	1 pt.	4 qts.	=	1 gal.

Appendix A: Measurement Equivalents and Edible Yield %

Scoops: The number of the scoop shows the number of scoops needed to equal 1 quart

#6	2/3 cup
#8	1/2 cup
#10	3/8 cup
#12	1/3 cup
#16	1/4 cup
#20	3 1/3 tablespoons
#24	2 tablespoons

Ladles: The number on the ladle refers to the number of fl. ounces it holds.

1 ounce	=	1/8 cup
2 ounce	=	1/4 cup
4 ounce	=	1/2 cup
6 ounce	=	3/4 cup
8 ounce	=	1 cup
12 ounce	=	1.5 cups

Can Sizes: Approximate Weight or Volume

No. 10	96 oz.	to	117 oz.
No. 3 Cyl.	51 oz.	or	46 fl. oz.
No. 2 1/2	26 oz.	to	30 oz.
No. 2 Cyl.	24 fl. oz.		
No. 2	20 oz.	or	18 fl. oz.
No. 303	16 oz.	to	17 oz.
No. 300	14 oz.	to	16 oz.
No. 2 (vac)	12 oz.		
No. 1 (picnic)	10.5 oz.	to	12 oz.
8 oz.	8 oz.		

Appendix A: Edible Yields % after Cooking

One Pound As Edible (Cooked) Purchased	=	Yield %
Beef		
Brisket, Corned (boned)	=	70%
Brisket, Fresh (boned)	=	69%
Ground Meats (26% fat)	=	72%
Ground Meats (20% fat)	=	74%
Ground Meats (15% fat)	=	75%
Ground Meats (10% fat)	=	76%
Heart (trimmed)	=	57%
Roast, Chuck (without bone)	=	63%
Roast, Chuck (with bone)	=	54%
Rump (without bone)	=	68%
Rump (with bone)	=	62%
Steak, flank	=	73%
Steak, round (without bone)	=	63%
Stew meat	=	61%
Tongue	=	58%
Poultry		
Chicken Breast Halves	=	66% w/skin
(approx. 6.1 oz. with ribs)	=	56% w/o skin
Chicken Breast Halves	=	55% w/skin
(approx. 7.5 oz. with backs)	=	47% w/o skin
Turkey	=	53% w/skin
	=	47% w/o skin
Other Meats		
Lamb Chops, Shoulder with bone	=	46%
Lamb Roast (Leg) without bone	=	61%
Lamb Roast (Shoulder) without bone	=	54%
Lamb Stew Meat	=	65%
Veal cutlets	=	54%
Pork Chops Loin	=	54%
Pork Roasts (leg) without bone	=	57%
Pork Roasts (leg) with bone	=	46%
Pork Loin without bone	=	58%
Pork Loin with bone	=	45%
Shoulder/Boston Butt without bone	=	60%
Shoulder/Boston Butt with bone	=	52%
Shoulder/picnic without bone	=	57%
Shoulder/picnic with bone	=	42%
Canadian Bacon	=	69%
Ham without bone	=	63%
Ham with bone	=	53%

Appendix A: Edible Yield % of Fresh Vegetables and Fruits

One Pound Purchased	=	Edible Yield %
Apples	=	91%
Apricots	=	93%
Asparagus	=	53%
Avocados	=	67%
Bananas	=	65%
Beans, Green	=	88%
Beans, Lima	=	44%
Beans, Wax (Yellow)	=	88%
Beet Greens	=	48%
Beets	=	77%
Broccoli	=	81%
Brussels Sprouts	=	76%
Cabbage	=	87%
Cabbage, Red	=	64%
Cantaloupe	=	52%
Carrots	=	70%
Cauliflower	=	62%
Celery	=	83%
Chard, Swiss	=	92%
Cherries	=	98%
Chicory	=	89%
Collards	=	57%
Corn, cob	=	33%
Cranberries	=	95%
Cucumbers	=	84%
Eggplant	=	81%
Endive, Escarole	=	78%
Grapefruit	=	52%
Grapes	=	97%
Honeydew Melon	=	46%
Kale	=	67%
Kohlrabi	=	45%
Lemons	=	43% (3/4 cup juice)
Lettuce, head	=	76%
Lettuce, leaf	=	66%
Lettuce, Romaine	=	64%
Limes	=	47% (7/8 cup juice)
Mangoes	=	69%
Mushrooms	=	98%
Mustard Greens	=	93%
Nectarines	=	91%
Okra	=	87%
Onions, Green	=	83%
Onions	=	88%
Oranges	=	71%

One Pound Purchased	=	Edible Yield %
Papaya	=	67%
Parsley	=	92%
Parsnips	=	83%
Peaches	=	76%
Pears	=	92%
Peas, Green	=	38%
Peppers, Green	=	80%
Pineapple	=	54%
Plantains, Green	=	62%
Plantains, Ripe	=	65%
Plums	=	94%
Potatoes, White	=	81%
Pumpkin	=	70%
Radishes	=	94%
Raspberries	=	96%
Rhubarb	=	86%
Rutabagas	=	85%
Spinach	=	88%
Squash, Summer	=	95%
Squash, Zucchini	=	94%
Squash, Acorn	=	70%
Squash, Butternut	=	84%
Squash, Hubbard	=	64%
Strawberries	=	88%
Sweet Potatoes	=	80%
Tangerines	=	74%
Tomatoes	=	99%
Tomatoes, Cherry	=	97%
Turnips, Greens	=	70%
Turnips	=	79%
Watercress	=	92%
Watermelon	=	57%

Success in Business Mathematics (The Percentage Formula Triangle)

The following is a tool to help even the "non-math lover" to succeed in solving business math problems.

The Percentage Formula

When working with percentages, it is important to first understand the parts of the equation before you try so solve the equation. If you understand how to identify each part and what each part represents, you will be able to solve any kind of problem that involves percentages.

There are three parts to every equation involving percentages: the Base, the Portion, and the Rate. Equations usually have two parts that are given and a third that is unknown. Before the problem solver actually sets up the equation to solve the unknown, he/she must first identify the two given numbers. The first step in solving a percentage equation is to identify the Base, the Portion, and the Rate. The following definitions can help.

The Base is identified as the whole, or total available. If there are 38 students in a classroom, the 38 students are the whole (or the total). When a guest check totals $120, the total of the guest check is the whole or the Base. If a business brings in $4,500 in sales, the $4,500 is the whole. Unless you are analyzing different types of sales dollars (food sales, beverage sales, room sales), sales will always be identified as the base. When looking at an equation or a word problem and having difficulty in determining the base number, look for the word "of," which always introduces the base to the problem solver.

The Portion is identified as part of the whole. Of the 38 students in the classroom mentioned above, there are 20 women. The 20 women are the Portion or part of the whole. If a guest check totals $120, and the guest wants to leave an $18 tip, the amount of the tip is part of the whole. If a business spends $1,350 in labor cost to produce $4,500 in sales, the $1,350 in labor cost is the Portion or part of the whole. Unless the problem solver is analyzing different categories of the same type of costs (labor cost: line cooks, prep cooks, dishwashers), costs will always be identified as a portion. When looking at an equation or a word problem and having difficulty in determining which is the portion, look for the word "is" or the "=" sign. "Is" or "equal to" will either introduce the portion or immediately follow the numeral that represents the Portion.

The Rate is identified as the percentage that corresponds to the part of the whole. It is always a percent, which may also be represented in decimal form. For example, 35% has the decimal equivalent of .35.

To change a decimal to a percent, the decimal is multiplied by 100 (.35 × 100 = 35%, the equivalent of moving the decimal point two places to the right). Decimal to Percent: move two places to the right (D to P: P is to the right of D in the alphabet therefore move the decimal point to the right two decimal places).

To change a percent to a decimal, the percent is divided by 100 (35% ÷ 100 = .35, the equivalent of moving the decimal point two places to the left). Percent to Decimal: Move two places to the left (P to D: D is to the left of P in the alphabet therefore move the decimal point to the left two decimal places).

If there are 20 women in a class of 38 students, what percent are women? (52.6%) When leaving a gratuity of $18 on a guest check of $120, what is the percent left? (15%) If sales are $4,5000, and $1,350 is spent on labor costs, what percent of sales is attributed to labor cost? (30%) At this point do not be concerned about how these answers are derived. Instead, concentrate on how to identify the Base, the Portion, and the Rate.

In the following problems, identify the Base, the Portion, and the Rate. Do not try to solve these problems. Try only to identify the parts of the equation. This process is the foundation to all business analysis.

Example 1: A recipe costs a foodservice operation $3.50 to prepare, and the business wants to maintain a 28% food cost. What is the minimum sales price that must be charged to maintain the desired Food Cost %? Identify:
the Base.
the Portion.
the Rate.

Example 2: 8% of $132 is? Identify:
the Base.
the Portion.
the Rate.

Example 3: A guest check total is $125.00, and the guest leaves a $30.00 gratuity. What percent gratuity did the customer leave? Identify:
the Base.
the Portion.
the Rate.

The base, rate, and portion of the preceding problems are listed below.

	Base:	**Portion:**	**Rate:**
Example 1:	(?)	$3.50	28%
Example 2:	$132.00	(?)	8%
Example 3:	$125.00	$30.00	(?)

Now that the Base, Portion, and Rate have been identified, set up the equation solving for the unknown.

When solving for Base:	Base	=	Portion	÷	Rate
When solving for Portion:	Portion	=	Base	×	Rate
When solving for Rate:	Rate	=	Portion	÷	Base

All three of these equations can be housed within a tool called the Percentage Formula Triangle.

Example 1—Solving for Base. Cover the letter B as the Base is the unknown. Covering the B will leave P ÷ R. Now insert the identified numbers and solve.

B = P ÷ R

B = $3.50 ÷ 28%

B = $3.50 ÷ .28 (28% ÷ 100)

B = $12.50

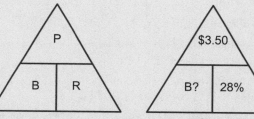

Example 2—Solving for Portion. If you cover the letter P on the triangle, the formula to solve for Portion is identified as B × R. Post the appropriate numbers and solve.

B × R

P = B × R

P = $132.00 × 8%

P = $132.00 × .08 (8% ÷ 100)

P = $10.56

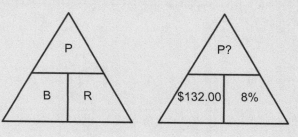

Example 3—Solving for Rate. Cover the letter R on the triangle, the formula to solve for Rate is identified as P ÷ B.

R = P ÷ B

R = $30.00 ÷ $125.00

R = .24 × 100

R = 24%

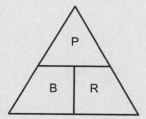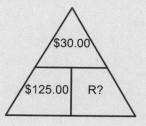

Other variations of this percentage formula triangle can be just as helpful.

C (Cost $) = Portion   Is   identifies Portion
S (Sales $) = Base   Of   identifies Base
C% (Cost %) = Rate   %   always is Rate

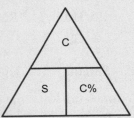

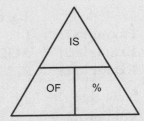

Practice identifying the Base, Rate, and Portion. The Percentage Formula is a tool that can be applied to almost every cost control formula used in the industry. The better the Base, Rate, and Portion concept is understood, the easier the math formulas will be to calculate.

Problems

Please round off your answers to the nearest cent and nearest .1%

1. 16 is what percent of 48?

2. 125 is what percent of 50?

3. Four college friends go out and spend $60 on lunch. They all pitch in and leave a $10 gratuity. What percent gratuity do they leave?

4. 40% of 300 is?

5. 150% of 20 is?

6. A guest check totals $152.50. The foodserver adds a 6% Sales Tax. How much is the Sales Tax?

7. 50 is 10% of?

8. $3.25 is 28% of?

9. Labor cost normally represents 35% of the sales dollar. If a restaurant expects to pay $4,200 in Labor Cost this week, what is the amount of sales needed to maintain a 35% labor cost?

10. A foodservice operation brings in $75,000 in food sales in January and wants to increase its food sales by 8% next month. What is the dollar amount of food sales needed in February?

Appendix C

Sample Chart of Accounts

A partial listing of accounts taken from the sample Chart of Accounts numbering system for the income and expense classifications (as seen in the Appendix of the seventh edition of the *Uniform System of Accounts for Restaurants* created by the National Restaurant Association, 1986) follows. The purpose of the Chart of Accounts system is to guide foodservice operations in organizing income and expense data using a consistent format so that foodservice operations may compare their results to those of other foodservice establishments. The purpose of this numbering system is to provide a solid foundation concerning expenses that are incurred by foodservice operations. It is strongly recommended that you become very familiar with this Chart of Accounts numbering system and that you purchase the *Uniform System of Accounts for Restaurants* from the National Restaurant Association.

Chart of Accounts

(4000)	Sales	**7200**	**Employee Benefits**
4100	**Food Sales**	7205	FICA
4200	**Beverage Sales**	7205	Federal Unemployment Tax
(5000)	Cost of Sales (Detailed sub-accounts,	7210	State Unemployment Tax
	if desired, will vary by type of	7215	Workmen's Compensation
	restaurant)	7225	Group Insurance
5100	**Cost of Sales: Food**	7230	State Health Insurance
5200	**Cost of Sales: Beverage**	7245	Accident and Health Insurance
(6000)	Other Income	7250	Hospitalization, Blue Cross, Blue
(7000)	Operating Expenses		Shield
7100	**Salaries and Wages**	7255	Employee Meals
7105	Service	7260	Employee Instruction and
7110	Preparation		Education
7115	Sanitation	7265	Employee Parties
7120	Beverages	7270	Employee Sports Activities
7125	Administrative	7285	Awards and Prizes
7130	Purchasing and Storing	7290	Transportation and Housing
7135	Other		

Chart of Accounts (continued)

7300	**Occupancy Cost**
7305	Rent, minimum or fixed
7310	Percentage rent
7315	Ground rental
7320	Equipment rental
7325	Real Estate Taxes
7330	Personal Property Taxes
7335	Other Municipal Taxes
7340	Franchise tax
7345	Capital stock tax
7350	Partnership or corporation license fees
7355	Insurance on building and contents
7370	Depreciation
7371	Buildings
7372	Amortization of leasehold
7373	Amortization of leasehold improvements
7374	Furniture, fixtures, and equipment
7400	**Direct Operating Expenses**
7402	Uniforms
7404	Laundry and Dry Cleaning
7406	Linen Rental
7408	Linen
7410	China and Glassware
7412	Silverware
7414	Kitchen Utensils
7416	Auto and Truck expense
7418	Cleaning Supplies
7420	Paper Supplies
7422	Guest Supplies
7424	Bar Supplies
7426	Menus and Wine Lists
7428	Contract Cleaning
7430	Exterminating
7432	Flowers and Decorations
7436	Parking Lot Expense
7438	Licenses and Permits
7440	Banquet Expenses
7498	Other Operating Expenses

7500	**Music and Entertainment**
7505	Musicians
7510	Professional entertainers
7520	Mechanical music
7525	Contracted wire service
7530	Piano rental and tuning
7535	Films, records, tapes, and sheet music
7540	Programs
7550	Royalties to ASCAP, BMI
7560	Meals to Musicians
7600	**Marketing**
7601	Selling and Promotion
7604	Direct Mail
7605	Telephone
7606	Complimentary Food and Beverage
7607	Postage
7610	Advertising
7611	Newspaper
7612	Magazines and Trade Journals
7613	Circulars, brochures, post cards, other mailing
7614	Outdoor Signs
7615	Radio and Television
7616	Programs, directories, and guides
7620	Public Relations and Publicity
7621	Civic and Community Projects
7622	Donations
7623	Souvenirs, favors, treasure chest
7630	Fees and Commissions
7640	Research
7641	Travel in connection with research
7642	Outside Research agency
7643	Product testing
7700	**Utilities**
7705	Electric
7710	Electric Bulbs
7715	Water
7720	Waste Removal
7725	Other Fuel

Chart of Accounts (continued)

7800	**Administrative and General Expenses**	**8100**	**Interest**
7805	Office Stationary	8105	Notes Payable
7810	Data Processing	8110	Long-term debt
7815	Postage	8115	Other
7820	Telegrams and Telephones	**8200**	**Corporate or Executive Office Overhead**
7825	Dues and Subscriptions		
7830	Traveling Expenses	**9000**	**Income Taxes**
7835	Insurance—general	9010	Federal
7840	Credit card commissions	9020	State
7845	Provisions for Doubtful Accounts		
7850	Cash over or <short>		
7855	Professional Fees		
7860	Protective and Bank Pick Up Service		
7865	Bank Charges		
7870	Miscellaneous		
7900	**Repairs and Maintenance**		
7902	Furniture and Fixtures		
7904	Kitchen Equipment		
7906	Office Equipment		
7908	Refrigeration		
7910	Air Conditioning		
7912	Plumbing and Heating		
7914	Electrical and Mechanical		
7916	Floors and Carpets		
7918	Buildings		
7920	Parking Lot		
7922	Gardening and Grounds Maintenance		
7924	Building Alterations		
7928	Painting, Plastering, and Decorating		
7990	Maintenance Contracts		
7996	Autos and Trucks		
7998	Other		
(8000)	Interest and Corporate Overhead		

Non-Computerized Sales Controls

Non-Computerized (manual, hand-prepared) controls are slowly becoming "a thing of the past". The hand-prepared control tools mentioned here are still sound control practices, although they do not offer the speed and accuracy of computer systems. While effective, non-computerized controls are time consuming.

Hand Prepared Guest Checks

Even though foodservice operations are using computerized cash register systems more frequently, we will examine the steps needed to assure sales control of Hand Prepared Guest Checks. It is usually small businesses that cannot afford a computerized cash register system, or very old businesses that have not yet changed with the times, that use hand prepared guest checks. Hand prepared guest checks are purchased from paper supply companies and are usually produced using NCR paper (No Carbon Required), which has a soft paper top sheet (the dupe), and a light cardboard customer copy. The foodserver takes the order from the customer and records it on the original form, which simultaneously transfers on to the hard bottom copy. The soft form is then removed and taken to the kitchen to place the order. The hard copy is kept by the foodserver to be tallied and presented to the customer when the dining experience is complete.

When a foodservice operation uses hand prepared guest checks, extra steps must be taken to ensure proper control. Having the foodservice operation's logo printed on the check is a good control measure. Although more costly, it helps to keep track of guest checks and deters outside checks from finding their way into your restaurant.

Foodservice operators must develop a standard procedure to control guest checks, in order to ensure that all are returned either paid for or unused. The foodservice operator must also develop a procedure to review guest checks and to guarantee that they have been used appropriately by sales personnel (the correct price charged, all items are charged for, etc.).

Figure D.1

Guest Check Issuance Inventory

University Inn Guest Check Issuance						Date:		March 3, 20XX	
SERVER NO.	CHECKS ISSUED	NO. ISSUED	RETURNED UNUSED	NO. UNUSED	NO. USED	TOTAL	NOTES		
24	02345-02359	15	02354-02359	6	9	15	n/a		
35	03768-03782	15	03780-03782	3	12	15	n/a		
36	03821-03835	15	None	0	15	15	n/a		
39	02522-02541	20	02539-02541	3	17	20	n/a		

Issuing Guest Checks

It is important that hand prepared guest checks have machine imprinted sequential numbers on them. The machine imprinted sequential numbering system helps foodservice managers to account for the guest checks used by the foodserver. Guest checks should be issued and used in numerical sequence. The numbers of the guest checks issued to each foodserver should be recorded per shift on a *Guest Check Issuance Sheet* (Figure D.1). A Foodserver Check Out Sheet should accompany the issued guest checks so that the foodserver is aware of the sequence of guest checks assigned to him/her (Figure D.2). It is important that the foodserver inspect the guest checks received to be certain that the numbers on the checks issued correspond to the numbers that have been recorded as issued. This inspection should occur prior to the start of the shift. During the shift, the foodservers must be certain to use the guest checks in sequential order. At the end of the shift, it is the foodservers responsibility to record all checks that were used and to return all unused checks. The check numbers are also recorded in the space provided on the Foodserver Check Out Sheet. Knowing the checks that have been issued, the checks used, and the checks returned unused, allows the chefs/managers to know that foodservers and bartenders are not walking away with checks.

Figure D.2
Foodserver Check Out Sheet

FOODSERVER CHECK OUT SHEET			
			Date:
Server:	Susan-24	Meal Period B L D	
Series Checks Issued:	02345-02359		
Number Checks Issued	15		
Series Checks Returned Unused	02356-02359		
Number Checks Returned Unused	4		
Number Checks Returned Used	11		
Total Checks Returned	15		
Steak Count: Filet		Desserts Sold	
Steak Count: Sirloin		Coffee Sold	
Steak Count: London		Promo Items	
Notes to Bookkeeper:			

The foodserver check out sheet may also include other sales control information that is invaluable to the operation. It may include data concerning the number of covers, or the sale of certain food and beverage items that the restaurant wants to monitor. Keeping track of the number of desserts sold, the number of sirloins, or even the number of cups of coffee and tea, is often regarded as useful information. If the foodservice operation had a computerized cash register

Figure D.3
Guest Check Audit

Date	Server	Checks Unused	Checks Used	Checks Missing	Errors Hard/Soft	Errors Pricing	Errors Tax	Errors Compute	Uninitialed Crossouts	Total Under/ Over Charge	Explanation
3/3	#24	6	9	0	0	$0.50	0	$0.00	0	$0.50	overcharged customer
3/7	#35	3	12	0	0	$0.00	0	$1.00	0	($1.00)	
3/12	#36	0	15	0	0	$0.00	0	$0.00	0	$0.00	
3/15	#39	3	17	0	1	$0.00	0	$0.00	0	($3.50)	didn't charge

system, this information would be provided automatically by taking a register reading. When a foodservice operation is not computerized, management must implement other measures such as foodserver check out sheets, to gather important sales control information.

Guest Check Audit

Another Hand Prepared guest check control is the Guest Check Audit (Figure D.3). Depending upon the size of the foodservice operation, this process may be used daily for all service personnel, or performed randomly, by selecting a few service personnel to audit. The purpose of the *Guest Check Audit* is to guarantee that the guest checks have been used correctly. Management compares prices on guest checks with the prices on the menu looking for any discrepancies (undercharges, overcharges). Soft and hard copies of each foodserver's used guest checks are also examined to see if everything ordered has been charged for (remember that no food or beverage item should leave the production area unless it has been documented on a dupe). It is also important that the soft copy of hand-prepared checks not be returned to the foodserver. A dishonest employee might be tempted to substitute similar guest checks and pocket the money. It is obvious that guest check control prior to a computerized Point of Sales cash register system was very time consuming. Even though most foodservices are now utilizing computerized systems, those that are not using a computer system must implement safeguards to insure proper sales controls.

In a foodservice operation that utilizes hand prepared guest checks, the number of covers served and the customer's menu item choices can be attained by thoroughly preparing the information area of the guest check. A Foodserver Check Out Sheet (Figure D.2), or a Seating Control Sheet (Figure D.4), can be used to track the number of customers served, while a Menu Scatter Sheet (Figure D.5) can be utilized to record the selections each customer makes.

Figure D.4
Seating Control Sheet

UNIVERSITY INN
Weather: Dry, Cool Evening
Hostess:

Date: March 3, 20xx
Meal: Dinner
Page: 2

Name of Party	Description	#Party	Time In	Smoke/Non	Est.Wait	Time Seat	Table	Server #
Johansen	Red Tie	4	6:05	NS	-0-	6:05	A-2	#24
Smith	Cute Child	6	6:10	NS	-0-	6:10	B-14	#35
Schwenk	Dark Hair	2	6:10	NS	-0-	6:10	A-1	#24
Diana	All Women	3	6:10	S	20	6:25	C-22	#36
Tom	Nice Coat	2	6:15	NS	25	6:40	B-15	#35
Marra	Chef	4	6:30	NS	30			
Flynn	Blue Dress	2	6:35	NS	30			

Figure D.5
Menu Scatter Sheet

Weekly Menu Scatter Sheet								
Meal Category: Dinner			Time Period/Dates			April 1 - April 8		
A	C	D	E	F	G	H	I	J
Menu Item	Monday	Tuesday	Wednesday	Thursday	Friday	Saturday	Sunday	Totals
Chicken Wings	10	8	12	28	32	25	28	143
Mozzarella	12	11	8	30	18	14	10	103
California Rolls	2	5	0	22	18	11	11	69
Florentine Bruchetta	23	27`	32	30	43	26	17	171
Calamari	37	25	31	33	38	18	18	200
Shrimp	0	0	0	6	22	18	11	57
Nachos	38	35	37	28	14	8	11	171
Quesadilla	6	13	3	8	8	11	8	57

Manual, hand-prepared control systems can be effective when closely monitored, and can adequately serve a foodservice operation until it has the capital to invest in a Point of Sale Computer system.

Appendix E

Sample Federal Income Tax Tables

SINGLE Persons—WEEKLY Payroll Period

SINGLE Persons—**WEEKLY** Payroll Period

If the wages are-		And the number of withholding allowances claimed is—										
At least	But less than	0	1	2	3	4	5	6	7	8	9	10
		The amount of income tax to be withheld is—										
$0	$55	0	0	0	0	0	0	0	0	0	0	0
55	60	1	0	0	0	0	0	0	0	0	0	0
60	65	2	0	0	0	0	0	0	0	0	0	0
65	70	2	0	0	0	0	0	0	0	0	0	0
70	75	3	0	0	0	0	0	0	0	0	0	0
75	80	4	0	0	0	0	0	0	0	0	0	0
80	85	5	0	0	0	0	0	0	0	0	0	0
85	90	5	0	0	0	0	0	0	0	0	0	0
90	95	6	0	0	0	0	0	0	0	0	0	0
95	100	7	0	0	0	0	0	0	0	0	0	0
100	105	8	0	0	0	0	0	0	0	0	0	0
105	110	8	1	0	0	0	0	0	0	0	0	0
110	115	9	2	0	0	0	0	0	0	0	0	0
115	120	10	2	0	0	0	0	0	0	0	0	0
120	125	11	3	0	0	0	0	0	0	0	0	0
125	130	11	4	0	0	0	0	0	0	0	0	0
130	135	12	5	0	0	0	0	0	0	0	0	0
135	140	13	5	0	0	0	0	0	0	0	0	0
140	145	14	6	0	0	0	0	0	0	0	0	0
145	150	14	7	0	0	0	0	0	0	0	0	0
150	155	15	8	0	0	0	0	0	0	0	0	0
155	160	16	8	1	0	0	0	0	0	0	0	0
160	165	17	9	1	0	0	0	0	0	0	0	0
165	170	17	10	2	0	0	0	0	0	0	0	0
170	175	18	11	3	0	0	0	0	0	0	0	0
175	180	19	11	4	0	0	0	0	0	0	0	0
180	185	20	12	4	0	0	0	0	0	0	0	0
185	190	20	13	5	0	0	0	0	0	0	0	0
190	195	21	14	6	0	0	0	0	0	0	0	0
195	200	22	14	7	0	0	0	0	0	0	0	0
200	210	23	15	8	0	0	0	0	0	0	0	0
210	220	25	17	9	2	0	0	0	0	0	0	0
220	230	26	18	11	3	0	0	0	0	0	0	0
230	240	28	20	12	5	0	0	0	0	0	0	0
240	250	29	21	14	6	0	0	0	0	0	0	0
250	260	31	23	15	8	0	0	0	0	0	0	0
260	270	32	24	17	9	2	0	0	0	0	0	0
270	280	34	26	18	11	3	0	0	0	0	0	0
280	290	35	27	20	12	5	0	0	0	0	0	0
290	300	37	29	21	14	6	0	0	0	0	0	0
300	310	38	30	23	15	8	0	0	0	0	0	0
310	320	40	32	24	17	9	1	0	0	0	0	0
320	330	41	33	26	18	11	3	0	0	0	0	0
330	340	43	35	27	20	12	4	0	0	0	0	0
340	350	44	36	29	21	14	6	0	0	0	0	0
350	360	46	38	30	23	15	7	0	0	0	0	0
360	370	47	39	32	24	17	9	1	0	0	0	0
370	380	49	41	33	26	18	10	3	0	0	0	0
380	390	50	42	35	27	20	12	4	0	0	0	0
390	400	52	44	36	29	21	13	6	0	0	0	0
400	410	53	45	38	30	23	15	7	0	0	0	0
410	420	55	47	39	32	24	16	9	1	0	0	0
420	430	56	48	41	33	26	18	10	3	0	0	0
430	440	58	50	42	35	27	19	12	4	0	0	0
440	450	59	51	44	36	29	21	13	6	0	0	0
450	460	61	53	45	38	30	22	15	7	0	0	0
460	470	62	54	47	39	32	24	16	9	1	0	0
470	480	64	56	48	41	33	25	18	10	2	0	0
480	490	65	57	50	42	35	27	19	12	4	0	0
490	500	67	59	51	44	36	28	21	13	5	0	0
500	510	68	60	53	45	38	30	22	15	7	0	0
510	520	71	62	54	47	39	31	24	16	8	1	0
520	530	74	63	56	48	41	33	25	18	10	2	0
530	540	77	65	57	50	42	34	27	19	11	4	0
540	550	80	66	59	51	44	36	28	21	13	5	0
550	560	82	68	60	53	45	37	30	22	14	7	0
560	570	85	71	62	54	47	39	31	24	16	8	1
570	580	88	74	63	56	48	40	33	25	17	10	2
580	590	91	77	65	57	50	42	34	27	19	11	4
590	600	94	79	66	59	51	43	36	28	20	13	5

SINGLE Persons—WEEKLY Payroll Period

At least	But less than	0	1	2	3	4	5	6	7	8	9	10
		The amount of income tax to be withheld is—										
$600	$610	96	82	68	60	53	45	37	30	22	14	7
610	620	99	85	71	62	54	46	39	31	23	16	8
620	630	102	88	73	63	56	48	40	33	25	17	10
630	640	105	91	76	65	57	49	42	34	26	19	11
640	650	108	93	79	66	59	51	43	36	28	20	13
650	660	110	96	82	68	60	52	45	37	29	22	14
660	670	113	99	85	70	62	54	46	39	31	23	16
670	680	116	102	87	73	63	55	48	40	32	25	17
680	690	119	105	90	76	65	57	49	42	34	26	19
690	700	122	107	93	79	66	58	51	43	35	28	20
700	710	124	110	96	82	68	60	52	45	37	29	22
710	720	127	113	99	84	70	61	54	46	38	31	23
720	730	130	116	101	87	73	63	55	48	40	32	25
730	740	133	119	104	90	76	64	57	49	41	34	26
740	750	136	121	107	93	79	66	58	51	43	35	28
750	760	138	124	110	96	81	67	60	52	44	37	29
760	770	141	127	113	98	84	70	61	54	46	38	31
770	780	144	130	115	101	87	73	63	55	47	40	32
780	790	147	133	118	104	90	75	64	57	49	41	34
790	800	150	135	121	107	93	78	66	58	50	43	35
800	810	152	138	124	110	95	81	67	60	52	44	37
810	820	155	141	127	112	98	84	70	61	53	46	38
820	830	158	144	129	115	101	87	72	63	55	47	40
830	840	161	147	132	118	104	89	75	64	56	49	41
840	850	164	149	135	121	107	92	78	66	58	50	43
850	860	166	152	138	124	109	95	81	67	59	52	44
860	870	169	155	141	126	112	98	84	69	61	53	46
870	880	172	158	143	129	115	101	86	72	62	55	47
880	890	175	161	146	132	118	103	89	75	64	56	49
890	900	178	163	149	135	121	106	92	78	65	58	50
900	910	180	166	152	138	123	109	95	80	67	59	52
910	920	183	169	155	140	126	112	98	83	69	61	53
920	930	186	172	157	143	129	115	100	86	72	62	55
930	940	189	175	160	146	132	117	103	89	75	64	56
940	950	192	177	163	149	135	120	106	92	77	65	58
950	960	194	180	166	152	137	123	109	94	80	67	59
960	970	197	183	169	154	140	126	112	97	83	69	61
970	980	200	186	171	157	143	129	114	100	86	72	62
980	990	203	189	174	160	146	131	117	103	89	74	64
990	1,000	206	191	177	163	149	134	120	106	91	77	65
1,000	1,010	208	194	180	166	151	137	123	108	94	80	67
1,010	1,020	211	197	183	168	154	140	126	111	97	83	68
1,020	1,030	214	200	185	171	157	143	128	114	100	86	71
1,030	1,040	217	203	188	174	160	145	131	117	103	88	74
1,040	1,050	220	205	191	177	163	148	134	120	105	91	77
1,050	1,060	222	208	194	180	165	151	137	122	108	94	80
1,060	1,070	225	211	197	182	168	154	140	125	111	97	82
1,070	1,080	228	214	199	185	171	157	142	128	114	100	85
1,080	1,090	231	217	202	188	174	159	145	131	117	102	88
1,090	1,100	235	219	205	191	177	162	148	134	119	105	91
1,100	1,110	238	222	208	194	179	165	151	136	122	108	94
1,110	1,120	241	225	211	196	182	168	154	139	125	111	96
1,120	1,130	244	228	213	199	185	171	156	142	128	114	99
1,130	1,140	247	231	216	202	188	173	159	145	131	116	102
1,140	1,150	250	234	219	205	191	176	162	148	133	119	105
1,150	1,160	253	237	222	208	193	179	165	150	136	122	108
1,160	1,170	256	240	225	210	196	182	168	153	139	125	110
1,170	1,180	259	244	228	213	199	185	170	156	142	128	113
1,180	1,190	262	247	231	216	202	187	173	159	145	130	116
1,190	1,200	266	250	234	219	205	190	176	162	147	133	119
1,200	1,210	269	253	237	222	207	193	179	164	150	136	122
1,210	1,220	272	256	240	224	210	196	182	167	153	139	124
1,220	1,230	275	259	243	227	213	199	184	170	156	142	127
1,230	1,240	278	262	246	231	216	201	187	173	159	144	130
1,240	1,250	281	265	249	234	219	204	190	176	161	147	133

$1,250 □□□ □□□   □se Table 1□a□dr □ SINGLE □□□□□□on □age 34□Also see the instructions on □age 32□

MARRIED Persons—WEEKLY Payroll Period

MARRIED Persons—**WEEKLY** Payroll Period

If the wages are		And the number of withholding allowances claimed is—										
At least	But less than	0	1	2	3	4	5	6	7	8	9	10
		The amount of income tax to be withheld is—										
$0	$125	0	0	0	0	0	0	0	0	0	0	0
125	130	1	0	0	0	0	0	0	0	0	0	0
130	135	1	0	0	0	0	0	0	0	0	0	0
135	140	2	0	0	0	0	0	0	0	0	0	0
140	145	3	0	0	0	0	0	0	0	0	0	0
145	150	4	0	0	0	0	0	0	0	0	0	0
150	155	4	0	0	0	0	0	0	0	0	0	0
155	160	5	0	0	0	0	0	0	0	0	0	0
160	165	6	0	0	0	0	0	0	0	0	0	0
165	170	7	0	0	0	0	0	0	0	0	0	0
170	175	7	0	0	0	0	0	0	0	0	0	0
175	180	8	0	0	0	0	0	0	0	0	0	0
180	185	9	1	0	0	0	0	0	0	0	0	0
185	190	10	2	0	0	0	0	0	0	0	0	0
190	195	10	3	0	0	0	0	0	0	0	0	0
195	200	11	3	0	0	0	0	0	0	0	0	0
200	210	12	5	0	0	0	0	0	0	0	0	0
210	220	14	6	0	0	0	0	0	0	0	0	0
220	230	15	8	0	0	0	0	0	0	0	0	0
230	240	17	9	1	0	0	0	0	0	0	0	0
240	250	18	11	3	0	0	0	0	0	0	0	0
250	260	20	12	4	0	0	0	0	0	0	0	0
260	270	21	14	6	0	0	0	0	0	0	0	0
270	280	23	15	7	0	0	0	0	0	0	0	0
280	290	24	17	9	1	0	0	0	0	0	0	0
290	300	26	18	10	3	0	0	0	0	0	0	0
300	310	27	20	12	4	0	0	0	0	0	0	0
310	320	29	21	13	6	0	0	0	0	0	0	0
320	330	30	23	15	7	0	0	0	0	0	0	0
330	340	32	24	16	9	1	0	0	0	0	0	0
340	350	33	26	18	10	3	0	0	0	0	0	0
350	360	35	27	19	12	4	0	0	0	0	0	0
360	370	36	29	21	13	6	0	0	0	0	0	0
370	380	38	30	22	15	7	0	0	0	0	0	0
380	390	39	32	24	16	9	1	0	0	0	0	0
390	400	41	33	25	18	10	2	0	0	0	0	0
400	410	42	35	27	19	12	4	0	0	0	0	0
410	420	44	36	28	21	13	5	0	0	0	0	0
420	430	45	38	30	22	15	7	0	0	0	0	0
430	440	47	39	31	24	16	8	1	0	0	0	0
440	450	48	41	33	25	18	10	2	0	0	0	0
450	460	50	42	34	27	19	11	4	0	0	0	0
460	470	51	44	36	28	21	13	5	0	0	0	0
470	480	53	45	37	30	22	14	7	0	0	0	0
480	490	54	47	39	31	24	16	8	1	0	0	0
490	500	56	48	40	33	25	17	10	2	0	0	0
500	510	57	50	42	34	27	19	11	4	0	0	0
510	520	59	51	43	36	28	20	13	5	0	0	0
520	530	60	53	45	37	30	22	14	7	0	0	0
530	540	62	54	46	39	31	23	16	8	0	0	0
540	550	63	56	48	40	33	25	17	10	2	0	0
550	560	65	57	49	42	34	26	19	11	3	0	0
560	570	66	59	51	43	36	28	20	13	5	0	0
570	580	68	60	52	45	37	29	22	14	6	0	0
580	590	69	62	54	46	39	31	23	16	8	0	0
590	600	71	63	55	48	40	32	25	17	9	2	0
600	610	72	65	57	49	42	34	26	19	11	3	0
610	620	74	66	58	51	43	35	28	20	12	5	0
620	630	75	68	60	52	45	37	29	22	14	6	0
630	640	77	69	61	54	46	38	31	23	15	8	0
640	650	78	71	63	55	48	40	32	25	17	9	2
650	660	80	72	64	57	49	41	34	26	18	11	3
660	670	81	74	66	58	51	43	35	28	20	12	5
670	680	83	75	67	60	52	44	37	29	21	14	6
680	690	84	77	69	61	54	46	38	31	23	15	8
690	700	86	78	70	63	55	47	40	32	24	17	9
700	710	87	80	72	64	57	49	41	34	26	18	11
710	720	89	81	73	66	58	50	43	35	27	20	12
720	730	90	83	75	67	60	52	44	37	29	21	14
730	740	92	84	76	69	61	53	46	38	30	23	15

MARRIED Persons—WEEKLY Payroll Period

If the wages are		And the number of withholding allowances claimed is—										
At least	But less than	0	1	2	3	4	5	6	7	8	9	10
		The amount of income tax to be withheld is—										
$740	$750	93	86	78	70	63	55	47	40	32	24	17
750	760	95	87	79	72	64	56	49	41	33	26	18
760	770	96	86	81	73	66	58	50	43	35	27	20
770	780	98	90	82	75	67	59	52	44	36	29	21
780	790	99	92	84	76	69	61	53	46	38	30	23
790	800	101	93	85	78	70	62	55	47	39	32	24
800	810	102	95	87	79	72	64	56	49	41	33	26
810	820	104	96	88	81	73	65	58	50	42	35	27
820	830	105	98	90	82	75	67	59	52	44	36	29
830	840	107	99	91	84	76	68	61	53	45	38	30
840	850	108	101	93	85	78	70	62	55	47	39	32
850	860	110	102	94	87	79	71	64	56	48	41	33
860	870	111	104	96	88	81	73	65	58	50	42	35
870	880	113	105	97	90	82	74	67	59	51	44	36
880	890	116	107	99	91	84	76	68	61	53	45	38
890	900	118	108	100	93	85	77	70	62	54	47	39
900	910	121	110	102	94	87	79	71	64	56	48	41
910	920	124	111	103	96	88	80	73	65	57	50	42
920	930	127	113	105	97	90	82	74	67	59	51	44
930	940	130	115	106	99	91	83	76	68	60	53	45
940	950	132	118	108	100	93	85	77	70	62	54	47
950	960	135	121	109	102	94	86	79	71	63	56	48
960	970	138	124	111	103	96	88	80	73	65	57	50
970	980	141	127	112	105	97	89	82	74	66	59	51
980	990	144	129	115	106	99	91	83	76	68	60	53
990	1,000	146	132	118	108	100	92	85	77	69	62	54
1,000	1,010	149	135	121	109	102	94	86	79	71	63	56
1,010	1,020	152	138	123	111	103	95	88	80	72	65	57
1,020	1,030	155	141	126	112	105	97	89	82	74	66	59
1,030	1,040	158	143	129	115	106	98	91	83	75	68	60
1,040	1,050	160	146	132	118	108	100	92	85	77	69	62
1,050	1,060	163	149	135	120	109	101	94	86	78	71	63
1,060	1,070	166	152	137	123	111	103	95	88	80	72	65
1,070	1,080	169	155	140	126	112	104	97	89	81	74	66
1,080	1,090	172	157	143	129	114	106	98	91	83	75	68
1,090	1,100	174	160	146	132	117	107	100	92	84	77	69
1,100	1,110	177	163	149	134	120	109	101	94	86	78	71
1,110	1,120	180	166	151	137	123	110	103	95	87	80	72
1,120	1,130	183	169	154	140	126	112	104	97	89	81	74
1,130	1,140	186	171	157	143	128	114	106	98	90	83	75
1,140	1,150	188	174	160	146	131	117	107	100	92	84	77
1,150	1,160	191	177	163	148	134	120	109	101	93	86	78
1,160	1,170	194	180	165	151	137	123	110	103	95	87	80
1,170	1,180	197	183	168	154	140	125	112	104	96	89	81
1,180	1,190	200	185	171	157	142	128	114	106	98	90	83
1,190	1,200	202	188	174	160	145	131	117	107	99	92	84
1,200	1,210	205	191	177	162	148	134	120	109	101	93	86
1,210	1,220	208	194	179	165	151	137	122	110	102	95	87
1,220	1,230	211	197	182	168	154	139	125	112	104	96	89
1,230	1,240	214	199	185	171	156	142	128	114	105	98	90
1,240	1,250	216	202	188	174	159	145	131	116	107	99	92
1,250	1,260	219	205	191	176	162	148	134	119	108	101	93
1,260	1,270	222	208	193	179	165	151	136	122	110	102	95
1,270	1,280	225	211	196	182	168	153	139	125	111	104	96
1,280	1,290	228	213	199	185	170	156	142	128	113	105	98
1,290	1,300	230	216	202	188	173	159	145	130	116	107	99
1,300	1,310	233	219	205	190	176	162	148	133	119	108	101
1,310	1,320	236	222	207	193	179	165	150	136	122	110	102
1,320	1,330	239	225	210	196	182	167	153	139	125	111	104
1,330	1,340	242	227	213	199	184	170	156	142	127	113	105
1,340	1,350	244	230	216	202	187	173	159	144	130	116	107
1,350	1,360	247	233	219	204	190	176	162	147	133	119	108
1,360	1,370	250	236	221	207	193	179	164	150	136	122	110
1,370	1,380	253	239	224	210	196	181	167	153	139	124	111
1,380	1,390	256	241	227	213	198	184	170	156	141	127	113

$1,390 and over

Use Table 1(b) for a **MARRIED** person on page 34. Also see the instructions on page 32.

Worksheets and Project Forms

Corresponding Chapter

Form Name

Chapter 4

Standard Recipe Template

Standard Recipe Card
Recipe Name:

Standard Yield:
Standard Portion:

Menu Item:

Portion Control Tool:

Recipe		
Quantity	**Unit**	**Ingredient**

Method of Preparation

Equipment Required

Corresponding Chapter   **Form Name**

Chapter 4   Standard Formula Template

Standard Recipe Card
Recipe Name:

Menu Item:

Standard Yield:
Standard Portion:
Portion Control Tool:

Ingredient	U.S. Standard		Metric		Baker's
	QTY	UNIT	QTY	UNIT	%

Method of Preparation

Equipment Required

Corresponding Chapter   **Form Name**

Chapter 5   Yield Test Cost Form

Yield Test Standard Portion Cost Form   Menu Listing: [   ]

Product: [   ]   Standard Portion Size in oz.: [   ]

As Purchased Cost: [   ]   As Purchased Weight in Lbs: [   ]   As Purchased Cost/Lb. [   ]

Product Use	Weight Lbs	Yield %	Number of Portions	Edible Cost/Lb.	Edible Cost/Portion	Cost Factor per Lb.	Cost Factor per Portion
Total Weight:		100.0%					
Trim Loss:							
Edible Product:							

Chapter 5   Cooking Loss Cost Form

Cooking Loss Standard Portion Cost Form   Menu Listing: [   ]

Product: [   ]   Standard Portion Size in oz.: [   ]

As Purchased Cost: [   ]   As Purchased Weight in Lbs: [   ]   As Purchased Cost/Lb. [   ]

Product Use	Weight in Lbs	Yield %	Number of Portions	Edible Cost/Lb.	Edible Cost/Portion	Cost Factor per Lb.	Cost Factor per Portion
Total Weight:							
Trim Loss:							
Pre-Cooked Weight							
Loss in Cooking							
Trim After Cooking							
Edible Product:							

Corresponding Chapter   **Form Name**

Chapter 5   Standard Recipe Cost Form

Standard Recipe Cost Card

Recipe Name:

Standard Yield:

Standard Portion:

Portion Control Tool:

| Recipe | | EY% | As Purchased | | Ingredient | Invoice | | | Recipe | | Individual Ingredient Cost |
Quantity	Unit		Quantity	Unit		Cost	Unit		Cost	Unit	

Total Ingredient Cost:

Q Factor %:

Recipe Cost:

Portion Cost:

Additional Cost:

Additional Cost:

Additional Cost:

Total Plate Cost:

Desired Cost %:

Preliminary Selling Price:

Actual Selling Price:

Actual Cost %:

Corresponding Chapter   **Form Name**

Chapter 6   Income Statement

Name of Restaurant

Income Statement

For the Month/Year Ending _____

Sales

    Food Sales

    Beverage Sales

    Total Sales

Cost of Sales

    Food Cost

    Beverage Cost

    Total Cost of Sales

Gross Profit

Expenses

    Salaries and Wages

    Employee Benefits

    Direct Operating Costs

    Music & Entertainment

    Marketing

    Utility Services

    Repairs & Maintenance

    Occupancy Costs

    Depreciation

    General and Administrative

    Interest

    Total Operating Expenses

Net Profit Before Income Taxes

Corresponding Chapter   **Form Name**

Chapter 7   Product Specification

SPECIFICATION CARD	
Product Name:	
Intended Use:	
Purchase Unit:	
Quantity /Packaging Standards	
Quality Standards	
Special Requirements:	

SPECIFICATION CARD	
Product Name:	
Intended Use:	
Purchase Unit:	
Quantity /Packaging Standards	
Quality Standards	
Special Requirements:	

SPECIFICATION CARD	
Product Name:	
Intended Use:	
Purchase Unit:	
Quantity /Packaging Standards	
Quality Standards	
Special Requirements:	

SPECIFICATION CARD	
Product Name:	
Intended Use:	
Purchase Unit:	
Quantity /Packaging Standards	
Quality Standards	
Special Requirements:	

Corresponding Chapter **Form Name**

Chapter 7 Order Sheet

Inventory Order Sheets			
Food Category:		Day/Date:	
Ingredient	**On Hand**	**PAR**	**Order**

Corresponding Chapter   **Form Name**

Chapter 7   Purveyor Bid Sheet

Purveyor Bid Sheet				
		Date:		
Food Category:				
Ingredient	Purchase Unit	Purveyor 1	Purveyor 2	Purveyor 3

Purveyor 1: _____

Purveyor 2: _____

Purveyor 3: _____

Corresponding Chapter

Chapter 7

Form Name

Purchase Order

Purchase Order #

Purchase Order

Restaurant Address

Phone Number

Purveyor

Name
Address
City
Phone

Misc	
Date	
Requested Delivery:	
Sales Rep:	
FOB	

Quantity		Description	Unit Price	TOTAL
Ordered	Unit			
			SubTotal	
			Shipping	
		Tax Rate(s)		
			TOTAL	

Payment

Comments
Name
CC #
Expires

Office Use Only

Ordered by _____

Corresponding Chapter

Chapter 8

Form Name

Purchase Distribution Journal

PURCHASE DISTRIBUTION JOURNAL		Category:	Food			Month/Year:			
Date	Invoice #	Meats	Seafood	Poultry	Produce	Grocery	Dairy	Bakery	Other	Total
Totals										

Corresponding Chapter

Chapter 8

Form Name

Receiving Report Form

RECEIVING REPORT FORM				Month/Year:					Page:	
Date	Invoice #	Purveyor	Description	Food	Beverage	Other	$Directs	$Stores	General Info

Corresponding Chapter   **Form Name**

Chapter 9   Inventory Sheet

INVENTORY SHEET					
Category:				Location:	
QTY	UNIT	ITEM	COST	UNIT	EXTENSION
					Page Total	
					Total	

Corresponding Chapter

Form Name

Chapter 9

Bin Card

Bin Card

Stock #: _____

| Product Name: _____ | | | | Unit Size: _____ | | | |

Date		Storage In		Storage Out		Balance on Hand	
Month	Day	Units	Costs	Units	Costs	Units	Costs

Corresponding Chapter

Chapter 9

Form Name

Transfer Memo

Food and Beverage Transfer

Food and Beverage Transfer					
Day/Date: _____					
From Department: _____			To Department: _____		
Quantity	Unit	Item		Unit Cost	Total

Authorized by: _____

Corresponding Chapter

Form Name

Chapter 10

Daily Cost %—Simple Approach

				Simple Daily Food Cost % Form			
Day	Date	Daily Purchases	Daily Sales	Daily Cost %	To-Date Purchases	To-Date Sales	To-Date Cost %

Corresponding Chapter   **Form Name**

Chapter 10   Daily Food Cost %—Accurate Approach

Day	Date	Reqs	Direct Purchases	Transfers to Kitchen	Cost of Food Used	Transfers from Kitchen	Emp. Meals	IHP	Daily Cost of Food Sold	Daily Sales	Daily Cost %	To-Date Cost of Food Sold	To-Date Food Sales	To-Date Food Cost %

ACCURATE DAILY FOOD COST PERCENTAGE WORKSHEET

Corresponding Chapter

Chapter 10

Form Name

Daily Beverage Cost %—Accurate Approach

DAY	DATE	ISSUES	TRANSFER to BAR	ADDITIONS	COST OF BEVERAGES USED	TRANSFER FROM BAR		SIGNING PRIVILEGE	SUB-TRAC-TIONS	DAILY COST OF BEV. SOLD	DAILY BEVERAGE SALES	DAILY BEVERAGE COST %	TO-DATE COST OF BEV SOLD	TO-DATE BEVERAGE SALES
						BAR	IHP							

Corresponding Chapter

Chapter 11

Form Name

Menu Engineering Worksheet

Menu Engineering

Food Category: _____ Time Period/Dates: _____

Menu Item	# Sold	Sales Mix%	Selling Price	Food Cost	Contrib. Margin	Total Sales	Total Costs	Total CM	CM %	Sales Mix Category	CM Category	Item Classification

TOTALS

Desired Sales Mix % _____ $ _____   Average Contribution Margin   Potential Food Cost %:

Corresponding Chapter   **Form Name**

Chapter 12   Weekly Schedule

Employee	Monday	Tuesday	Wednesday	Thursday	Friday	Saturday	Sunday	Total Hours

Department:

Labor Schedule

Week of

Projected Covers

Corresponding Chapter

Chapter 12

Form Name

Payroll Ledger

| Employee | MS | WA | Hours Worked | | Wage Rate | | Total Wages | Weekly Salary | Tips & Service | Total Paid by Employer | Tips Declared | Wage/Hour Total | Deductions | | | | Total Deductions | Net Pay |
			Regular	OverTime	Regular	OverTime							FICA	Medicare	Federal Tax Withheld			

Bibliography

Adams, J. (January 24, 2014). Lehigh University Touts New Gluten-Free Dining Options. Retrieved January 25, 2014 from, http://www.celiac.com/articles/23512/1/Leigh-University-Touts-New-Gluten-Free-Dining-Options/Page1.html

http://www.annerobertsgardens.com Retrieved January 20, 2014.

Bauer, M (March 1, 2013). 6 Restaurants that grow own ingredients. Retrieved January 26, 2014 from, http://www.sfgate.com/restaurants/sixofakind/article/6-restaurants-that-grow-own-ingredients-4321687.php

Bell, R. (December 23, 2013). Chefs experiencing demand for locally- sourced, sustainably-grown products. Retrieved January 7, 2014 from, http://msue.anr.msu.edu/news/chefs_experiencing_demand_for_locally_sourced_sustainably_grown_products

Boston & surrounding towns-Gluten Free Boston Grill. Retrieved January 24, 2014 from, http://www.glutenfreebostongirl.com/restaurants-2/boston-surrouding-towns/
http://www.cafegratitude.com Retrieved January 7, 2014.
http://www.cafenormandie.com Retrieved January 20, 2014.

Celiac Disease & Gluten-free Diet Information at celiac.com. Retrieved January 25, 2014 from, www.celiac.com

Conducting a Feasibility Study for a New Restaurant. National Restaurant Association and Cini-Grissom Associate Inc. 1983, Washington D.C.

http://www.darden.com/sustainability/ Retrieved January 20, 2014.

Department of the Treasury. Internal Revenue Service. (2014). *Publication 15, Circular E, Employer's Tax Guide, Cat. No. 10000W.* Philadelphia: January 2014.

Dining Out Celiac Disease Foundation. celiac.org. Retrieved January 25, 2014 from, http://celiac.org/live-gluten-free/gluten-free-lifestyle/dining-out/

Dittmer, P. R. & Griffin, G.G. (1994). *Principles of Food, Beverage, and Labor Cost Controls.* (5th ed.). New York, NY: Van Nostrand Reinhold.

Drysdale, J. A. (1994). *Profitable Menu Planning.* Englewood Cliffs, NJ: Prentice-Hall Career & Technology Prentice-Hall Inc.

http://www.eastsidecafeaustin.com/menus/lunch-dinner.html. Retrieved January 16, 2014.

http://www.fishstorynapa.com Retrieved January 16, 2014.

Fleming, C. A., Miller, R.K., & Washington, K. (January 2008). "*The 2008 Restaurant & Foodservice Market Research Handbook.*"

http://www.flourandwater.com/friends/ Retrieved January 16, 2014.

http://he3533.wix.com/wokworks Retrieved January 28, 2014

Johnson & Wales University. (2010). *Culinary Fundamentals.* (2nd. ed.). Singapore: Imago.

Johnson & Wales University. (2009). *Baking & Pastry Fundamentals.* Upper Saddle River, NJ: Pearson Education, Inc.

Johnson, R. C. & D. L. Bridge. (1993). *The Legal Problem Solver for Foodservice Operators*, (6th. ed.). Washington D.C.: National Restaurant Association.

Jones, A. 6 Trends In Kids' Nutrition. Retrieved January 27, 2014 from, http://www.fona.com/sites/default/files/whitepaper-6trendsinkidsnutrition-trendresources-040412.pdf

Jones-Mueller, A. (July 23, 2010). Childhood obesity: 10 ways your restaurant can make a difference. Retrieved January 6, 2014 from, http://www.restaurantnutrition.com/NRNs-Skinny-on-Nutrition/Childhood-obesity—10-ways-your-restaurant-can-mak.aspx

Kasavana, M. L., & Smith, D. I. (1990). *Menu Engineering: A Practical Guide to Menu Analysis*. Okemos, Michigan: Hospitality Publications, Inc.

Katz, J. A. & Green, R. P., II. (2011). *Entrepreneurial Small Business*. (3rd ed.). New York, NY: McGraw-Hill/Irwin.

Keister, Douglas C. (1977). *Food and Beverage Control*. Englewood Cliffs, NJ: Prentice-Hall, Inc.

Kids LiveWell Program –National Association. Restaurant.org. Retrieved January 22, 2014 from, http://www.restaurant.org/industry-impact/food-healthy-living/kids-livewell-program

Kotschevar, L. H. & M. R. Escoffier. (1994). *Management by Menu*. (3d. ed.). The Educational Foundation of the National Restaurant Association.

Laube, J. & Shuster, B. K. (2012). *The Uniform System of Accounts for Restaurants*. (8th ed.) Washington, D.C.: National Restaurant Association.

Laventhol & Horvarth. (1990). *Uniform System of Accounts for Restaurants*. (6th ed.). Washington, D.C.: The National Restaurant Association.

Legal Sea Foods Quality Control Center. legalseafood.com. Retrieved January 7, 2014 from, http://www.legalseafoods.com/index.cfm/page/Quality-Control-Center/pid/44423

Levinson, C. (1989). *Food and Beverage Operation*. (2d. ed.). Englewood Cliffs, NJ: Prentice-Hall, Inc.

Market Mobile: Farm-to-Biz Delivery for Rhode Island and Massachusetts. Retrieved January 18, 2014 from, www.farmfresh.org/hub/

Melamed, S. (January 3, 2014). Jewish foods, non-wheat noodles top 2014 trends. Retrieved January 7, 2014 from, http://articles.philly.com/2014-01-03/food/45802295_1_food-trends-vedge-michael-solomonov

Motagna at the Little Nell. Retrieved January 8, 2014 from, http://www.epicurious.com/articlesguides/diningtravel/restaurants/farmtotable_montagna

National Digestive Diseases Information Clearinghouse (NDDIC) Retrieved January 25, 2014 from, http://www.digestive.niddk.nih.gov/ddiseases/pubs/celiac/

National Restaurant Association, (1983). *Conducting a Feasibility Study for a New Restaurant, A Do It Yourself Handbook*.

Olmsted, L. (December 6, 2013). Best farm-to-table-movement restaurants. Retrieved January 7, 2014 from, http://www.usatoday.com/story/experience/food-and-wine/best-of-food-and-wine/food/2013/12/06/best-farm-to-table-restaurants/2703405/

On The Menu: Restaurant Nutrition Initiatives 2013 Report. Retrieved January 27, 2014 from, https://www.restaurant.org/getattachment/Industry-Impact/Food-Healthy-Living/Nutrition-Report_Final_low.pdf

Overview of FDA Proposed Labeling Requirements for Restaurants. Retrieved from, http://www.fda.gov/Food/IngredientsPackagingLabeling/LabelingNutrition/ucm248732.htm

Palo Alto Software, Inc. Rutabaga Sweets Business Plan. Retrieved April 3, 2014 from http://paloalto.com

Powers, S. (July 13, 2013). Food Hubs Try To Grow Local Farms. Retrieved January 6, 2014 from, http://harvestpublicmedia.org/article/food-hubs-try-grow-local-farms

Robitaille, J. (2014). Personal Interview. Johnson & Wales University, Larry Friedman International Center for Entrepreneurship.

Seaberg, A. G. (1990). *Menu Design Merchandising and Marketing*. (4th ed.). New York: John Wiley & Sons, Inc.

Schwartz, W.C. (April 9, 1984). Eliminating Poor Receiving Habits. *Nation's Restaurant News*.

7 Tips for healthful kids 'meals. Retrieved January 6, 2014 from, http://www.restaurant.org/Manage-My-Restaurant/Food-Nutrition/Nutrition/7-tips-for-healthful-kids-meals

Shoukas, D. (June 24, 2013). Innovations in Pasta, Noodles, Grains and Rice. Retrieved January 7, 2014 from, http://www.specialtyfood.com/news-trends/featured-articles/article/innovations-pasta-noodles-grains-and-rice

Social Responsibility Sustainable Seafood. Retrieved January 7, 2014 from, http://www.rubios.com/socialresponsibility/sustainableseafood

Sodexo to Serve Eco-Labeled Seafood, Improve Supply Chain Sustainability. Retrieved January 6, 2014 from http://www.environmentalleader.com/2013/04/08/sodexo-to-serve-eco-labeled-seafood-improve-supply-chain-sustainability/

Stefanelli, J. M. (1992). *Purchasing: Selection and Procurement for the Hospitality Industry*, (3d. ed.). New York, NY: John Wiley and Sons, Inc.

Sustainability at the top of 2014 What's Hot Survey. Retrieved January 6, 2014 from, http://www.restaurant.org/News-Research/News/Sustainability-at-top-of-2014-What%E2%80%99s-Hot-survey

http://www.tululasgarden.com. Retrieved January 8, 2014.

http://www.tedsmontanagrill.com. Retrieved January 20, 2014.

The United States Small Business Administration. Create Your Own Business Plan. Retrieved February 15, 2014 from http://www.SBA.Gov.com/starting &managing-a-business/start-a- business/create-your-business-plan.

Top 10 Seafood Restaurants in the U.S. Retrieved January 7, 2014 from, http://travel.yahoo.com/ideas/top-10-seafood-restaurants-u-204141052.html

Uchi Philosophy. Retrieved January 8, 2014 from, http://uchiaustin.com/uchi-philosophy

http://www.vernickphilly.com/pdf/Vernick%20Food%20Menu.pdf Retrieved January 28, 2014.

http://www.vignolamaine.com Retrieved January 8, 2014.

What's Hot in 2014 Culinary Forecast. Retrieved January 7, 2014 from, http://www.restaurant.org/News-Research/Research/What-s-Hot

Woodfire Grill. Retrieved January 8, 2014 from, http://www.epicurious.com/articlesguides/diningtravel/restaurants/farmtotable_woodfiregrill

Zavatto, A (September 14, 2012). Farm-to-menu restaurants that grow their own. Retrieved January 26, 2014 from, http://www.foxnews.com/leisure/2012/09/14/backyard-farm-to-menu-restaurants-that-are-trying-to-grow-their-own/

http://www.zazukitchen.com Retrieved January 28, 2014.

Index